Dedicated to our colleague and mentor of many years, James L. McKenney.

Preface

Corporate Information Strategy and Management examines how information technology (IT) enables organizations to conduct business in radically different and more effective ways. The commercialization of the Internet has created a seismic change in the business environment. New channels of supply and distribution are emerging. New electronic marketplaces and exchanges are being created. The infrastructures of firms and the industries within which they operate have been permanently altered.

This is a fast-moving and global phenomenon. For established companies, the resulting challenges have been deep and pervasive. In many cases, the changes have threatened not just a firm's competitiveness but also its survival. Executives bear an enormous burden as they attempt to understand the challenges, keep abreast of events, and make intelligent decisions and plans.

The objective of this book is to provide readers with a better understanding of the influence of 21st-century technologies on business decisions. The book discusses today's challenges from the point of view of the executives who are grappling with them. It recounts stories of success and failure, focusing on the issues faced and the decisions made by executives in companies around the world.

The information presented here is organized in an Introduction, four modules, and a Conclusion. The first module is aimed at understanding the impact of IT on industries and markets. It discusses issues of strategic positioning and explains how 21st-century IT provides opportunities to alter market/industry structure, power, and relationships. The second module shifts the focus from the external environment to the internal organization. It explores new organizational capabilities, management/leadership principles, and sources of value that arise within networked companies. The third module turns the reader's attention to operational issues at the interface of business and technology as it examines approaches to designing and managing open-standard, networked technology infrastructures. The fourth module concentrates on leadership and management of IT activities, focusing on the issues that arise at the boundary as four key constituents—business executives, IT executives, users, and IT partners—work together to leverage technology to create a sustainable advantage. The Conclusion summarizes key frameworks, insights, and themes.

The material presented here is the outgrowth of field-based research we have conducted at the Harvard Business School since the early 1970s. To both Dean John McArthur and Dean Kim Clark we express our appreciation for making the time and resources available for us to complete this work.

We are particularly indebted to the executives who provided so much time and insight during the course of our research. Without the cooperation of many executives, the preparation of this book would not have been possible.

We are grateful as well for the many valuable suggestions and insights provided by our Harvard Business School colleagues, especially Jim Cash, Alan MacCormack, Andrew McAfee, Jim McKenney, Richard Nolan, Kash Rangan, and David Upton. In addition, we acknowledge the valued work of our doctoral students, fellows, and research assistants. Our heartfelt thanks go to Nancy Bartlett, Alastair Brown, Meredith Collura, Mark Cotteleer, Melissa Dailey, LeGrand Elebash, Cedric Escalle, Evelyn Goldman, Kristin Kohler, David Lane, Marc Mandel, Felipe Monteiro, Tom Rodd, Mary Rotelli, Deb Sole, George Westerman, and Fred Young. We also acknowledge the support of the directors of Harvard Business School research centers, including Christina Darwall of the California Research Center; Gustavo Herrero, Director of the Latin America Research Center; Camille Tang Yeh, Director of the Asia Pacific Center; and Carin Knoop, Executive Director of Global Research. Thanks go to Alan Murray, a superlative friend and former colleague, who provided important reviews of technical details, especially in the chapter on computer security. Finally, we express our appreciation to our editor, Tom Cameron, and to Jennifer Chalfin, Maureen Donovan, Brooke Spangler, and Maurie SuDock, who provided administrative support.

Lynda M. Applegate

Robert D. Austin

F. Warren McFarlan

658.L038 APP

Corporate Information Strategy Management

**The Chal...
in a Netw...**

...plegate
...ıstin
...:Farlan

Business

Boston   Burr Ridge, IL   Dubuque, IA   Madison, WI   New York   San Francisco   St. Louis
Bangkok   Bogotá   Caracas   Kuala Lumpur   Lisbon   London   Madrid   Mexico City
Milan   Montreal   New Delhi   Santiago   Seoul   Singapore   Sydney   Taipei   Toronto

McGraw-Hill Higher Education

*A Division of The **McGraw-Hill** Companies*

CORPORATE INFORMATION STRATEGY AND MANAGEMENT: THE CHALLENGES OF MANAGING IN A NETWORK ECONOMY

Published by McGraw-Hill/Irwin, a business unit of The McGraw-Hill Companies, Inc., 1221 Avenue of the Americas, New York, NY, 10020. Copyright © 2003, 1999, 1996, 1992, 1988, 1983 by The McGraw-Hill Companies, Inc. All rights reserved. No part of this publication may be reproduced or distributed in any form or by any means, or stored in a database or retrieval system, without the prior written consent of The McGraw-Hill Companies, Inc., including, but not limited to, in any network or other electronic storage or transmission, or broadcast for distance learning.

Some ancillaries, including electronic and print components, may not be available to customers outside the United States.

This book is printed on acid-free paper.

domestic   1 2 3 4 5 6 7 8 9 0 FGR/FGR 0 9 8 7 6 5 4 3 2
international   1 2 3 4 5 6 7 8 9 0 FGR/FGR 0 9 8 7 6 5 4 3 2

ISBN 0-07-245665-5

Publisher: *George Werthman*
Senior sponsoring editor: *Rick Williamson*
Editorial assistant: *Jennie Yates*
Marketing manager: *Greta Kleinert*
Media producer: *Greg Bates*
Senior project manager: *Kari Geltemeyer*
Production supervisor: *Debra R. Sylvester*
Design team leader: *Mary L. Christianson*
Senior supplement producer: *Rose M. Range*
Senior digital content specialist: *Brian Nacik*
Typeface: *10.5/12 Times New Roman*
Compositor: *Carlisle Communications, Ltd.*
Printer: *Quebecor World Fairfield Inc.*

Library of Congress Cataloging-in-Publication Data

Applegate, Lynda M.
    Corporate information strategy and management : the challenges of managing in a network economy / Lynda M. Applegate, Robert D. Austin, F. Warren McFarlan.—6th ed.
        p. cm.
    Rev. ed. of: Corporate information systems management : the challenges of managing in an information age. 5th ed. c1999.
    Includes bibliographical references and index.
    ISBN 0-07-245665-5 (alk. paper)—ISBN 0-07-112291-5 (international : alk. paper)
    1. Management information systems. I. Austin, Robert D. (Robert Daniel), 1962- II. McFarlan, F. Warren (Franklin Warren) III. Applegate, Lynda M. Corporate information systems management. IV. Title
    HD30.2 .A653 2003
    648.4'038'011—dc21   2002026560

INTERNATIONAL EDITION ISBN 0-07-112291-5

www.mhhe.com

Contents

MODULE 2
BUILDING THE NETWORK ECONOMY: CAPABILITIES AND ORGANIZATION   77

Chapter 3
Building Networked Businesses   79

Chapter 4
Making the Case for Networked Business   115

MODULE 3
MANAGING NETWORKED INFRASTRUCTURE AND OPERATIONS   149

Chapter 5
Understanding Internetworking Infrastructure   151

Chapter 6
Assuring Reliable and Secure IT Services   179

Introduction
Challenges of Managing
in a Network Economy

Information technology (IT) has always been a wild card in business, a source of opportunity and uncertainty, advantage and risk. Business executives have often viewed the IT function with apprehension, seeing it as the province of technocrats primarily interested in new features that may have little relevance to real-world business problems. Technology executives have often considered business managers to be shortsighted, lacking the vision to exploit all that technology has to offer. Both struggle as they attempt to implement increasingly complex systems in the face of rapid change in business and technology.

And yet we have, since the inception of business computing, tightened our embrace of IT, and for good reason. Despite exasperating moments, technology has become embedded in the way we define and execute strategy, the way we organize and lead businesses, and the way we define a unique value proposition.

Indeed, the pace of IT evolution has been both dramatic and disconcerting (see Figure I.1). The coevolution of technology, work, and the workforce over the last 40 years has dramatically influenced our concept of organizations and the industries within which they compete. No longer simply a tool to support "back-office" transactions, IT has become a strategic part of most businesses, enabling the redefinition of markets and industries and the strategies and designs of firms competing within them. Today's supersonic jets cross the Atlantic in three hours or less, and global communication networks carry information around the world in seconds. Distance and time have become much less significant determinants of market and organizational structures and processes.[1] Moreover, information has become a major economic good, frequently exchanged in concert with, or even in place of, tangible goods and services.

[1] R. Miles and C. Snow, "Organizations: New Concepts for New Forms," *California Management Review,* 28:62–73, 1986; T. Malone, J. Yates, and R. Benjamin, "Electronic Markets and Electronic Hierarchies: Effects of Information Technology on Market Structure and Corporate Strategies," *Communications of the ACM* 30(6):484–497, 1987 R. Johnston and P. Lawrence, "Beyond Vertical Integration—The Rise of the Value-Adding Partnership," *Harvard Business Review,* July–August, 1988; W. Powell, "Neither Market nor Hierarchy: Network Forms of Organization," *Research on Organizational Behavior* 12:295–336, 1990.

FIGURE I.1
**Evolution of
Computing
Performance**

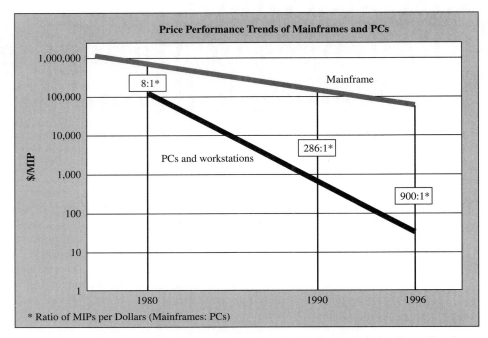

Price Performance Trends of Mainframes and PCs

Source: Adapted from J. McKenney, *Waves of Change: Business Evolution through Information Technology* (Boston: Harvard Business School Press, 1995).

The last decade has added considerably to the mystique and magic of IT. Something dramatic happened to technology in the 1990s, although it is probably too early to discern the full impact. Many of us remember the first time we opened a browser and gained access to the World Wide Web (WWW). For some executives who had lived their lives avoiding technology, a light went on, and they glimpsed the potential of what previously had lain deep within the silicon switches that processed data in the basement of the organization. Others ventured forth only to become mired in a sea of useless information and broken links that convinced them that although the technology was more appealing to the eye, the same old flaws remained.

Then came the boom of the late 1990s, when the capital markets caught the fever. Stories of "20-something" billionaires who only a few years earlier had plotted their business ideas on napkins grabbed our attention. Stories of investors who pushed entrepreneurs to take more money and spend it more quickly challenged our view of the blood, sweat, and tears that used to define how a new business was built from the ground up. Stories of newly public firms with market capitalizations in the billions of dollars, yet with no discernible path to profitability, caused us to question the fundamental economic principles that guided how we built and managed companies.

As the new century dawned, the "bubble" burst. The tech-heavy Nasdaq lost more than half its value within months, and spending for IT equipment and services dropped. The world economy headed into a downward spiral that, when this book was written in early 2002, threatened to continue into 2003.

Some young executives began their careers during the boom, and for a time it seemed they would have an advantage. When the dot-com bubble burst, executives young and old found themselves in pretty much the same situation as they attempted to understand which opportunities were real and which were nothing more than the hype that surrounds all new inventions.

Some things are clear. The world is forever changed. IT has burst forth from its safe containment in the basements of corporations. Business executives have begun to wrest control from IT executives who have failed to step up to the challenge of entering the boardroom. Technology has become a core enabler and, in some cases, the primary channel through which business is done. The world is smaller, and the "global village" is quickly becoming a reality. Physical location matters less than it once did. Borders and boundaries, ownership and control have become less rigid. The last decade has offered examples of IT-enabled "virtual" organizations in which many small, independent agents (or firms) band together as nodes on an information network to achieve dramatic increases in scope and scale. Such arrangements challenge both our legal and our social definitions of an organization as business practice outpaces legal and regulatory policy—especially in areas such as international competitiveness and trade, intellectual property, privacy, security, family, community, education, and culture. And yet there are still new frontiers to explore, new challenges to meet, and new magic in store.

Because so much has changed so quickly, because the ups and downs have come in such a short interval, this is a difficult time to engage in sense making. Yet that is precisely what we are doing in this book. We're attempting to relate what we know from decades of study to what we are learning from those who are creating the future. The last five years have provided the richest vein of potential learning we have ever been positioned to mine. It has been a period of intense experimentation. Many new models have been tried, and many of them have failed. We would be remiss if we did not attempt to understand it all—the successes and the failures.

Our objective is to help business executives who find themselves paralyzed by confusion and uncertainty to begin to take the important first steps on the path of transformational change. At the same time, we wish to help IT executives assume leadership positions, not just in defining and executing technology strategy but also in defining and executing business strategy. As we work toward these dual objectives, we draw on years of research and experience, much of it in the field with executives who have accepted the challenge and are venturing forward into uncharted waters.

The insights presented in *Corporate Information Strategy and Management* expand the thinking presented in a companion book, *Creating Business Advantage in the Information Age.*[2] These insights are organized around the following key themes,

[2]L. M. Applegate, R. D. Austin, and F. W. McFarlan, *Creating Business Advantage in the Information Age* (New York: McGraw Hill, 2002). Visit the website http://www.mhhe.com/catalogs/0072523670.mhtml for more information.

which are introduced briefly in the remainder of this Introduction and then expanded upon throughout the book.

1. As 21st-century IT expands processing capacity; enables convergence of voice, video, and data; encourages real-time transactions and interactivity; and dramatically increases connectivity and access, we are confronted with new choices for designing and building industries, markets, and organizations.
2. The business models that dominated the Industrial Economy are evolving to take advantage of the capabilities of the new technologies and business practices of the Network Economy, giving rise to new sources of power and differentiation.
3. The types of opportunities pursued and the technology employed strongly influence the approach taken to developing, operating, and managing IT.
4. As IT infrastructure becomes more standardized, modular, and scalable, we see a shift in IT investment priorities and decisions from a cost-avoidance, project-centered approach to an asset-based, strategic option approach.
5. The time required for successful organizational learning and assimilation of rapidly changing technologies limits the practical speed of change.
6. External industry, internal organizational, and technological changes are increasing the pressure on organizations to "buy" rather than "make" IT applications and services.
7. The ability to exploit 21st-century technology successfully demands high levels of engagement and cooperation among four key constituencies: business executives, IT executives, users, and technology providers/partners.
8. The ability to ensure high levels of security, privacy, reliability, and availability is a core capability that determines an organization's ultimate success and survival.
9. Over the past decade there has been a fundamental shift in IT that has dramatically changed the way people access and use technology, the way organizations exploit it, and the way it is developed and managed.

Theme 1: Market Structure and Industry Dynamics

Every day managers hear claims about how the new technologies of the 21st century (for example, the Internet, the WWW, browsers, and wireless devices) are radically changing the way we work, play, interact, learn, and build businesses. While these new technologies have dramatically expanded the opportunities that can be pursued, the fundamental economic theories that define how markets, industries, and organizations are built continue to guide executive decision making and actions.

In fact, most 21st-century organizations continue to operate as they always have—as members of a business network of suppliers, producers, distributors, and partners that work together to design, deliver, market, and sell products and services for business customers and consumers. Yet while the basic roles remain unchanged, executives today have numerous options for how to organize these activities and manage relationships among multiple parties.

FIGURE I.2
The Value
Chain Defines
Industry
Structure and
Relationships

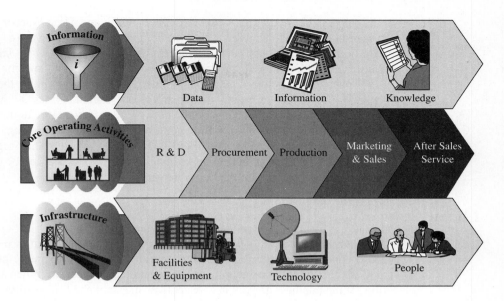

The primary value activities that define how raw materials, information, and labor are used to create products and services for business customers and consumers used to be structured as a *sequential* "value chain" (see Figure I.2). Value chain activities inside most Industrial Economy firms were organized within functional units (for example, R&D, procurement, production, marketing, sales, and service), and relationships among those functional units were often "transactional" in nature (for example, when R&D finished a new product design, it was "thrown over the wall" to production, and so on down the chain). These well-defined roles, responsibilities, and relationships were governed by standardized policies, procedures, and agreements. Because of the difficulty of managing and controlling all but the most routine activities, Industrial Economy executives traditionally chose to locate everything except the most routine activities within their organizational boundaries, and this resulted in the rise of vertically integrated firms as the key power broker within most industries.

Today's executives are faced with a myriad of organizational and market choices. They may continue to operate within industries with clearly defined boundaries and relationships. Alternatively, they may operate within an industry in which boundaries are becoming fluid and relationships are increasingly based less on structured transactions and contracts and more on partnerships that require trust and cooperation. Many believe that the ability to conduct business electronically, integrating supply and distribution channels by using IT systems that enable access to the real-time information needed to closely monitor core activities that take place outside organization boundaries, will give rise to virtually integrated industries. Yet the same benefits also can be achieved inside the organization.

Consider the merger of America Online (AOL) and Time Warner, which is discussed in Module 1. The newly merged company is testing the limits of "virtual integration" *inside a vertically integrated governance structure.* The AOL Time Warner networked model stands in sharp contrast to that of Covisint—the collaborative partnership between auto industry manufacturers, suppliers, distributors, and technology providers. Covisint demonstrates how executives across an industry have chosen to cooperate on the design of a networked infrastructure upon which all parties in the industry will do business while simultaneously competing on price, quality, and product innovation. The choices facing executives as they organize to conduct business within market networks and the frameworks that can be used to inform those choices are discussed in depth in Chapters 1 through 3.

Theme 2: Evolving Business Models

As technology redefines opportunities and the choices executives make to exploit those opportunities, the business logic traditionally used to frame how executives made decisions and took actions has been called into question. When asked the question "What business are you in?" executives in established firms often reply with the name of the industry within which their company competes and the role or roles the firm plays within the industry. For example, they might say: "We're a telecommunications service provider" or "We're a consumer products manufacturer." For most people, these industries and roles have become so familiar that this shorthand description is all that is needed to communicate what the firm does, its position within an industry, and how it makes money.

On the other hand, most executives have a very hard time answering the question "What is your business model?" This is especially true if a company has adopted one of the emerging online business models (for example, portals or application service providers, also called ASPs). After some prodding, these executives begin to provide a more detailed picture of the activities that their company performs, the customers to whom they sell, and the suppliers from whom they buy. They talk about channels to market, competitors, and the economics of the business (including the cost structure and revenue models). These details are the components of a business model (see Figure I.3).

Why is a focus on business models so important today? If you think about it, we spent nearly a century building and perfecting the Industrial Economy business models that defined how companies conducted business throughout most of the 1900s. The Internet and the associated technologies of the Network Economy are enabling us to exploit new opportunities and build new capabilities. As a result, we are able to evolve current business models and, in some cases, build new ones. We have not yet developed a shorthand way to describe the emerging networked business models that are revolutionizing business and society in the 21st century. Chapter 2 provides this shorthand system as it examines changes in structure, relationships, and power among players in the personal financial services, business logistics, and entertainment/media industries.

FIGURE I.3
Components of
a Business
Model

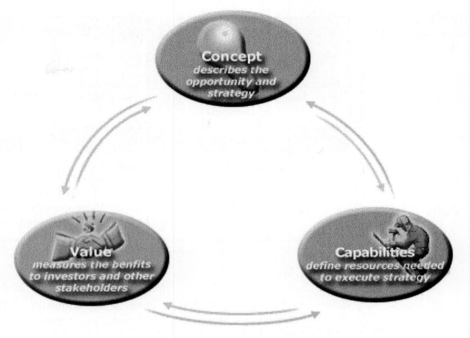

Theme 3: IT Impact

The goal for technology use strongly influences the approach to developing, operating, and managing technology. Two key dimensions must be considered: (1) the impact of IT on core operations and (2) the impact of IT on core strategy. These dimensions help frame the decisions that executives make in organizing and managing IT.

The first dimension assesses the impact of IT on core operations. In some firms, such as Nasdaq, reliable, zero-defect operation of IT is critical to performing core value activities inside the firm and across the global securities industry. Failure for even a few seconds can bring the entire securities industry to its knees. In other firms, for example, some law firms, the impact of a day-long IT failure would be much less immediate and severe.

The second dimension assesses the strategic impact of IT on the core strategy of a firm. In some firms, such as PSA and American Express, a steady stream of technological innovations drives strategy evolution. In these firms, IT development activities are inextricably linked to the strategy of the firm and IT investment decisions are made in the boardroom by those charged with assuring the success and survival of the firm. In other firms, IT development priorities are targeted toward incremental, operational improvements that may improve a firm's cost profile but do little to change its position or power in the industry. The "strategic grid" depicted in Figure I.4 defines four categories of IT impact that

FIGURE I.4
The Impact of IT

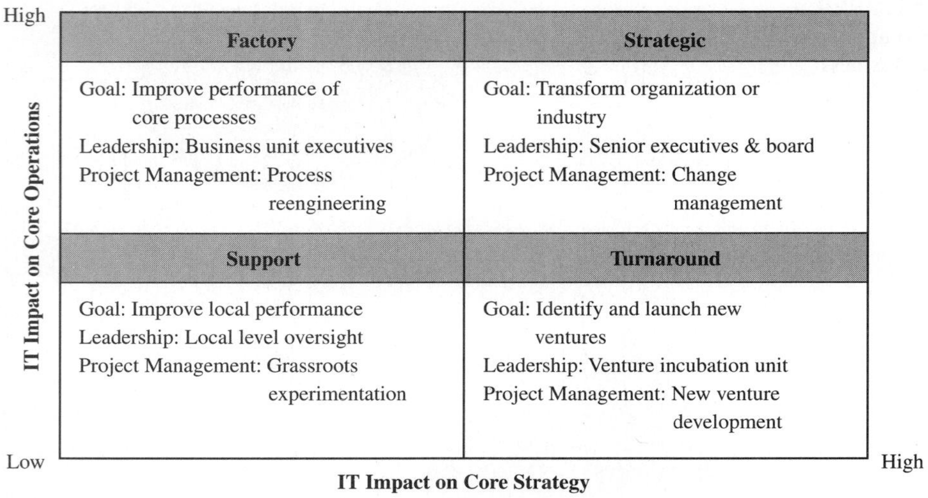
High
Factory
Goal: Improve performance of core processes
Leadership: Business unit executives
Project Management: Process reengineering
Strategic
Goal: Transform organization or industry
Leadership: Senior executives & board
Project Management: Change management
Support
Goal: Improve local performance
Leadership: Local level oversight
Project Management: Grassroots experimentation
Turnaround
Goal: Identify and launch new ventures
Leadership: Venture incubation unit
Project Management: New venture development
IT Impact on Core Operations
Low
High
IT Impact on Core Strategy

help determine the approach used to identify opportunities, define and implement IT-enabled business initiatives, and organize and manage IT assets and professionals. (Appendix A provides a more detailed description of the four categories of IT impact depicted on the strategic grid.)

IT-enabled activities that fall squarely within the "Support" quadrant of the grid are often designed, implemented, and managed by IT specialists with the help of end users. IT-enabled activities that fall within the "Factory" quadrant are designed, implemented, and managed by business unit executives in partnership with IT executives. IT-enabled activities that are designed to exploit opportunities that represent emerging strategic opportunities (the "Turnaround" quadrant) are often designed, implemented, and managed through partnerships between business development and emerging technologies groups inside an organization or within technology partner firms. Finally, firms that have moved into the "Strategic" quadrant have made a commitment to use IT to enable both core operations and core strategy. In these firms, IT initiatives are often defined, implemented, and managed at the top levels of the corporation. These four approaches to IT investment decision making and management are examined throughout Modules 1 through 4.

Theme 4: Prioritizing IT Investments

Few would dispute the fact that 21st-century technologies are pervading and shaping industries, markets, and organizations. Yet many managers treat IT as a budgeted expense to be justified on a project-by-project basis and are then disappointed with the returns. They would do better, we argue, to think of IT as an investment that must deliver benefits today and in the future. These benefits are of two main types and may be targeted inside or outside the firm (see Table I.1).

TABLE I.1   Making the Case for IT

Categories of Benefits	Goals and Measures	
	Internal	External
Type I: Benefits from Investments in Networked IT Infrastructure		
Functionality and flexibility	Improve infrastructure performance; increase the functionality and range of strategic options that can be pursued	Create an efficient, flexible online/offline platform for doing business with customers, suppliers, and partners
	Sample measures: Decrease the cost and/or improve the performance of internal IT operations; enable new IT applications to be created at lower cost, in less time, and with less risk; expand the range of internal IT initiatives	*Sample measures:* Decrease the cost and/or improve the performance of doing business online; decrease the time, cost, and risk of launching new online business initiatives; expand the reach of existing IT-enabled businesses and the range of business opportunities that can be pursued
Type II: Benefits from Doing Business on a Networked IT Infrastructure		
Commerce	Improve internal operating efficiency and quality	Streamline and integrate channels to market, create new channels, and integrate multiple online/offline channels
	Sample measures: Internal process performance and work flow improvements; cost savings or cost avoidance; increased quality; decreased cycle time	*Sample measures:* Supply chain or distribution channel performance improvements; cost savings or cost avoidance for the organization and its customers, suppliers, or partners; decrease time to market or just-in-time order replenishment; enable new channels to market and/or extend the reach and range of existing channels
Content/knowledge	Improve the performance of knowledge workers and enhance organizational learning	Improve the performance of knowledge workers in customer, supplier, and partner organizations; add "information value" to existing products and services; create new information-based products and services

(continued)

TABLE I.1 *(continued)*

Categories of Benefits	Goals and Measures	
	Internal	**External**
Content/knowledge *(continued)*	*Sample measures:* Enable individuals to achieve and exceed personal performance goals; increase the speed and effectiveness of decision making; increase the ability of the organization to respond quickly and effectively to threats and opportunities	*Sample measures:* Provide information to customers, suppliers, and partners that enables better decision making; charge a price premium for products and services based on information value added; launch new information-based products and services; increase revenue per user and add new revenue streams
Community	Attract and retain top talent; increase satisfaction, engagement, and loyalty; create a culture of involvement, motivation, trust, and shared purpose	Attract and retain high-quality customers, suppliers, partners, and investors; increase external stakeholders' satisfaction, engagement, and loyalty
	Sample measures: Length of time to fill key positions; attrition rate, trends in hiring and retaining top talent (over time, by industry, by region)	*Sample measures:* Customer, supplier, partner satisfaction and lifetime value; average revenue per customer and trends over time; level of personalization available and percentage that use it; churn rate

Type I benefits arise from improvements in IT infrastructure, including computers, databases, and networks. Most large, established companies assembled their IT infrastructure in a piecemeal fashion over the last 20 to 30 years. They adopted new technologies as they became available and added them to their existing IT infrastructure without considering how the different technologies might need to work together in the future.

By the early 1990s, the IT infrastructure in most established companies had become a hodgepodge of incompatible and inefficient technologies that were costly and difficult to manage and maintain. At the same time, managers recognized that the ability to integrate these technologies had become a competitive necessity. These trends converged and stimulated the transition to the network era.

Today's networked technology infrastructures are built around open standards. They are more flexible and scalable, are easier to access and use, have significantly expanded reach, and yet cost less to run. These new infrastructures enable executives to shift IT investment priorities from a project-centered, one-time cost avoidance approach to an ongoing stream of investments in the development and exploitation of "reuseable information assets" that we call the "strategic option" value of IT.

With a flexible and robust IT networked platform in place, a company is poised to pursue the type II benefits that accrue when an organization exploits new IT-enabled business opportunities that take advantage of the infrastructure.

Commerce benefits are created when a company uses IT to improve its internal and external operations. Internally, a company can use IT to streamline, integrate, and synchronize key operating processes such as procurement, order fulfillment, and customer service. Then it can extend these IT-enabled processes to improve the efficiency and effectiveness of supply or distribution channels.

Content benefits are created when a company harnesses information and knowledge located inside or outside an organization to improve the performance of individuals and groups as they make decisions and take actions. The individuals and groups may belong to the same organization or may be customers, suppliers, or business partners. As well as helping people "work smarter," information and expertise can be used to create new products and services or to add value to existing ones, thus increasing the flow of revenues and improving a company's competitive position.

Community benefits are created when a company uses networked technologies to increase the commitment and loyalty of internal and external stakeholders. Inside the organization, e-mail, groupware, and intranets can be used to link employees around the world to information resources and expertise, improve the performance of virtual work teams, and create communities of interest. Outside the company, the same technologies can be used to establish a position at the center of an electronic market around which a "virtual community" of customers, suppliers, and business partners can grow.

The ideal IT project, at least to begin with, often streamlines highly leveraged, resource-intensive processes while layering in important components of reusable infrastructure to produce measurable results within a short period of time. These projects often have a clearly defined scope. As the project unfolds, however, astute managers must be on the lookout for follow-on projects that leverage reusable components of the infrastructure (e.g., databases, networks, processing power, user access devices) to increase the value of IT assets and enable a steady flow of value-creating IT-enabled business opportunities. Chapter 3 discusses the organizational capabilities required to exploit a robust and flexible networked IT infrastructure. Chapter 4 discusses the IT investment framework. Chapters 5 through 7 address the design, operation, and management of the networked IT infrastructure required to achieve these benefits.

Theme 5: Assimilation and Organizational Learning

Successful implementation of a new technology often requires that users learn new ways of interacting and working. When strategic technologies transform organizations and industries, the need for individuals to assimilate and learn how to use them to achieve the intended benefits extends throughout an organization to encompass

FIGURE I.5
Identifying and Assimilating IT

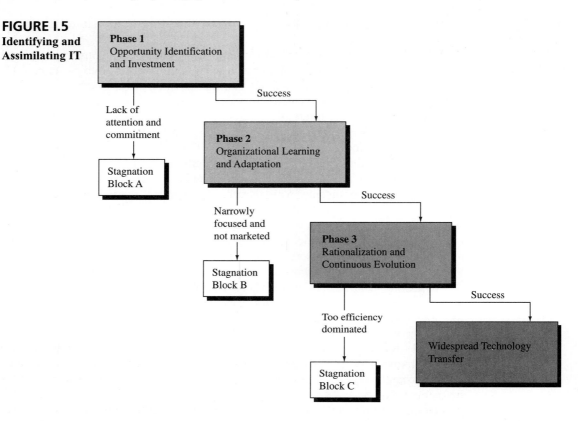

users within customer, supplier, and partner firms. To achieve the benefits of IT, users must adopt new mental models that frame decision making and behavior. Chris Argyris calls the process of organizational adaptation to new ideas, inventions, and technologies "double loop learning."[3] Jim Cash and Poppy McLeod apply this organizational learning theory to the technology innovation and diffusion process.[4] Three phases of the process are depicted in Figure I.5.

Phase 1. Opportunity Identification and Investment

This phase involves identifying an IT-enabled business opportunity and funding pilot projects. Often this requires "grassroots" experimentation by local business and IT professionals who are in the best position to identify the potential uses and benefits of the new technology. Because the implementation remains local, so does the risk. The challenge is to identify those technologies that show promise beyond the local level.

[3]C. Argyris, "Double-Loop Learning in Organizations," *Harvard Business Review,* September–October 1977.
[4]J. Cash, and P. McLeod, "Managing the Introduction of Information Technology in Strategically Dependent Companies," *Journal of Management of Information Systems* 1:5–23, 1985.

Phase 2. Organizational Learning and Adaptation

This phase occurs when stories of the success of grassroots efforts catch the attention of senior executives, who then fund broader levels of investment. Opportunities for follow-on investment often occur along two evolutionary paths. Technologies that have enabled streamlining and simplification of work often evolve into full-scale business process redesigns that will extend across organizational boundaries inside and outside the firm. As will be seen in later modules, this was a key approach used by Cisco. American Express followed an alternative evolutionary path as its grassroots experimentation efforts evolved into a new business unit, American Express Interactive, and several joint ventures.

Phase 3. Rationalization and Continuous Evolution

This phase occurs when a new technology becomes embedded within the core operations or strategy of the business. The challenge during this phase is to develop appropriate organizational structures and controls to ensure efficient widespread deployment and management while not stifling further experimentation and innovation. Chapters 3, 5, 7, and 10 address the assimilation of IT-enabled business opportunities.

Theme 6: Buy versus Make

During the mid-1980s and early 1990s, business professionals and executives at all levels in a firm adopted personal computers (PCs) and user-friendly personal software packages (e.g., word processing, spreadsheets). As the use of personal technologies increased, IT professionals were commonly asked: "If I can buy a word-processing package, why can't I buy an order fulfillment package?" During this same period, pressure to shed nonperforming assets and focus on core capabilities caused executives to ask a second question: "Do I really need to keep all these IT assets on my books? Can I outsource my data centers, networks, help desks, and PC support?" As standardized, modular, open-access networks and software became available during the late 1990s, a third question was asked: "Can I replace many of my off-the-shelf IT applications with subscriptions to IT services run by network and hosting services and ASPs?"

By the late 1990s, the preference of most executives had shifted from make to buy, rent, or subscribe. This significantly influenced how IT systems and assets were implemented, operated, and managed. In so doing, it also dramatically changed the role of IT professionals and executives. When strategic IT systems are outsourced, relationships with IT vendors and service providers must be managed as strategic alliances. Alignment of short-term and long-term goals and incentives becomes institutionalized within interorganizational structures such as executive governance boards, advisory boards, and cross-boundary liaison positions and operating teams. At times, shared equity in joint ventures helps align incentives and controls. At other times, short-term service-level agreements and contracts are combined with real-time online and face-to-face information sharing, coordination, and control. Given high levels of uncertainty and the rapid pace of technological and business change, the decision to enter into a long-term strategic relationship involves long periods of "due diligence," focusing on the intents, interests, capabilities, and viability of all the parties. Formal contracts contain provisions for joint planning processes that are designed to identify and address strategic uncertainties and for changing terms to deal with unforeseen opportunities and risks. Provisions for "death" and "divorce" become critical in outsourcing strategic IT system development or operation. More recently, the move toward standardized, modular, open access technology has been making it easier to change vendors, which is putting pressure on vendors to reduce the length of contracts and provide more favorable terms. Factors to consider as executives struggle with outsourcing decisions are presented in Table I.2.

Chapters 5 through 7 address the issues faced in outsourcing the 21st-century networked infrastructures and applications delivered by service providers. Chapter 9 examines the issues and challenges of outsourcing major segments of the IT function.

Theme 7: Partnership among Key Constituencies as IT Evolves

Much of the complexity of managing IT arises from the conflicting pressures of dealing with four different and vitally concerned stakeholder groups: business executives, IT executives, users, and IT vendors/partners. All may have conflicting goals, interests, and incentives. All use a different language to define opportunities, describe implementation approaches, and manage benefits and risks. The ability to align goals, incentives, and activities must begin with the development of a shared understanding and a shared language.

The task of business executives and users is to develop a working knowledge of the capabilities and management challenges of today's technology. They must understand how these technologies differ from past technologies and the expected timing and trajectory of their future evolution. Comfort with technology can come only when business executives become active players rather than delegating technology decisions to IT executives or vendors. An appropriate analogy is as follows: While many executives would not consider themselves finance professionals, they would never delegate all oversight and control of the financial performance of the organization to the chief financial office (CFO). Instead, they must be actively involved, questioning experts when they don't understand highly technical details until they have sufficient understanding to make informed business decisions.

Lou Gerstner, chief executive officer (CEO) and chairman of IBM, provides an excellent example of how a senior executive ensured that he had sufficient knowledge of IT to lead IBM successfully through a difficult transition. Upon assuming control of the company, Gerstner immediately asked that all senior executives be provided with the latest model of IBM PC, connected to the most sophisticated IBM network, utilizing state-of-the-art executive information-reporting and communication software. The firsthand view of the company's technology, from the perspective of an executive user, provided the senior executive team with important data that were used to evolve the company's products, services, and business strategy, which included the purchase of Lotus.

TABLE I.2 Factors to Consider in Make versus Buy Decisions

Decision Criteria	Pressure to Make/Own	Pressure to Buy/Rent/Subscribe
Business strategy	IT application or infrastructure provides proprietary competitive advantage.	IT application or infrastructure supports strategy or operations but is not considered strategic in its own right.
Core competencies	Business or IT knowledge/expertise required to develop or maintain an application is considered a core competency of the firm.	Business or IT knowledge/expertise required to build or maintain an IT application or infrastructure is not critical to the firm's success.
Information/process security and confidentiality	The information or processes contained within IT systems or databases are considered highly confidential.	Failure of routine security and confidentiality measures, while problematic, would not cause serious problems.
Availability of suitable partners	There are no reliable, competent, and/or motivated partners that could assume responsibility for the IT application or infrastructure.	Reliable, competent, and appropriately motivated vendors (or other partners) are available.
Availability of packaged software or solutions	The IT application or infrastructure required by the firm is unique.	Packaged software or solutions are available that would meet the majority of business requirements.
Cost-benefit analysis	The cost of purchasing the product or service and/or coordinating and controlling interorganizational relationships and operations is greater than the cost of performing the service in-house.	The cost of purchasing and managing the service is significantly lower than the cost of performing the service in-house.
Time frame for implementation	There is sufficient time available to develop internal resources and skills, implement the IT application, and/or develop the IT infrastructure required by the firm.	The time required to develop internal resources and expertise and/or to implement the IT application or infrastructure project exceeds the organization's demand for the product or service.
Evolution and complexity of the technology	The firm is able to attract, retain, and develop the range of IT experts needed to implement IT applications and infrastructures at a reasonable cost.	The firm is unable to keep pace with the rapidly changing and increasingly complex technologies required.
Ease of implementation	Software development tools that provide rapid IT application development are available.	Tools to support rapid application development are not available or are viewed as insufficient or ineffective.

FIGURE I.6
Three Eras of IT Evolution

	Administrative Framework	Target for IT Use	Justification/Benefits
Era I Mainframe	Regulated monopoly	Back-office automation	Organizational productivity
Era II Microcomputer	Free market	Individual decision making and productivity	Individual effectiveness
Era III Internetworking	Shared partnership	Electronic integration and learning	Business advantage

Many IT executives, having progressed through the ranks over the last several decades, have faced the same steep learning curve as their business counterparts. As they moved higher in the organization, IT executives often lost touch with the latest technologies. Adherence to outdated mind-sets blinded them to the potential opportunities and risks presented by emerging technologies and at times delayed dialogues with new IT partners. Figure I.6 provides an overview of the three eras of technology evolution and the 'mind-sets' that accompany each one. At the time of this book, IT executives in many large, established firms needed to simultaneously manage IT resources and relationships within all three eras.

Chapters 5, 7, 8, and 9 focus on the challenges of creating and managing partnerships among multiple constituencies within evolving IT paradigms.

Theme 8: Protecting IT Assets and Managing Risks

In the age of the Internet and broadband, customers expect "always on" service performance. Fully capturing the economic advantages of new technologies requires "always up," reliable, secure IT infrastructures. Open access networks such as the Internet dramatically increase our ability to share information, communicate, and transact business. They also dramatically increase the risk of doing business online. These risks include accidents as well as sophisticated and malicious cyberterrorism and attacks.

Success in embedding IT in core operations has brought with it a host of new and challenging issues. For a number of firms, an interruption of service means immediate and significant economic loss. When e-Bay's systems failed three times in 2000, in each case for a period of six or more hours, the company's plight made the front page of *The Wall Street Journal*. Within hours, the stock price began to drop and the company's market value declined.

Just like electricity, we now expect and demand that network and information services be available 24 hours per day, 7 days per week. Once we design our lives and work around technology, we can no longer tolerate even short failures. Chapters 6 and 10 address issues of security, reliability, privacy, and risk management.

Theme 9: Pervasive Computing: Opportunities and Risks

Not long ago it was rare that anyone but technology specialists ever bothered to use IT. While some futurists envisioned a world where IT devices and networks would become commonplace in the home, in schools, and in offices around the world, most never gave IT technology a thought. The widespread belief was that IT was for those who crunched data or crunched numbers. Executives might receive reports generated by IT systems or enter data into them, but the majority of us never thought that IT would dramatically influence our lives.

As we enter the 21st century, that picture has changed. By year end 2001, over 350 million people around the world were connected to the Internet and in the United States people spent more on personal computers than they did on televisions, a ubiquitous household appliance.[5] Teenagers in Japan conversed regularly on i-mode phones that enabled them to stay in touch and stay connected to friends and online acquaintances anytime, anywhere, and anyplace. Advertisers and retail store owners found that this geographic connectivity enabled the delivery of targeted promotions designed to draw those most likely to purchase into nearby stores. Executives found that they could carry PCs and Internet-enabled personal digital assistants (PDAs) with them and connect to information and people on airplanes, in hotels, and during the morning and evening commute. Truly, IT had become both mobile and pervasive.

The next 10 years promise to bring equally profound changes. Indeed, predicting what the future user interface will be is difficult. Some see a "television-like" device that will connect to a broadband network that integrates voice, video, data, and services to enable individuals to access vast stores of information, entertainment, and e-commerce/communication services. Others see the evolution of cell phones, pagers, and network devices in cars, airplanes, and trains that will render us constantly online and constantly in touch in an increasingly boundaryless world. Whether we will find ubiquitous technology helpful or intrusive in our daily lives remains to be seen; we expect it will be both. These issues are discussed in Chapters 5 through 7.

Summary

In combination, these themes create a very complex and challenging managerial environment. They form the backdrop for the discussions of specific frameworks and managerial approaches in the succeeding chapters of this book (see Table I.3). Below are questions that senior executives can ask to assess the health of their IT activity.

---

[5] Statistics on worldwide Internet penetration are available from Jupiter Research Center (www.jup.com).

TABLE I.3 Summary of Key Themes

	Market Structure and Industry Dynamics	Evolving Business Models	IT Impact	Prioritizing IT Investments	Assimilation and Organizational Learning	Buy versus Make	Partnership among Key Constituencies as IT Evolves	Protecting IT Assets and Managing Risks	Pervasive Computing: Opportunities and Risks
Chapter 1: Creating Business Advantage with IT	✓		✓						
Chapter 2: Crafting Business Models	✓	✓	✓						
Chapter 3: Building Networked Businesses	✓		✓	✓	✓				
Chapter 4: Making the Case for Digital Business			✓	✓					
Chapter 5: Understanding Internetworking Infrastructure			✓	✓	✓	✓	✓		✓
Chapter 6: Assuring Reliable and Secure IT Services			✓	✓		✓		✓	✓
Chapter 7: Managing Diverse IT Infrastructures	✓	✓	✓	✓	✓	✓	✓		✓
Chapter 8: Managing and Leading the IT Organization			✓				✓		
Chapter 9: Managing IT Outsourcing			✓		✓	✓	✓	✓	
Chapter 10: A Portfolio Approach to IT Projects			✓						

1. How important is IT to our success and survival? Are we missing opportunities that, if properly executed, would give us a sustainable advantage?
2. Are we prioritizing IT investments and targeting our development efforts in the right areas? Are we spending money efficiently and effectively?
3. Are we managing IT assets and infrastructure efficiently and effectively? Is leadership of the wide range of IT activities at the right level, given the goals for its use? Are we organized to identify, evaluate, and assimilate emerging technologies on a timely basis?
4. Is our IT infrastructure sufficiently insulated against the risks of a major operational disaster? Are the appropriate security, privacy, and risk management systems in place to ensure "always on" and "always up" service?
5. Are IT and business leaders capable of defining and executing IT-enabled strategies? Have we opened an effective dialogue among business executives, IT executives, users, and partners?

We hope you enjoy the book and find it useful as you attempt to leverage the opportunities and address the challenges of managing in a network economy.

Appendix A

Analyzing the Strategic Impact of IT

The "strategic grid" depicted in Figure I.4 and discussed under Theme 3 defines four categories of IT impact. These four categories help frame the approach used to identify opportunities, define and implement IT-enabled business initiatives, and organize and manage IT assets and professionals. Examples of firms operating in each of the four categories are discussed in this Appendix.

Support

Until recently, the impact of IT on the core operations and strategy of most professional services firms (e.g., law firms and consulting firms) was quite small. For example, despite a consulting company spending $30 million in the early 1990s to equip each of its 2,000 consultants with laptop computers, consultants in the firm were able to continue serving the needs of their clients during a major IT failure that lasted over 24 hours. In addition, IT had little impact on the

firm's strategy. By the late 1990s, this picture had changed. The same consulting firm had begun to use IT to provide consulting advice to its global customers. Consulting reports were advertised and sold on Amazon.com. Clearly, IT had moved from the back office to the front office, offering new channels to previously untapped markets and generating new revenue streams. These new IT initiatives shifted the impact of IT within this consulting firm toward the Turnaround quadrant on the strategic grid.

Turnaround

As seen in the consulting firm example, while some firms do not depend on uninterrupted, highly reliable IT service to ensure strategic success, new IT projects can cause a firm to move from the Support to the Turnaround quadrant of the strategic grid. A rapidly growing manufacturing firm provides a good example.

Until the mid-1990s, the IT used in this mid-size company, although important, was not absolutely vital to the firm's success and survival. In the late 1990s, however, the company began the development of a new IT system that would coordinate all aspects of the firm's operations, including how supplies were ordered, products were manufactured and sold, orders were fulfilled, and customers were served. The new system was required to enable executives and local business managers to gain control of the company's operations as it launched new products and rapidly expanded into multiple international locations. Another new IT application enabled the company to centralize key customer data and integrate those data with production scheduling information from over 60 plants and two customer service call centers. These new applications enabled the firm to improve service dramatically, lower administrative costs sharply, and decrease the cost of operations significantly.

With the launch of these new projects, the company entered the Turnaround quadrant of the strategic grid. As it did this, the approach to running the IT function changed. A senior business unit executive was appointed to head the IT function, and involvement in IT planning by the firm's executive committee increased substantially. Once implemented, the new IT-enabled operations became critical to the firm's success, shifting the focus from the Turnaround to the Factory quadrant.

Factory

By the 1990s, a growing number of firms had invested in IT to ensure cost-effective, totally reliable operations. Even minutes of system downtime caused major organizational disruption that in turn generated customer dissatisfaction and significant financial problems.

The CEO of an investment bank, for example, became fully aware of the high level of operational dependence of his firm on IT when a flood above the data center brought all securities trading to a halt. Failure to ensure the presence of an off-site redundant data center crippled the bank's trading operations and caused massive financial losses. Needless to say, the CEO developed a new appreciation for the importance of IT in running critical areas of business operations, and a redundant data center was constructed shortly after the incident. The devastation caused at the World Trade Center on September 11, 2001, and the subsequent IT-enabled operating challenges faced by many financial services firms brought global attention to the importance of IT security, reliability, and availability for organizational success and survival.

Strategic

As we enter the 21st century, most executives recognize that IT is an essential component of current and future strategy and operations. Going forward, banks, insurance companies, auto manufacturers, and major retail chains have embedded IT in their core operations and core strategy. Within strategically IT-dependent firms, IT executives are members of the executive committee.

Building the Network Economy: Markets and Models

by Lynda M. Applegate

Today's Internet technologies build upon and revolutionize computing and communication platforms introduced decades earlier. As we enter the 21st century, we are experiencing an intense period of technology-enabled innovation, creativity, and excitement that has been spurred by the commercialization of several core technologies and associated changes in work and society. Exploiting these opportunities while avoiding the pitfalls requires vision, sound execution, and the ability to respond quickly. It also requires imagination—and a little luck.

The chapters in this module enable discussion of the approaches executives use, the decisions they make, and the issues they face as they build businesses for a Network Economy. The focus of the module is on understanding the impact of IT on industries and markets. It discusses issues of strategic positioning and how 21st-century IT provides opportunities to alter market/industry structure, power, and relationships.

Chapter

1

Chapter

Creating Business Advantage with IT[1]

As the century closed, the world became smaller. The public rapidly gained access to new and dramatically faster communication technologies. Entrepreneurs, able to draw on unprecedented scale economies, built vast empires. Great fortunes were made. . . Every day brought forth new technological advances to which old business models seemed no longer to apply. . . . A prophecy for the 21st century? No. You have just read a description of what happened one hundred years ago when the 20th century industrial giants emerged.[2]

As this quote implies, new technologies sometimes can catch us off guard. In fact, when Rutherford B. Hayes, the 19th president of the United States, saw a demonstration of the telephone in the late 1800s, he reportedly commented that while it was a wonderful invention, businessmen would never use it. Hayes believed that people had to meet face to face to conduct substantive business affairs, and he was not alone in that assessment.

Few of Hayes's contemporaries could foresee the profound changes that would be ushered in by the telephone and other technologies of the day, including steam engines and production machinery; railroads, automobiles, and other transportation technologies; and communication technologies such as the telegraph and telephone (see Figure 1.1). The exodus of people from rural to urban areas, the shift

[1]This chapter is adapted from papers and materials for Professor Applegate's course, Building Business in a Network Economy. The chapter draws on earlier work by Professor F. Warren McFarlan and James L. McKenney, which is summarized in F. W. McFarlan, J. L. McKenney, and P. Pyburn, "Information Archipelago: Plotting a Course," *Harvard Business Review,* January 1983.
[2]C. Shapiro and H. Varian, *Information Rules: A Strategic Guide to the Network Economy* (Boston: HBS Press, 1998).

FIGURE 1.1
The Impact of Technology on Business and Society during the Industrial Revolution

Source: Reprinted with permission from Duke University Rare Book, Manuscript, and Special Collections Library.

from craft-based work to mass production, and the decline of small, owner-operated firms in favor of large, vertically integrated multinationals—these transitions marked the shift from an agricultural to an industrial economy. In fact, while technological innovation served as one of many stimuli to change, it was the confluence of technological, business, and social changes that enabled passage from the agricultural era to the industrial era.

In retrospect, these changes were revolutionary, but they evolved incrementally through periods of evolution punctuated by intense periods of revolution.[3] Similarly, the shift from an industrial economy to an information economy began with a period of intense technological innovation during the 1940s, 1950s, and 1960s that built upon, yet significantly altered, the technologies of the industrial revolution.[4] Today's Internet technologies both build upon and revolutionize computing and communication platforms introduced decades earlier. For example, the Internet servers that power Network Economy businesses evolved from early mainframe computers and microprocessors that were commercialized in the mid-1950s and the 1960s. In addition, the new computing and communication devices used to access the Internet to shop, pay bills, trade stocks, do business, and communicate with others around the

---

[3]C. Gersick, "Revolutionary Change Theories: A Multilevel Exploration of Punctuated Equilibrium Paradigm," *Academy of Management Review,* 16:10–36, 1991 and L. M. Applegate, "In Search of a New Organizational Model," *Shaping Organization Form* ed. DeSanctis and Fulk (Sage Publications, 1999).
[4]Interestingly today's sophisticated computers actually trace their roots to the mechanical tabulating machines and typewriters that heralded the start of the industrial revolution during the 1800s.

FIGURE 1.2
Technology,
Business, and
Societal
Evolution
during the 20th
Century

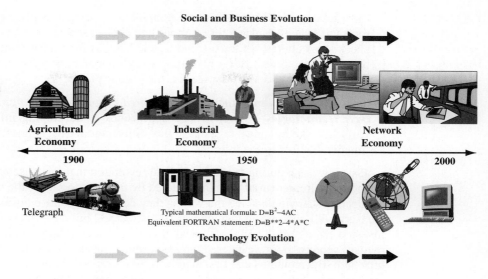

world evolved from personal computers and cell phones introduced in the 1970s and
1980s (see Figure 1.2).

As we enter the 21st century, we are once again experiencing an intense period of
technology-enabled innovation, creativity, and excitement that has been spurred by
the commercialization of several core technologies and associated changes in work
and society. The technological changes include the following:

- The *Internet* and *broadband networks*—low-cost, standardized, global alternatives to the expensive, specialized, and proprietary communication platforms of
  the 1970s and 1980s. These technologies enable the transmission of multimedia
  digital information on a common communication channel.

- The *World Wide Web (WWW)* and *high-performance servers*—flexible, standardized, powerful platforms for creating and storing information in all its many
  forms (for example, text, data, voice, and video) on high-performance computers
  that can be located anywhere in the world.

- The *Uniform Resource Locator (URL)* and *browser*—common approaches for
  identifying and locating information anywhere on the Internet and easy-to-use
  tools for accessing, packaging, and displaying multimedia information.

- *Multimedia digital devices*—portable Internet access devices that provide a single point of entry to voice, television, and information. Today's new devices include laptop computers, palm pilots, interactive television set-top boxes, and
  game consoles.

- *Wireless networks* and *protocols*—the technology and supporting business infrastructure to enable access to the Internet, untethered by physical wires. While initially limited by a lack of common standards, performance, and useful applications,

this "go anywhere" form of access is rapidly becoming a reality, especially in Europe and Asia. In Finland, for example, cell phone users can send e-mail, pay bills, check stock quotes, get traffic reports, and buy gas from a gas pump or buy a cup of espresso at a local café—all through a cell phone or wireless device. In Japan, the hottest new accessory for teens is the i-mode phone.

- *Java, Jini, XML,* and other *object-oriented programming language and database technologies*—powerful new approaches to developing information systems that take full advantage of the flexibility, modularity, connectivity, and multimedia features of the Internet.

Just as we saw during the technological revolution that gave rise to the Industrial Economy, entrepreneurial firms, unfettered by the need to satisfy the expectations of entrenched shareholders, led the way as they defined innovative business models for the Network Economy. In fact, during 1999, over $32 billion—90 percent of the total invested by venture capitalists—was invested in technology (including Internet-related) ventures.[5] As we entered the 21st century, investor confidence had hit an all-time high. But as annual and first quarter earnings reports for newly public "dot-com" businesses hit the streets, momentum buying was replaced by momentum selling and stock prices plummeted.[6] Venture capital investments in business-to-consumer (B2C) e-commerce, which had garnered 40 to 50 percent of private equity dollars during 1999,[7] declined to less than 3 percent of venture investments by the second quarter of 2000.[8] E-commerce companies that only months earlier had been awarded valuations in excess of $1 billion went out of business in record numbers. In fact, over 780 Internet firms went out of business between January 2000 and January 2002.[9]

While most were slow to get started, by 2001 established firms began to take advantage of the decreased strength of new entrants and take a lead role in defining the Network Economy for the 21st century. Pioneering high-tech firms such as Cisco, IBM, Microsoft, and Intuit and established players in non-high-tech industries such as General Electric, Charles Schwab, American Express, and Ford aggressively pursued Internet business initiatives, often building on online business foundations that had begun decades earlier. Non-U.S. firms (such as France Telecom, Vivendi Uni-

[5]M. Mowrey, "Financial Spotlight: Inside the Dot-Com VC Billions," *The Standard* (www.thestandard.com), February 21, 2000. This study reports the findings of three venture capital studies conducted by Price Waterhouse (www.pwcglobal.com), Venture Economics (www.ventureeconomics.com), and Venture One (www.ventureone.com).
[6]"NASDAQ's Near Meltdown," *The Standard* (www.thestandard.com), April 4, 2000; J. Boudreau, "New Economy Reality Check," *SiliconValley.com* (www.sjmercury.com/svtech/news/indepth), April 16, 2000; S. Lorh, "Stocks' Slide May Spark Dot-Com Shakeout," *New York Times on the Web,* (www.nytimes.com), April 17, 2000; P. Wallace, "The Dog Days of E-Commerce," *The Standard* (www.thestandard.com), June 1, 2000.
[7]Mowrey, op cit.
[8]P. Bonanos, "Net VC: Past Its Prime?" *The Standard* (www.thestandard.com), August 28, 2000.
[9]See Webmergers.com (www.webmergers.com) for a detailed report of dot-com mergers, acquisitions, and failures. The data presented here were collected on April 4, 2002.

versal, and Bertelsmann in Europe; Li & Fung, Cosco, and PSA in Asia; and Telefonica and UOL in Latin America, to name just a few) were also actively creating the global Network Economy.

This chapter draws on over two decades of research on the impact of information technology (IT) on industries, markets, and the organizations that operate within them. It examines the forces that shape strategic decision making in the 21st century and presents frameworks to analyze the impact of the Internet and associated technologies on competitive and market forces.

Forces That Shape Business Strategy

Companies that have deployed Internet technology have been confused by distorted market signals, often of their own creation. It is understandable, when confronted with a new business phenomenon, to look to marketplace outcomes for guidance. But in the early stages of the rollout of any important new technology, market signals can be unreliable. New technologies trigger rampant experimentation, by companies and their customers, and the experimentation is often economically unsustainable. As a result, market behavior is distorted and must be interpreted with caution.[10]

When the business environment is stable, strategic decision making is like a game of chess. One player studies an opponent's moves and then makes countermoves. During periods of business innovation, however, a competitor's moves may not necessarily reflect rational and reasonable business thinking. It then becomes necessary to return to the fundamental analyses of the forces that shape strategy.

In this section, we present three frameworks that can be used to guide analysis of the impact of IT on strategy. Michael Porter's "value chain" and "industry and competitive analysis" (ICA) frameworks, although not originally developed to examine the impact of the Internet and IT on strategic decision making, have proved very useful in this regard.[11,12] The third framework, Warren McFarlan's strategic grid (also discussed in the Introduction to this book), is a tool for characterizing the roles the Internet and IT may play in specific firms and industries and for deriving appropriate IT-related strategies and management practices.

Value Chain Analysis

For decades, the value chain framework (see Figure 1.3) has been a powerful tool for identifying and analyzing the stream of activities through which products and services are created and delivered to customers. Once activities are defined, it becomes

---

[10]M. Porter, "Strategy and the Internet," *Harvard Business Review,* March 2001.
[11]M. Porter, *Competitive Advantage: Creating and Sustaining Performance* (New York: Free Press, 1985). See Porter, op cit., for a value chain analysis of Internet opportunities.
[12]Early pioneering work on the use of Porter's frameworks for analyzing the impact of IT on industries, markets, and firm strategies was conducted by Professors Jim Cash, Warren McFarlan, Jim McKenney, and Mike Vitale. The work was summarized in: J. I. Cash, F. W. McFarlan, and J. L. McKenney, *Corporate Information Systems Management: The Issues Facing Senior Executives,* 3rd ed. (New York: McGraw Hill-Irwin, 1988).

FIGURE 1.3
The Value Chain

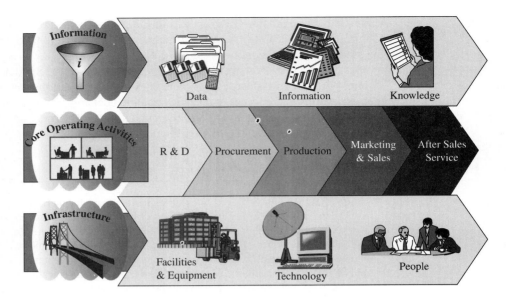

possible to analyze the economics at each step in the chain by identifying both the costs incurred and the value created. These activities can be located inside a firm or across firm boundaries. In the latter case, activities may involve customers, suppliers, partners, or other stakeholders. Accompanying the physical value chain is a related information value chain through which the involved parties coordinate and control activities.

Participants within a business market assume one or more of four primary roles to carry out these value-creating activities (see Figure 1.4). The point within a value chain where maximum economies of scale and scope are created determines market power. *Economies of scale* are achieved when a market participant or a network of participants is able to leverage capabilities and infrastructure to increase its revenues and profitability within a single product line or market. *Economies of scope* are achieved when a market participant or a network of participants is able to leverage capabilities and infrastructure to launch new product lines or businesses or enter new markets.

Industrial Economy business innovations favored producers. The innovations included physical/analog production and distribution technologies (machines, railroads, steam engines, telephones), an operating model (the assembly line, marketing, sales, and after-sales service channels), a management model (the hierarchy), and a social/regulatory system (specialized work, pay-for-performance incentives, worker education, unions, antitrust laws).

As we enter the 21st century, Network Economy pioneers such as eBay, covisint, and AOL Time Warner are defining new business models that are reshaping the global business landscape and redefining power. Once again, emerging models exploit the power of technological, business, and social innovations within a regulatory and policy framework that emerges over time.

Creating Business Advantage with IT

FIGURE 1.4
Market Roles

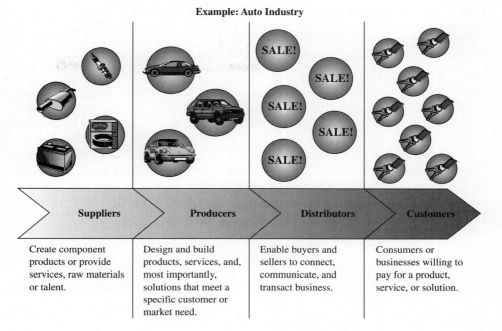

Example: Auto Industry

Suppliers	Producers	Distributors	Customers
Create component products or provide services, raw materials or talent.	Design and build products, services, and, most importantly, solutions that meet a specific customer or market need.	Enable buyers and sellers to connect, communicate, and transact business.	Consumers or businesses willing to pay for a product, service, or solution.

Network Economy business innovations include digital production and distribution technologies (broadband and wireless networks, multimedia content creation, flexible/real-time knowledge access and management), a networked operating model (integrated supply chains and buy chains), a networked management model (teams, partnerships, consortia), and social/regulatory systems (ownership incentives, freelancing, virtual work, distance learning, digital copyright laws).

Although Industrial Economy markets and power bases were built on proprietary infrastructure, participants in Network Economy markets leverage a shared *digital business infrastructure* to enable new entrants and established firms to create and exploit network economies of scale and scope. *Network economies of scale* are achieved when a "community" of firms shares its infrastructure, capabilities, and customer base to produce and distribute products faster, better, and cheaper than competitors can. *Network economies of scope* are achieved when the community uses its shared infrastructure to produce and distribute new products and services, enter new markets, or launch new businesses more quickly, at less cost, and more successfully than competitors can.

As we will see later in this section, the interorganizational IT systems of the 1980s and early 1990s (e.g., American Airlines' Sabre reservation system and American Hospital Supply Corporation's ASAP system) foreshadowed how network economics could create value. Because they were built using proprietary technologies, access, reach, and flexibility were limited. Table 1.1 compares Industrial Economy and Network Economy models.

TABLE 1.1 **Comparison of the Industrial Economy and Network Economy**

Characteristics	Industrial Economy	Network Economy
Criteria for economic success	Internal, proprietary, and specialized economies of scale and scope; economies of scope are limited by the level of infrastructure specialization required	External, networked, and shared economies of scale and scope; economies of scale and scope are increased dramatically by the ability to build new businesses on the nonproprietary, flexible, shared, and ubiquitous Internet infrastructure
Technological innovations	Production, communication, and distribution technologies	Distribution, communication, and information technologies; the ability to "assemble" component pieces
Operating innovations	Standardization of work; job specialization; assembly line operations; value chain industry structure	Knowledge work; job expansion; work teams (face to face and virtual); extended enterprise; outsourcing and partnerships; value networks
Management innovations	Hierarchical coordination and supervision; compliance-based control; pay-for-performance incentives; centralized planning and control	Networked coordinating and supervision; ownership incentives; information-based ("learning") models of control; distributed planning and control
Societal/regulatory innovations	Urban growth; mass transportation; social security and welfare; unions, federal regulations; domestic economy	Work at home; self-employment; personal pension and savings programs; global economy
Length of time to achieve economies of scale and scope	Decades	Uncertain
Dominant industry power	Producers	Solution assemblers and channel managers

Industry and Competitive Analysis

Porter's ICA framework postulates that economic and competitive forces in an industry are the result of five basic forces: (1) bargaining power of suppliers, (2) bargaining power of buyers, (3) threat of new entrants, (4) threat of substitute products or services, and (5) competitive intensity and positioning among traditional business rivals. Figure 1.5 presents the ICA framework.

Porter describes three *generic strategies* for achieving proprietary advantage within an industry: cost leadership, differentiation, and focus. Each generic strategy embodies two key choices: (1) Should we lower cost or differentiate our products

FIGURE 1.5
Forces
Influencing
Industry and
Competitive
Advantage

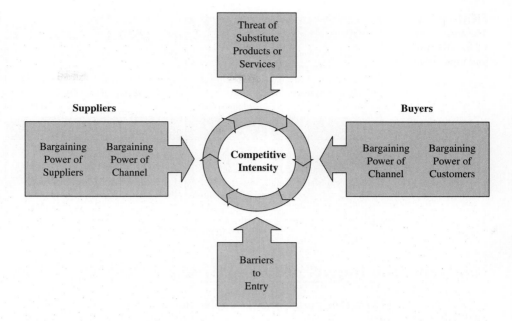

and services (this is known as the "competitive mechanism"); and (2) Should we target a broad market or a narrow one (this is known as "competitive scope")? Specific actions required to implement each generic strategy vary widely from industry to industry, as do feasible generic strategies within a particular industry. Selecting and implementing the appropriate strategy are central to achieving long-term competitive advantage in an industry.

Strategic Grid Analysis

The value chain and industry competitive analyses discussed above help frame strategic decision making along the two dimensions depicted on McFarlan's strategic grid in Figure 1.6.

Along the vertical axis, executives assess the impact of IT on operations. As was discussed in the Introduction of this book, for some organizations, the second-by-second, utterly reliable, precision execution of IT operations is crucial to survival. Even small interruptions in service or disruptions in quality have a profound impact. For other organizations, it would take a significant disturbance in IT operations over an extended period to have a major impact on an organization's ability to execute.

Along the horizontal axis of the strategic grid, executives assess the strategic impact of IT on market forces that influence future sustainable business advantage. For some organizations, IT-enabled business initiatives are critical to future strategic positioning. For others, new IT applications provide local improvements but do not affect business strategy.

FIGURE 1.6
The Impact of
IT on Strategy
and Operations

	Factory	**Strategic**
High	Goal: Improve performance of core processes Leadership: Business unit executives Project Management: Process reengineering	Goal: Transform organization or industry Leadership: Senior executives & board Project Management: Change management
	Support	**Turnaround**
Low	Goal: Improve local performance Leadership: Local level oversight Project Management: Grassroots experimentation	Goal: Identify and launch new ventures Leadership: Venture incubation unit Project Management: New venture development

IT Impact on Core Operations (vertical axis)

IT Impact on Core Strategy (Low ... High)

Analyzing the Impact of IT on Strategic Decision Making

Plotting the portfolio of IT applications and their impact within the strategic grid enables executives to choose the appropriate approach to organizing and managing IT-enabled business activities. Five key questions can be used to guide strategic decision making when one is evaluating the impact of networked IT on core operations and core strategy.

- Can IT be used to reengineer core value activities and change the basis of competition?

- Can IT change the nature of relationships and the balance of power among buyers and suppliers?

- Can IT build or reduce barriers to entry?

- Can IT increase or decrease switching costs?

- Can IT add value to existing products and services or create new ones?

Can IT Be Used to Reengineer Core Value Activities and Change the Basis of Competition?

At their core, IT systems are used to automate activities whether those activities take place inside an organization or across its boundaries. In the 1950s and 1960s, when IT was first introduced for commercial use, the primary target of IT applications was to automate routine, information-intensive "back-office" transactions such as payroll processing, accounting, and general ledger postings. The primary goal was to increase efficiency and productivity.

Businesses quickly learned to apply those benefits to "front-office" activities that involved transactions with suppliers, distributors, customers, and other value chain participants. In fact, benefits increased dramatically when businesses used IT not just to *automate* but also to *transform* and *inform*. A streamlined and integrated value chain helped businesses eliminate redundancies, reduce cycle times, and achieve even greater efficiency and productivity. Information, a by-product of automation, also enabled executives, employees, partners, and other stakeholders to better understand fast-cycled operations. Moreover, real-time information could be used to improve coordination and control, personalize products and services, add value to—and differentiate—existing products and services, and create IT-enabled products and services that would attract new market participants and generate new revenue streams.

American Hospital Supply Corporation (AHSC) and American Airlines (AA) are two early examples of using IT to reengineer value activities and transform the basis of competition.[13] The story began during the late 1960s when an entrepreneurial sales manager at AHSC created a system that enabled hospital purchasing clerks to order supplies over telephone lines by using punch cards and primitive card-reading computers. At about the same time, enterprising sales managers at AA were paving new ground by giving large travel agencies computer terminals that allowed them to check airline schedules posted within American's internal reservation systems. Indeed, from these entrepreneurial actions grew two legendary strategic IT applications that changed the basis of competition in their respective industries.

Both AHSC and AA built their strategic systems upon internal systems that originally were designed to automate back-office transaction processing. AHSC, for example, first installed computers to manage internal inventory and order processing activities; AA used computers to manage its internal reservation process. In both cases, the value of these early systems came from the ability to structure, simplify, and unify internal operations. But once they had simplified and structured activities inside the firm, both AHSC and AA recognized that they could allow customers to "self-serve" without fear of reducing quality. Because each firm had built its system with proprietary technology, AHSC and AA owned the platform on which business was conducted, and they also owned the information flowing from the automated transaction systems. This information enabled executives and front-line workers in both firms to coordinate and control activities whether those activities took place inside or outside the firm. By harnessing the power of the information, both firms were able to differentiate existing services and offer new information-based services.

The benefits of conducting business online were so great that AHSC gave hospitals the card readers required to do business electronically and taught hospital supply clerks how to use them.[14] AHSC even helped hospital personnel redesign their internal purchasing processes to fit the new online process. AA did the same thing when it gave travel agents the computer reservation system terminals. Neither AHSC

[13]See J. L. McKenney and D. G. Copeland, *Waves of Change* (Boston: HBS Press, 1995), and L. M. Applegate, "Electronic Commerce," in *The Technology Management Handbook,* ed. Richard C. Dorf (CRC Press, 1999), for an in-depth discussion of the evolution of early strategic systems.
[14]By 1985, AHSC saved over $11 million per year through online ordering and generated $4 million to $5 million per year in additional revenue.

nor AA charged its customers for the computer equipment or the training. Why? The benefits of self-service more than offset the cost of giving away the terminals.

The AHSC and AA examples demonstrate how two firms used IT to fundamentally alter the basis of competition in their respective industries. This occurred when executives implemented strategies that radically changed the cost structure for the industry and at the same time differentiated the product/service offering, causing massive shifts in market share and demand.

As we enter the 21st century, Internet pioneers are using today's technological innovations to reengineer value chains and fundamentally change the basis of competition. Charles Schwab provides an example of how a firm built upon existing capabilities and technology infrastructure to radically transform the financial services industry. Founded in 1975, Schwab accomplished this feat not once but twice. Initially Schwab executives placed a bet that a growing number of individual investors would prefer to save money and time by using low-cost local branch office brokerage services rather than high-priced personal brokers. They were correct, and by 1997 revenues for Schwab's discount brokerage business had reached $2.3 billion. The industry was forced to adjust its practices in reaction to this new entrant, although full-service brokerages remained strong.

When the commercial Internet appeared in the mid-1990s, Schwab was poised to segment the market again. Routine customer service requests (quotes, balances, positions) already had migrated from Schwab branches to the telephone and a proprietary online service. By the time Schwab rolled out its Internet online brokerage capabilities in January 1998, only 5 percent of routine customer service was handled at a brokerage office. The Web-based service provided access to online and offline brokerage services for a single fee of $29.95 per trade (compared to an average of $80 per trade for full-service brokerage commissions). Within less than a year, sales were up 19 percent, and since the online self-service business lowered costs dramatically, profits were up 29 percent.

Full-service brokers such as Merrill Lynch were initially skeptical. But as the market penetration (and market value) of Charles Schwab soared, even the most stalwart critics were forced to launch their own online/offline integrated channels.

Can IT Change the Nature of Relationships and the Balance of Power among Buyers and Suppliers?

As was mentioned earlier, AHSC rose to power within the hospital supplies industry by streamlining channels, dramatically decreasing cost, improving order accuracy, and increasing speed of fulfillment between suppliers (for example, Johnson & Johnson, Baxter, and Abbott) and hospital buyers. Initially, AHSC used traditional offline processes to buy supplies from manufacturers and store them in AHSC-owned warehouses. But once it succeeded in getting a large number of customers to buy online, AHSC sought to streamline the supply chain further. Sensing that they were at risk of being excluded from the market and lacking the money, expertise, and time to respond, suppliers succumbed to the pressure to put their catalogs online and join the electronic market. Once electronic links to suppliers had been established, AHSC customers could order directly from supplier inventory. This enabled further reductions in cost and cycle time for all the members of the online market.

Customers encouraged channel consolidation. They recognized the value of a multivendor marketplace but were unwilling to put up with the problems of using multiple different supplier systems to conduct business. Within a short time, AHSC became a powerful channel manager within the hospital supply industry, controlling both the physical and information channels for conducting business. In fact, this neutral, third-party distributor created such a significant shift in the balance of power away from hospital suppliers that in 1985 it was bought by Baxter Healthcare Corporation, a hospital supplier in the industry. A few years later, responding to pressure from market participants, Baxter was forced to spin out the distribution business it had purchased.

Initially, many believed that the Internet might similarly shift power from producers (manufacturers and service providers) to channel players (wholesalers, distributors, and retailers). Indeed, during the late 1990s, Internet-based channel players flourished, especially within fragmented markets and industries. Chemdex, for example, attracted much attention (and investment) by establishing a neutral, third-party virtual marketplace for the life sciences industry.[15] Likewise, software services firms such as CommerceOne, Oracle, and Ariba developed and operated electronic marketplaces that linked buyers and suppliers across multiple industries. By mid-2000, however, many independent marketplaces, such as Chemdex, were struggling or had closed, and software services firms were suffering from weakened demand. As neutral, independent channel players faltered, established players, including both suppliers and buyers, exploited the shared Internet online business infrastructure to launch initiatives to defend their respective positions. Once again, the health-care industry provided an excellent view into these shifting power dynamics.

In March 2000, five of the largest health-care suppliers—Abbott, Baxter, GE Medical, Johnson & Johnson, and Medtronic—launched the Global Healthcare Exchange, LLC (GHX).[16] GHX promised to eliminate inefficiencies in every step in

---

[15]Chemdex was launched in November 1998 to serve as an independent marketplace through which buyers and suppliers in the life sciences business could conduct business. In March 2000, the founders of Chemdex created a new corporate parent, Ventro, with the goal of creating multiple marketplaces. By late 2000, Chemdex had been forced to shut down and Ventro was struggling. See M. Collura and L. M. Applegate, *Ventro Corporation: Builder of B2B Businesses* (HBS Publishing) (Order No. 801–042).

[16]In addition to serving as a leading producer within a number of industries (for example, medical, appliances, lighting, power systems, capital/financial services), General Electric served as an online marketplace software and services firm through its Global Exchange business. GE Global Exchange assumed responsibility for building, deploying, and hosting the Global Healthcare Exchange. Learn more about the Global Healthcare Exchange by visiting the company website at www.ghx.com.

the health-care supply chain, from placing orders to tracking delivery. These ineffi-ciencies accounted for an estimated $11 billion in unnecessary purchasing costs.[17] The five founding companies supplied over 70 percent of all the products and serv-ices purchased by hospitals and health-care providers and did business with over 90 percent of the potential buyers. By early 2001, over 70 additional suppliers had signed on. As participation grew and the network expanded, GHX greatly increased the bargaining power of suppliers.

Even before the launch of GHX, however, health-care buyers had begun to form technology-enabled coalitions called Group Purchasing Organizations (GPOs). Healthcare Purchasing Partners International (HPPI) was an example of a GPO es-tablished to provide Veteran's Health Administration (VHA) and University Health System (UHS) member health-care providers with the highest-quality supplies, equipment, and other services at the most competitive prices. During 2001, HPPI managed over $18 billion in annual purchases for over 6,200 hospitals and health-care providers around the world. Purchasing through HPPI was reported to have saved member firms over $750 million.[18]

As we entered the 21st century, the race was on to determine whether buyer-led or supplier-led coalitions would achieve a dominant position within health-care electronic commerce markets. Interestingly, by 2001, buyer-led coalitions such as HPPI had begun to do business with supplier-led coalitions such as GHX. In fact, GHX executives publicly stated that they considered the new GPOs to be important members of the exchange not just as customers but also as partners.

Several actions in late 2001 clarified GHX's strategic intent to grow through part-nerships with other coalitions. On August 29, 2001, GHX and Neoforma signed a definitive agreement to provide comprehensive, integrated supply chain solutions for the global health-care industry. At the time of the agreement, Neoforma operated marketplaces for some of the largest buyer-led group purchasing organizations in the health-care industry, including MedBuy, a Canadian GPO that united over 100 hospitals in 11 regions across Canada, and Healthcare Purchasing Partners Interna-tional, described above. How buyer-seller power relationships will eventually stabi-lize in the health-care industry and other industries is not yet clear. What is abun-dantly clear, however, is that enabling technologies have had a significant impact on buyer-supplier power and that executives around the world are being forced to re-think strategic priorities, relationships, and decisions.

Can IT Build or Reduce Barriers to Entry?

Companies erect entry barriers by offering customers and other market participants attractive products and services at a price and level of quality that competitors can-not match. Before the rise of the commercial Internet, first movers such as AHSC and AA spent hundreds of millions of dollars over decades to establish a dominant

[17]R. Winslow, "Baxter International, Others Plan Net Concern for Hospital Purchases," *Wall Street Journal Interactive,* March 30, 2000.
[18]For more information on HPPI, visit the website at www.hppigo.com. Data obtained on March 10, 2002.

position within electronic markets. The sheer magnitude of the investment to build and operate proprietary networks, transaction systems, and databases created significant barriers to entry. For example, American Airlines and archrival United Airlines each spent hundreds of millions of dollars during the late 1970s and early 1980s to build the proprietary networks and computer systems required to launch and run online customer reservation systems. By the time other airlines recognized the situation, they were forced to tie into those two dominant online channels or risk being cut off from customers.[19]

Over time, however, these technology-based advantages decreased. The more sustainable advantage came from second-order barriers to entry created by exploiting the value of information generated by the technology and the value of the loyal community of suppliers, customers, and partners that did business by using the company's proprietary digital infrastructure.

Today many believe that the overall impact of Internet technologies will be to lower entry barriers for all players in online markets.[20] This belief arises from the fact that Internet technologies dramatically lower the cost of participating in an electronic market. In addition, the shared, nonproprietary nature of the Internet makes it easy for market participants to link to a common, shared platform for conducting business online and, more important, to sever ties with one firm and link to another.

Indeed, the low cost and ease of penetration decrease the benefits to any one participant unless people within the firm are capable of learning and responding more quickly and more effectively than others, are able to build proprietary capabilities that are not easily replicable, and can attract a large, loyal community that remains connected despite the availability of seemingly comparable alternatives. As we saw in the past, these "knowledge and community barriers" provide a more sustainable entry barrier within Internet-based electronic markets. In most cases, we see that incumbent firms with large investments in proprietary infrastructure and channels to market are at a particular disadvantage relative to new entrants when they attempt to create and quickly deploy second-order barriers to entry.

Amazon.com, one of the most celebrated new entrants of the dot-com era, provides an example of how new technology can lower entry barriers in an established industry. But as we will see, while entry barriers were initially low, Amazon's e-retail business model required the company to take ownership of physical inventory. This in turn required significant investment in building a "click and mortar" online/offline retail infrastructure. While building and deploying the infrastructure delayed profitability, by January 2002 the company had found ways to capitalize

---

[19]During the late 1980s and early 1990s, new entrant Southwest Airlines offered a regional service that provided a significant decrease in price and a corresponding increase in the number of flights to popular destinations within a local area. This niche market strategy enabled it to achieve a sustainable competitive advantage without tying into online reservation systems. By early 2000, Southwest was able to offer its own online reservation system that enabled customers to bypass travel agents and buy directly from Southwest.

[20]Porter, op cit.

on the infrastructure it had built, the community it had connected, and what it had learned.

In July 1995, Jeff Bezos, Amazon's chief executive officer (CEO) and founder, launched his online bookstore from a 400-square-foot warehouse (about the size of a one-car garage) with only a few servers and a high-speed connection to the Internet. The company quickly became the number one online bookstore. Just two years after launch, sales had reached $148 million and the number of customers exceeded 2 million.

During its third year, Amazon executives demonstrated that the initial success in quickly dominating the online book market could be repeated. During the summer and fall of 1998, Amazon opened new online music and video "stores" and achieved the number one position in online music sales within four months and the number one position in online video sales within a record 45 days.[21]

At that point, Amazon had demonstrated how the Internet could lower entry barriers to the detriment of established players. But there was also a deeper lesson. Established competitors, such as Barnes & Noble, Borders, and Bertelsmann (in Europe), were not blind to Amazon's early success; they invested heavily but were unable to catch up. Why? Many erroneously believed that Amazon's dominance came from its first-mover advantage. While this was important, in other instances first movers have been crushed quickly. CDNow, for example, was overtaken by Amazon.com in short order.

The secret to Amazon's success in entering and dominating multiple industries was the transaction, information, and community infrastructure that Amazon.com executives built *behind* its website. In fact, during 1999 and 2000, Amazon executives spent almost $500 million building a sophisticated, Web-based order fulfillment capability that enabled the company to fulfill orders for over 31 million units during the six-week 2000 holiday period from mid-November to the end of December. Over 99 percent of orders arrived on time.

The transaction infrastructure fed valuable information into a sophisticated knowledge management infrastructure that allowed executives and employees at all levels to develop a real-time understanding of the dynamics of the marketplace and the needs of market participants. Amazon used that knowledge to coordinate and control operations not only inside the firm but also across organizational boundaries. More important, it used its growing understanding of customer preferences to personalize its online services in a way that could not be matched by competitors and to feed valuable information to suppliers. The number of loyal customers increased quickly, and by late 2000 over 25 million people shopped on Amazon. These *proprietary* transaction, knowledge, and community infrastructures (which united people and technology) enabled Amazon to develop powerful barriers to entry that, to date, competitors have been unable to match.

By mid 2001, however, many wondered whether those proprietary advantages would be enough. After the rapid decline in the price of Internet stocks during 2000

---

[21]See L. M. Applegate, *Amazon.com 2000* (HBS Publishing) (Order No. 801–194).

and the loss of investor confidence in online business models, the company found that sources of financing for growth had dried up. Amazon executives moved the company's strategy and business model away from a dependence on retail product sales and toward a services model in an effort to reach profitability more quickly. This new strategy paralleled the approach used by AHSC and AA during the 1980s, as both firms shifted from selling products to selling services and expertise.

By early 2002, Amazon had successfully attracted a number of established "brick and mortar" retailers (including ToysRus, Borders, Egghead.com, Circuit City, Target, and CatalogCity) that wished to tap into online markets while avoiding the risk and time required to develop, deploy, and manage equivalent capabilities. Those firms signed multiyear outsourcing contracts that over time began to shift the Amazon.com business model from a pure-play e-retailer to an online/offline logistics services provider. As evidence of the value of Amazon's proprietary networked business infrastructure, in summer 2001, AOL Time Warner, anticipating a need to dramatically expand its e-commerce capabilities, invested $100 million in Amazon.com. While it was still unclear whether Amazon would be able to successfully integrate these multiple established company operations before it ran through its rapidly dwindling cash reserves, the company posted its first profit in the fourth quarter of 2001.

Can IT Increase or Decrease Switching Costs?

To provide a sustainable source of revenues, an IT system ideally should be easy to start using but difficult to stop using. Customers drawn into the system through a series of increasingly valuable enhancements should willingly become dependent on the system's functionality. Once the use of the system becomes ingrained within day-to-day activities, switching to another system becomes difficult and costly.

In the past, when proprietary technologies were the norm, switching costs were high because switching usually required buying into different proprietary networks and systems owned and operated by an online channel manager, such as American Airlines in the travel services industry, American Hospital Supply in the hospital supplies industry, or Wal-Mart in the retail industry. On the narrowband, public Internet, however, the cost to connect is relatively low and the technologies required to participate are not proprietary.[22] Switching costs are, therefore, substantially reduced. For example, the cost to a customer of switching from shopping at Amazon.com to shopping at the Barnes & Noble online store is merely a few keystrokes of effort. Easy switching makes for easy price comparisons, which suggests that over time it will be difficult to achieve strong customer loyalty.

While there appears to be a certain inevitability to this logic, savvy executives, for example, Scott Cook at Intuit, have identified ways to exploit the power of the Internet to increase, rather than decrease, switching costs. Launched in 1983, Intuit provided low-cost financial services software (Quicken, TurboTax, and QuickBooks) designed to be easy to use by individuals with little on no background in finance or

---

[22]It is important to note that over the next few years, switching costs for broadband Internet channels are expected to be much higher than those associated with the narrowband, public Internet.

technology. Initially, the products "hooked" the user by providing a much simpler and easier way to complete time-consuming and repetitive tasks. By also providing a simple way to store personal information, which would have to be reentered if a customer switched to a different product, the company kept users hooked over time. Intuit quickly became the market leader for individual and small business financial software, with over 80 percent market share across its product line and over 90 percent retention rates. The company continues to maintain this position despite aggressive competition from Microsoft.

A decade after launching its first software product, the company launched an online financial services portal, Quicken.com, to complement and extend its packaged software offerings. By linking its Internet business to the company's traditional desktop software, Intuit has been able to transition users from its desktop product line to its Internet product line while also offering an even easier to use and more useful set of services. By 2001, consumers and small business owners could pay bills and bank online, calculate and pay taxes, and manage a portfolio of investments. Small business owners also could manage payroll, inventory, and customer accounts and purchase supplies. As these features were added to the service and as customers gained from their value and convenience, switching became more difficult. Changing an online bill-paying service, for example, involved setting up relationships between the new online bill-paying service and each company to be paid.

Intuit used the lessons learned from its successful software business to guide the launch and evolution of its Internet business. Careful attention was paid to creating a service offering that provided a unique value proposition for customers and then "hooked" them to the company by providing a simple and easy-to-use way to complete time-consuming and repetitive tasks. Once users invested the effort to store personal information and set up online transaction relationships, it became much harder to switch. Using these principles, within less than one year of launch, Intuit's online version of its TurboTax software gained over 80 percent market share in the highly competitive market for online tax preparation and filing.

Can IT Add Value to Existing Products and Services or Create New Ones?

In addition to lowering cost, improving quality, and changing power dynamics, IT can add value to existing products or services and create new ones. For example, grocery stores used to be in the business of selling packaged goods and fresh food, but now they are also in the business of selling information. Many market research firms purchase scanner data on consumer shopping behavior from large supermarket chains, analyze the data, and then sell information back to the supermarkets along with aggregate competitor, industry, and demographic data from a wide variety of sources.

The information content of existing products has also increased markedly. Many are unaware that by 2000 there were more computer chips in a late-model car than there had been in the entire U.S. National Defense Department in 1960. Not only do these chips control everything from internal air temperature to the braking system, they also provide valuable information to service mechanics and auto manufacturers to guide after-sales service and future product design.

Information technologies can alter or even completely transform a product from an analog to a digital form. Products particularly well-suited to digitization include books, magazines, and other printed materials, such as music, video, and games. Over the last two years, established firms such as Sony and Bertelsmann, Internet start-ups such as RealNetworks[23] and Amazon.com's e-books, and new coalitions of firms such as MusicNet and Duet have suggested that digital distribution of books, music, and video will dramatically alter existing publishing and entertainment industries.[24]

Summary

Exploiting the opportunities afforded by IT in the 21st century while avoiding the pitfalls requires vision, sound execution, and the ability to respond quickly. It also requires imagination and a little luck. This chapter has presented frameworks for analyzing the impact of IT on the core operations and core strategy of a firm. Executives are encouraged to ask five key questions as they assess potential strategic uses of IT: (1) Can we use IT to reengineer key value activities and change the basis of competition? (2) Can we use IT to change the nature of relationships and the balance of power among buyers, suppliers, business partners, and competitors? (3) Can we use IT to build or reduce barriers to entry? (4) Can we use IT to increase or decrease switching costs? (5) Can we use IT to add value to existing products and services or create new ones?

An understanding of strategic opportunities must be combined with an understanding of strategic risks. Risks increase when executives (1) have a poor understanding of sources of competitive dynamics in the industry within which their firm competes, (2) fail to fully understand the long-term implications of a strategic system that they have launched or one launched by a competitor or another industry participant, (3) launch a system that brings on litigation or regulation to the detriment of the innovator, and (4) fail to account for the time, effort, and cost required to ensure user adoption, assimilation, and effective utilization.

When an organization invests in a new technology, it is important to assess candidly whether the investment will result in a sustainable advantage or will simply maintain the current industry and competitive dynamics at an increased level of cost. Finally, the movement of IT personnel between firms often results in rapid proliferation of strategic ideas. This can put the pioneering firm under pressure to keep innovating and evolving the IT-enabled strategy. The following questions can be used by executives to assess IT-enabled business opportunities and risks:

---

[23]L. M. Applegate, *RealNetworks: Converging Technologies/Expanding Opportunities* (HBS Publishing) (Order No. 399–025).
[24]On April 2, 2001, AOL Time Warner, Bertelsmann, EMI Group, and RealNetworks announced the formation of MusicNet, a joint venture that would create a "breakthrough platform" for an online music subscription service. On April 6, 2001, Yahoo! announced a nonexclusive partnership arrangement with Sony and Universal to make those companies' Duet online music service available through Yahoo!. See M. Cavallaro, "Yahoo and Duet: Déjà Vu All Over Again," *The Standard* (www.thestandard.com), April 6, 2001.

1. What business are we in? Who are our customers, suppliers, and business partners? What value do we provide to these key constituencies (including employees and owners)? What are the competitive dynamics and balance of power within the industry? Can IT be used to create value and change the basis of competition?

2. Who are our biggest competitors today? Who will they be in the future? How easy (or difficult) is it for new players to enter our markets, offering a unique value proposition and/or substitute products and services? How easy (or difficult) would it be for customers, suppliers, or partners to switch?

3. How efficient and effective are our core operating activities and processes? How easy (or difficult) is it for customers, suppliers, and partners to do business with us? How easy (or difficult) is it for employees to exceed performance standards and continuously improve our products and services and the way we do business?

4. Are there any big changes looming on the horizon? Are we in a position to capitalize on these changes? Do we want to lead the industry or be a fast follower?

5. Will changes in related industries (or even in unrelated industries) influence our industry? Can we not only enhance what we do today but also expand into new products or markets and extend into new businesses?

6. Have we accurately identified the strategic risks the organization faces today and in the future? Do we have the systems and processes in place to manage risks?

7. Have we appropriately prioritized our business investments? Does our planning and budgeting process enable us to identify and effectively respond to strategic opportunities and threats?

2

Crafting Business Models[1]

> Some of the best innovations involve a paradigm shift, a real mental change of assumptions and certainties. In fact, the process of innovating and entrepreneuring is much less about invention or new ideas. It's much more about rethinking and questioning the assumptions people already make . . . The ability to rethink fundamental assumptions and take what people accept as certain and question it [is the central] talent of being a great entrepreneur.[2]

Few would dispute the fact that the rapid technological advancements of the second half of the 20th century have spawned dramatic worldwide socioeconomic changes. By the mid-1990s, a new economic paradigm was emerging that many called the Network Economy. Its promise caused established firms to embark upon business transformation designed to shed the static, rigid structures, processes, and mind-sets that remained as a legacy of the Industrial Economy. Today, as we stand at the gateway to a new millennium, the Internet and its associated technologies form the foundation on which new businesses are being built. Initially, entrepreneurs and executives in established firms approached the Internet in much the same way that fortune seekers of the 1800s prospected for gold. Although there are still frontiers to explore, the "gold rush" mentality has given way to a search for frameworks and analytic tools to guide us in building successful—and sustainable—Network Economy businesses.

---

[1]This chapter is adapted from papers and materials from Professor Applegate's course entitled *Building Businesses in a Networked Economy.*
[2]Scott Cook, founder of Intuit Inc., address to executives, September 15, 1998.

This chapter analyzes how emerging Network Economy business models are revolutionizing the conduct of business around the world. Portals, aggregators, exchanges, and marketplaces are only a few of the models examined here. The in-depth analysis provides the foundation for a discussion of business strategy, capabilities, value creation, and business model evolution in a number of companies, including a long-established firm—American Express—and a more recently launched independent Internet venture—Amazon.com.

Business Models: Something Old and Something New

> If there is one lesson we can learn from continuing evolution of work and competition in the new economy, it's this . . . Change the question and you change the game . . . The old question was "What business am I in?" The new question is "What is my business model?"[3]

Why is a focus on business models so important today? If you think about it, we spent nearly a century building and perfecting Industrial Economy models that defined how companies conducted business through most of the 1900s. As a result, we knew what it meant if someone said, "I sell insurance" or "I sell cars." We had developed a shorthand way of describing how a business was structured, what types of people were needed, and what roles they filled. That shorthand told us how our company interacted with others in the industry and, most important, how it made money and delivered value to customers, suppliers, partners, employees, and owners. It also told everyone who did business with us what to expect. The Industrial Economy business models became so familiar that they no longer required explanation.

In contrast, emerging networked technologies enable us to create new business models and redefine existing ones. Technology can provide a flexible channel for procuring and distributing products and services as well as the tools to create and package content in all its many forms, including data, voice, and video. This highly interactive and engaging channel offers new opportunities and enables the development of new capabilities that were difficult to achieve before the commercialization of the Internet. Figure 2.1 shows the building blocks of a business model and the relationships among them. These components link to the financial model of an organization (see Figure 2.2). Appendix 2A summarizes revenue, cost, and asset options.

As you review the business model framework, it is important to recognize that the components and relationships depicted here are not new. Indeed, this basic approach has been used for decades to analyze a wide variety of Industrial Economy business models. What is new are the business rules and assumptions that form the *mental models* that guide how we make decisions and take actions. As we define new models, we do not immediately throw out the old ones. In fact, the best inventions leverage old paradigms, relaxing assumptions to define new models that are familiar yet decidedly superior to the old ones.[4]

---

[3]A. Slywotsky and D. Morrison, *Profit Patterns* (New York: New York Times Business, 1999).
[4]T. Kuhn, *The Structure of Scientific Revolution* (Chicago: University of Chicago Press, 1970).

FIGURE 2.1
Business Model Components

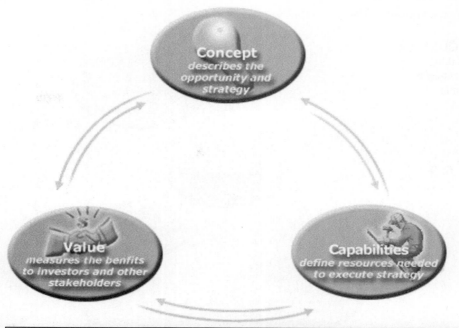

What is it?	How will we?
An organization's **business concept** defines its strategy. The concept is based on analysis of: • Market opportunity • Product and services offered • Competitive dynamics • Strategy for capturing a dominant position • Strategic options for evolving the business	• Attract a large and loyal community? • Deliver value to all community members? • Price our product to achieve rapid adoption? • Become #1 or #2? • Erect barriers to entry? • Evolve the business to "cash in on strategic options?" • Generate multiple revenue streams? • Manage risk and growth?
An organization's **capabilities** define resources needed to execute strategy. Capabilities are built and delivered through its: • People and partners • Organization and culture • Operations • Marketing/sales • Leadership/Management process • Business development/Innovation process • Infrastructure/Asset efficiency	• Achieve best-in-class operating performance? • Develop modular, scalable. and flexible infrastructure? • Build and manage strong partnerships with employees and the community? • Increase the lifetime value of all members of the community? • Build, nurture, and exploit knowledge assets? • Make informed decisions and take actions that increase value? • Organize for action and agility?
A high-performing organization returns **value** to all stakeholders. This value is measured by: • Benefits returned to stakeholders • Benefits returned to the firm and its owners • Market share and performance • Brand and reputation • Financial performance	• Deliver value to all stakeholders? • Claim value from stakeholder relationships and transactions? • Increase market share and drive new revenues off existing customers? • Increase brand value and reputation? • Generate confidence and trust? • Ensure strong growth in earnings? • Generate positive equity cash flow? • Increase stock price and market value?

FIGURE 2.2
Linking
Strategy to
Value

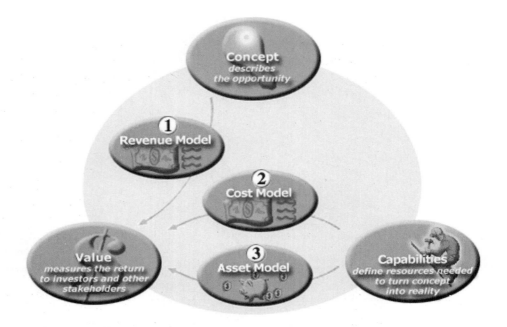

Classifying Business Models

Consumers are looking for the ability to bundle the products they want in a fashion unique to each individual, and the Web will provide this capability . . . We believe that vertical portals will do the best job of providing the consumer empowerment that the Internet makes possible . . . Not only will vertical portals have a profound effect on traditional distribution networks, but in information industries like financial services, they may also pose a threat to specialty [producers] that choose to downplay the significance of the Internet channel.[5]

For decades, executives have used the value chain framework discussed in Chapter 1 to describe the set of activities through which a product or service is created and delivered to customers.[6] These customers may be either individuals or businesses willing to pay for a product, service, or solution. In selling to business

[5]U.S. Internet and Financial Services Equity Research Team, "The Internet and Financial Services," Morgan Stanley Dean Witter, August 1999.
[6]M. Porter, *Competitive Advantage: Creating and Sustaining Superior Performance* (New York: Free Press, 1985).

customers, individual consumers—the actual end users—are often located inside the customer firm. Often this fact creates a two-stage adoption cycle: First the business must decide to purchase a product or service, and then individuals must decide to use it.

There are two key value chain roles that market participants may assume. *Producers* design and build products and services that meet specific customer or market needs. They may sell, service, and support the product or may leave selling and maintaining to others within an industry or outside traditional industry boundaries. Sometimes producers function as suppliers, selling parts, components, or services to other businesses. Alternatively, producers may sell finished equipment or solutions to business users or consumers, in which case they sometimes are called original equipment manufacturers (OEMs).

The second key value chain role is that of a *distributor.* Distributors enable buyers and sellers to connect, communicate, and transact business. Distributors may assume control of inventory and resell a product, solution, or service (retailers, wholesalers). Or they may simply act as agents, connecting buyers and suppliers but not assuming control of inventory (aggregators, marketplaces, and exchanges).

A company need not confine itself to operating within a specific role. A vertically integrated industry structure results when a single player adopts multiple roles within an industry.

Although networked business models adopt the same basic roles, the classification framework presented here extends producer and distributor roles in some important ways (see Figure 2.3).

First, the framework distinguishes between the networked business models for companies that do business on the Internet and associated networks. We then discuss businesses that provide the networked infrastructure. While these two classes of models are separated for simplicity, we recognize that the lines between them are becoming increasingly blurred. For example, Microsoft used to be solely in the business of delivering technology infrastructure. Today it is also a consumer portal and an online financial services provider; at one time it was even an online travel service.

The networked business model framework also distinguishes between *focused distributors* and *portals.* While both can be classified as distributors, the business model for online focused distributors is much like the business model of offline distributors. Portals, in contrast, serve as gateways offering access to a broad array of content, products, services, and solutions through online or multichannel distribution networks. For example, as an independent company, InsWeb is a focused distributor for the insurance industry. InsWeb also operates as the insurance distributor within the Yahoo! Finance vertical portal.

Because companies gained the most far-reaching economic benefits of the Internet and its associated technologies by connecting with customers, suppliers, and business partners, many of the earliest networked business models redefined the roles of distributors, including focused distributors and portals. As a result, we begin with a discussion of focused distributors and portals before moving on to producer models.

FIGURE 2.3
Classifying
Network
Business
Models

Create and package products,
services, and solutions

Enable buyers and sellers to connect,
communicate, and transact business

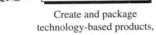

Create and package
technology-based products,
services, and solutions

Enable technology
buyer and sellers to
transact business

Enable consumers and
businesses to access online
services and information

Businesses Built on a Networked Infrastructure

Focused Distributors

Focused distributors provide products and services related to a specific industry or market niche. For example, in 2000, InsWeb and E-Loan operated as focused distributors offering products and services within the financial services industry and Staples.com was a focused distributor for office products and supplies. The five types of focused distributor business models—retailers, marketplaces, aggregators, exchanges, and infomediaries—are differentiated from each other by the following characteristics (see Table 2.1):

- Does the business assume control of inventory?

- Does the business sell online?

- Is the price set outside the market, or is online price negotiation and bidding permitted?

- Is there a physical product or service that must be distributed?

Retailers such as ToysRus.com and Staples.com assume control of inventory, set a nonnegotiable price to the consumer, and sell physical products online.[7] The primary revenue model is based on product/service sales, and the cost model includes procurement, inventory management, order fulfillment, and customer service (including returns). Because e-retailers assume control of physical goods, their ratio of

[7]See M. Collura and L. M. Applegate, *Amazon.com: Exploiting the Value of a Digital Business Infrastructure* (HBS Publishing) (No. 800-330), for a more detailed analysis of the evolution of the online retailer business model.

TABLE 2.1 Focused Distributor Business Models

| Model and Examples | Model Differentiators | | | | Likely Revenues | Likely Costs |
	Own Inventory	Sell Online	Price Set Online	Physical Product or Service		
Retailer ToysRus.com Staples.com	Yes	Yes	No	Yes	Product/service sales	Advertising and marketing; physical facilities; inventory and customer service; R&D; IT infrastructure
Marketplace Eloan.com InsWeb.com	Possibly	Yes	No	No	Transaction fees; service fees; commissions	Advertising and marketing; R&D; IT infrastructure
Aggregator Autoweb.com	No	No	No	Possibly	Referral fees; advertising and marketing fees	Advertising and marketing; R&D; IT infrastructure
Infomediary Internet Securities	No	Yes	Yes	No	Subscription fees; advertising fees	Advertising and marketing; R&D; IT infrastructure; content aquisition
Exchange eBay.com Freemarket.com	Possibly	Possibly	Yes	Possibly	Depends on model	Advertising and marketing; staff support for auctions (especially B2B); inventory and logistics if inventory control; R&D; technical infrastructure

Focused distributor business model trends
- Focused distributors that do not allow customers and the business community to transact business online are losing power.
- Aggregators are evolving into marketplaces and/or vertical portals.
- Multiple business models are required to ensure flexibility and sustainability.
- Focused distributors are aligning closely with vertical and horizontal portals or are evolving their model to become vertical portals.

tangible to intangible assets often is much higher than that which would be found in a firm that does not assume control of physical inventory.

Marketplaces such as E-Loan and InsWeb sell products and services—loans and insurance, respectively[8]—but do not take control of physical inventory. They do, however, sell products with a nonnegotiable price and complete sales online. Their revenue model is based on a commission or transaction fee on each sale. Because sales transactions take place online, e-marketplaces often electronically link to supplier databases and transaction systems to ensure that transactions can be completed and revenue can be recognized. This is reflected in the cost model; for example, in 2001 it took a team of information technology (IT) professionals up to two months to integrate Ins-Web's transaction systems and databases with those of its insurance carrier partners.[9] Because marketplace companies do not assume control of physical inventory, procurement and inventory management costs often are lower than those of retailers.

Aggregators such as Autoweb[10] provide information on products or services for sale by others in the channel. While a comparison of features and pricing is often provided, aggregators do not enable buyers and sellers to complete the final transaction. Therefore, the revenue model for these sites often is based on referral fees and advertising. Because transactions are not completed online, some aggregators, especially aggregators of physical products and services, find that consumers use the site to comparison shop but then go offline to make the purchase. As a result, aggregators may not be able to claim referral fees, which makes them highly dependent on advertising and other supplemental revenue sources.

Infomediaries such as Internet Securities[11] are a type of aggregator that unites sellers and buyers of information-based products, such as news, weather, sports, and financial information. Because no physical product is involved, the transaction can be completed online. Infomediaries, especially those that cater to business professionals, may charge individual users a subscription fee for the service. Business-to-business (B2B) infomediaries often charge a company a corporate subscription fee. Business-to-consumer (B2C) infomediaries may provide the information service free to consumers and make money from advertising revenues collected from sponsors or affiliates.

Because information is available elsewhere and the cost of packaging and delivering the information is relatively low, barriers to entry also may be low. As a result, in-

---

[8]See L. M. Applegate, *QuickenInsurance: The Race to Click and Close* (HBS Publishing) (No. 800-295), for a more detailed analysis of the evolution of the online marketplace business model.

[9]The decision to provide system integration services and to host the online insurance quoting, application, and sales transaction systems for carriers has enabled InsWeb to add two digital infrastructure provider models—application service provider (ASP) and system integrator and developer—which are discussed later in this chapter. These two models provide new revenue streams: IT consulting and development fees and ongoing hosting and maintenance fees. They also change the cost and asset models.

[10]A portion of the AutoWeb website enables dealers and consumers to auction cars. As a result, AutoWeb has adopted a hybrid business model that combines an aggregator model and an exchange model.

[11]See L. M. Applegate, *Internet Securities: Building a Business in Internet Time* (HBS Publishing) (No. 398-007), for a more detailed analysis of the infomediary business model.

fomediaries must do more than simply broker information. Some choose to develop unique value-added content and analytic tools; others extend their businesses by incorporating new models. Within the limits of privacy, ethics, and regulation, infomediaries must also leverage the economic value of the information they collect about market participants and how they do business. Over time, these intangible information assets become a major source of strategic differentiation and sustainability.

Exchanges such as eBay and FreeMarket may or may not take control of inventory—the tendency is to try to avoid assuming inventory carrying costs whenever feasible—and may or may not complete the final sales transaction online. The key differentiating feature of this model is that the price is not set; it is negotiated by the buyer and the seller at the time of the sale. The revenue, cost, and asset models vary depending on whether the online exchange assumes control of inventory and completes the transaction. B2B auction exchanges such as FreeMarket charge transaction fees and supplement revenues with fees for consulting services. B2C and consumer-to-consumer (C2C) exchanges often supplement transaction revenues with advertising revenues.

Portals

The *American Heritage Dictionary of the English Language* defines the term *portal* as "a doorway or gate—especially one that is large and imposing."[12] To many, this definition seems a fitting description of the portal business model that has emerged on the Web. Although the terminology is rather recent, the earliest online business portals (for example, American Hospital Supply's ASAP and American Airlines' Sabre) were first launched in the late 1960s and 1970s.[13] Online consumer portals (for example, America Online and CompuServe) emerged in the 1980s with the adoption of the personal computer. Built upon proprietary technology, these pre-Internet portals provided limited access. In fact, in late 1993, AOL's proprietary consumer portal had only 500,000 members. By mid-2001, the number had grown to over 30 million.[14] Three types of portal business models—horizontal, vertical, and affinity portals—are differentiated from each other by the following characteristics (see Table 2.2):

- Does the business provide gateway access to a full range of online information and services, including search, calendar, e-mail, instant messaging, chat, and other community-building tools?

- Does the business provide access to deep content, products, and services within a vertical industry (e.g., financial services, travel)?

- Does the business provide information and services for all types of users, or are the information and services specific to a well-defined affiliation group (e.g., women, people selling or buying a home).

[12]*American Heritage Dictionary of the English Language* (Boston: Houghton Mifflin, 1971).
[13]See L. M. Applegate, F. W. McFarlan, and J. L. McKenney, "Electronic Commerce: Trends and Opportunities," in *Corporate Information Systems Management* (New York: McGraw-Hill Irwin, 1999).
[14]Visit the AOL Time Warner company website (www.aoltimewarner.com) to examine a timeline of events in the evolution of the AOL Time Warner family of companies.

TABLE 2.2   Portal Business Models

Model and Examples	Model Differentiators			Likely Revenues	Likely Costs
	Gateway Access	Deep Content and Solutions	Affinity Group Focus		
Horizontal portals AOL.com Yahoo.com Quicken.com Small Business	Yes	Possibly; often through partnerships with vertical and affinity portals	Possibly; often through partnerships	Advertising, affiliation and slotting fees; possibly subscription or access fees	Advertising, marketing and sales; content/information asset management; R&D; IT infrastructure
Vertical portals WebMD.com Covisint.com	Limited	Yes	No	Transaction fees; commissions; advertising, affiliation, and slotting fees	Advertising, marketing, and sales; content/information asset management; R&D; IT infrastructure; legacy system integration to support transactions
Affinity portals Realtor.com iVillage.com	Possibly	Focused on affinity group	Yes	Referral fees; advertising, affiliation, and slotting fees	Advertising, marketing, and sales; content/information asset management; R&D; IT infrastructure

Portal business model trends
- Horizontal and vertical portals are emerging as dominant sources of power within consumer and business markets.
- Horizontal portals are joining forces with horizontal infrastructure portals to provide not just access to content and services but also access to network and hosting services.
- Large media and entertainment portals that represent the convergence of data, telephone, television, and radio networks are emerging in the consumer space. These portals unite content development, packaging, and distribution components of the value chain.
- B2B portals provide both horizontal access to business networks and vertical industrywide solutions.

Horizontal portals such as AOL.com, Yahoo!, and Quicken.com Small Business provide gateway access to the Internet's vast store of content and services. They also provide a broad range of tools for locating information and websites, communicating with others, and developing online communities of interest. Like the broadcast networks on which they were modeled, pure-play horizontal portals such as Yahoo! initially depended on advertising as the primary revenue source. Development, maintenance, and operation of infrastructure and content were the primary costs. But the "pure-play" horizontal portal model proved hard to sustain. As a result, Yahoo! and others have extended their models to include multiple vertical solution "channels" in an attempt to derive increasing revenues from transaction fees. In addition, horizontal portals that do not provide Internet access often form strategic alliances with dial-up and broadband Internet service providers (ISPs) to enable revenue sharing on access fees.[15] Reflecting its heritage as a proprietary online information provider, AOL.com operated as both a content portal and a network service provider before the Internet and maintained that model when it launched its Internet service in 1995. By 2000, AOL was generating approximately 70 percent of its $6.9 billion in revenue from subscription and access fees.[16] It also generated revenues from advertising (29 percent of 2000 revenues) and, with its purchase of Netscape, from software licensing, sales, and maintenance/integration fees (7.3 percent of 2000 revenues).

Vertical portals such as Covisint in the automobile industry and WebMD in the health-care industry provide deep content; a place to conduct business, learn, and shop; and communications and community-building tools. Like other networked businesses, vertical portals are often composed of a variety of business models, all of which generate separate revenue streams. The business models adopted by the vertical portal determine its revenue and cost models. For example, if the vertical portal does not allow individuals to complete transactions, revenues will be generated primarily through advertising and referral fees. However, if transactions are completed online, sales revenues, service fees, or transaction fees may be generated. Additionally, if the portal includes unique content, subscription revenues may be generated.

Affinity portals provide deep content, commerce, and community features such as those found in a vertical portal, but these offerings are targeted toward a specific market segment. Some, such as iVillage.com, are targeted toward a specific gender. Others, such as Realtor.com, are targeted toward a specific event, in this case, selling or buying a home. As with other vertical portals, the revenue, cost, and asset models are based on the business models adopted by the portal.

Producers

Producers design and make and also may directly market, sell, and distribute products, services, and solutions. Since the key technologies that created economic wealth in the Industrial Economy were production technologies, producers often

---

[15]On November 14, 2001, Yahoo! announced that it had entered into a strategic alliance with SBC Communications to develop a cobranded high-speed Digital Subscriber Line (DSL) broadband Internet service. See Yahoo! press release, November 14, 2001(www.yahoo.com).
[16]AOL annual report, 2000.

held the position of power in traditional business markets.[17] In contrast, the Internet and associated networked technologies of the Network Economy create wealth by connecting buyers and suppliers. Given these basic economic facts, many believed that distributors would become the dominant players in the Network Economy. While gaining control of distribution channels remains a key success factor in the 21st century, producers in a variety of industries have taken steps to reestablish positions of power. In some instances, producers are forming coalitions to develop online/offline supply or distribution channels to market. Examples of producer coalitions include Covisint in the automobile industry and Global Healthcare Exchange in the health-care industry. In others, vertically integrated megacorporations such as AOL Time Warner are uniting producers and distributors within the same firm. The six categories of producer business model—manufacturer, service provider, educator, adviser, information and news service, and producer portal—are differentiated from each other by the following characteristics (see Table 2.3):

- Does the business sell physical products and/or provide face-to-face services?

- Does the business sell information-based products and/or services?

- Does the business provide customized products and/or services?

Manufacturers such as Ford Motor Company and Procter & Gamble design, produce, and distribute physical products. Manufacturers include component or parts manufacturers that serve as suppliers to an industry and OEMs that produce finished goods. Given the physical nature of the product, the primary effect of the Internet and the associated networked technologies has been to streamline, integrate, coordinate, and control physical channels of production and distribution. These IT-enabled process redesign efforts often begin inside the firm and then extend to connect customers, suppliers, and partners.

Service providers such as American Express and Singapore Airlines offer a wide range of service offerings that may be delivered through multiple channels. Like manufacturers of physical products, service providers that offer physical services (e.g., car rental agencies, restaurants) often use IT to streamline, integrate, coordinate, and control service delivery and to connect and share information with customers, suppliers, and partners. Service providers that offer primarily information-based services (e.g., financial services) can use IT to digitize service delivery.

Educators such as Harvard University and Virtual University create and deliver online educational programs, products, and services. The ability to use the Internet and associated technologies to define new multimedia educational offerings and to customize those offerings to meet the learning needs of individuals and businesses is revolutionizing education. While community features of emerging networked technologies enhance interactive learning, it is widely believed that distance learning will never totally replace face-to-face education.

---

[17]It is important to note that communications technologies (for example, the telephone and telegraph) and distribution technologies (for example, the train and truck) were also key technological drivers of the Industrial Economy.

TABLE 2.3   Producer Business Models

| Model and Examples | Model Differentiators | | | Likely Revenues | Likely Costs |
	Sell Physical Product/ Service	Sell Information- Based Product/ Service	Level of Customization		
Manufacturers Ford Motor Company Procter & Gamble	Yes	Possibly	Low to moderate	Product sales; service fees	Advertising, marketing and sales; content/ information asset management; R&D; IT infrastructure
Service providers American Express Singapore Airlines	Yes	Possibly	Moderate to high	Commission, service, or transaction fees	Advertising, marketing, and sales; content/information asset management; R&D; IT infrastructure
Educators Harvard University Virtual University	Possibly	Possibly	Moderate to high	Registration or event fee; subscription fee; hosting fee	Content information asset management; R&D; IT infrastructure
Advisers McKinsey Accenture	Yes	Yes	Moderate to high	Service fee; registration or event fee; member- ship fee; commission, transaction, or sub- scription fee	Content/information asset management; IT infrastructure

(continued)

TABLE 2.3 Producer Business Models *(continued)*

Model and Examples	Model Differentiators			Likely Revenues	Likely Costs
	Sell Physical Product/Service	Sell Information-Based Product/Service	Level of Customization		
Information and news services					
Dow Jones Euromoney	Yes	Yes	Moderate to high	Subscription fee; commission, transaction, or service fee	Content/information asset management; advertising, marketing, and sales; IT infrastructure
Producer portals					
Covisint Global Healthcare Exchange	Possibly	Yes	High	Transaction or service fee; subscription or membership fee; consulting and integration fee; hosting fee	Content/information asset; IT infrastructure and R&D; software development logistics

Producer business model trends
- Producers must be best in class—the number one or number two brand—to survive.
- Some large full-service producers, such as American Express and Citigroup in the financial services industry and AOL Time Warner in the entertainment and media industry, are acquiring a full range of products and services and then integrating them to provide vertical solutions required by customers. These solutions are offered through company-owned portals and also through a wide variety of distribution agreements.
- Industry supplier coalitions are forming to enable virtually integrated B2B commerce within and across industry groups.

Advisers such as McKinsey and Accenture provide consulting and coaching services to businesses and individuals. These firms have found that online channels can be used to extend the nature of the relationship with customers from a one-time consulting project to an ongoing education and advisory service. Online channels can be used to disseminate knowledge, connect consultants with their clients, and create communities of interest.

Information and news services such as Dow Jones and Euromoney create, package, and deliver information through both online and offline channels and across multiple media formats. Because information in all its many forms can be digitized, stored, and delivered to meet personalized needs, we see convergence among publishing, television, radio, and information services industries.

Producer portals such as Covisint and Global Healthcare Exchange use the Internet and associated technologies to support all aspects of the production and distribution process.

Businesses That Provide Networked Infrastructure

Until recently, there was a distinct separation between businesses that were built *using* a digital technology infrastructure and businesses that primarily *developed and sold* the technology infrastructure, the latter of which were often referred to as the high-tech industry. As we entered the 21st century, digital infrastructure was becoming embedded within the very fabric of how organizations create, produce, and distribute products and services. As a result, it has become increasingly difficult to clearly categorize organizations as members of the high-tech industry. David Pottruck, co-CEO of Charles Schwab, emphasized this point:

> [Charles Schwab] is a technology company that just happens to be in the brokerage business. Everything we think about as we run our business has technology in the center of it with the goal of engineering costs down and service up . . . If you want to constantly increase service while decreasing the cost structure and the cost of service, then technology is the play. You have to be great at it. If we are going to be successful [against our competitors], technology will have to be built into our DNA in a way that's different.[18]

Networked infrastructure provider business models are classified by using the same producer/distributor categories that define digital businesses built on the Internet. Once again, powerful channel players—horizontal infrastructure portals (for example, AT&T and British Telecom) and vertical infrastructure portals (for example, IBM's E-Business Solutions and GE's Global eXchange Services)—are emerging.

Infrastructure Distributors

Infrastructure distributors enable technology buyers and sellers to transact business. The four categories of infrastructure distributor—infrastructure retailers, infrastructure

[18]Presentation by David Pottruck at a Harvard Business School executive program, October 22, 1999.

marketplaces, infrastructure aggregators, and infrastructure exchanges—are differentiated by the following characteristics (see Table 2.4):

- Does the business assume control of inventory?
- Does the business sell online?
- Is the price set outside the market, or is online price negotiation and bidding permitted?
- Is there a physical product or service that must be distributed?

Like their nontechnology counterparts, ***infrastructure retailers*** such as CompUSA and Egghead assume control of inventory, set a nonnegotiable price to the consumer, and sell physical products online. Therefore, the primary revenue model often is based on product/service sales and the cost model includes procurement, inventory management, order fulfillment, and customer service (including returns).

Infrastructure marketplaces such as Ingram Micro and Tech Data sell computer and network hardware and software. Unlike many low-tech counterparts, these marketplaces are often required by suppliers to take control of physical inventory and often offer custom configuration for large business customers. Given the competitive nature of the technology industry and the short useful life of technology products, product pricing may be negotiated with sales representatives. Alternatively, the price may be set for the duration of a contract. The revenue model includes product sales and may include a commission or transaction fee on each sale. Because sales transactions take place online, infrastructure marketplaces must often electronically link to supplier databases and transaction systems to ensure that transactions can be completed and revenue can be recognized. This is reflected in the cost model.

Infrastructure aggregators such as Cnet.com and ZDNet provide information on high-tech products and services that are sold by others in the channel. They enable comparison of features and pricing and provide product reviews and technical reports but do not enable users to complete the final transaction.

Infrastructure exchanges such as Converge (formerly NECX) auction new and used electronic, computer, and network equipment, software, and solutions.

Infrastructure Portals

Infrastructure portals provide consumers and/or businesses with access to a wide range of network, computing, and application hosting services. Before the commercialization of the Internet, many large firms developed and ran their own networks and data centers, often leasing telephone services and data lines from network service providers that were called common carriers or value-added network services (VANs) providers. Small to midsize businesses often bought low-end computers and packaged software from local retailers, national distributors, or a network of value-added resellers (VARs) that also provided services such as installation, integration, and help desk repair and trouble shooting.

In the network era of the 21st century, a new option has emerged: An increasing number of small to midsize and even large organizations are choosing to "rent," rather than lease or buy, their digital infrastructure, which is hosted by an infrastructure

TABLE 2.4 Infrastructure Distributor Business Models

Models and Examples	Model Differentiators					Likely Revenues	Likely Costs
	Control Inventory	Sell Online	Price Set Online	Physical Product or Service			
Infrastructure retailers CompUSA.com Egghead	Yes	Yes	Not usually	Yes		Product sales; service fees	Advertising and marketing; physical facilities, inventory and customer service; R&D; IT infrastructure
Infrastructure marketplaces Ingram Micro Tech Data	Usually	Yes	Not usually, but may be customized	Yes		Transaction fees; service fees; commission; channel assembly fee	Advertising and marketing; R&D; IT infrastructure
Infrastructure aggregators C/Net ZD Net	No	No	No	Possibly		Referral fees; advertising and marketing fees	Advertising and marketing; R&D; IT infrastructure
Infrastructure exchanges Converge	Possibly	Possibly	Yes	Yes		Depends on model	Advertising and marketing; staff support for auctions (especially B2B); inventory and logistics if inventory control; R&D; technical infrastructure

Infrastructure distributor business model trends

- The speed of obsolescence of the technology, coupled with the complexity of the solution and slim margins, has forced massive consolidation in network and computing technology channels. For many, service revenues are driving profitability.
- Those distributors that take ownership of inventory are searching for inventoryless, just-in-time business models.
- Distributors that have the capability for custom configuration of products and services are gaining power.

portal player. Infrastructure portals, like their business portal counterparts, may be either horizontal or vertical. They are differentiated by the following characteristics (see Table 2.5):

- Does the firm provide "gateway access" to networks, data centers, or Web services?

- Does the firm host, operate, and maintain networks, data centers, or Web services?

- Does the firm provide access to hosted application services?

Horizontal infrastructure portals include ISPs (for example, America Online and Earthlink), network service providers (for example, AT&T, British Telecom, NTT Docomo, and Time Warner Cable), data center outsourcing providers (for example, IBM and EDS), and Web hosting service providers (for example, Digex). Horizontal infrastructure portals provide gateway access to a wide range of network, data center, and hosting services. The revenue model includes access and maintenance fees, subscription services, and in some cases transaction fees. If combined with an online content business (e.g., AOL), the portal also may generate advertising revenues. The key costs include data and network operations, software development and maintenance, marketing, sales, and administration.

Vertical infrastructure portals such as IBM's E-Business Solutions and General Electric's Global eXchange Services may also be called ASPs. ASPs host and maintain software applications (rather than selling or licensing them), enabling businesses and individuals to log in and conduct business online. Because ASPs often operate as a business portal rather than a consumer portal, advertising is a less significant source of revenue. Instead, ASPs may generate revenues through hosting and maintenance fees, consulting fees, and system integration fees. Key costs are similar to those incurred by horizontal portals.

Infrastructure Producers

Infrastructure producers design, build, market, and sell technology hardware, software, solutions, and services. Producers may sell and provide after-sales service directly or may share this responsibility with online/offline channel partners, including retailers, distributors, and portals (see Table 2.6):

- Does the business manufacture computer or network components or equipment?

- Does the business develop packaged software?

- Does the business provide infrastructure services or consulting?

Equipment/component manufacturers such as IBM, Sony, Lucent, and Intel design, produce, and distribute computer and network hardware. Component manufacturers such as Intel serve as suppliers to the industry, and original equipment manufacturers (OEMs) produce the computers and networks that are purchased by individuals and business customers. Cost categories are similar to those of other manufacturers of physical products, but costs are magnified by the rapid pace of obsolescence (with correspondingly high levels of R&D cost) and the need for highly specialized, "clean" factories.

TABLE 2.5 Infrastructure Portal Business Models

Models and Examples	Model Differentiators		Likely Revenues	Likely Costs
	Internet/Network Access and Hosting	Hosted Applications and Solutions		
Horizontal infrastructure portals America Online British Telecom Digex	Yes	Through partnership with noninfrastructure portals and ASPs	Access fees; commission, service, or transaction fees; subscription fees; hosting fees	R&D; IT infrastructure; advertising, marketing, and sales
Vertical infrastructure portals IBM E-Business Solutions GE Global eXchange Services	Often through partnership with horizontal infrastructure portals	Yes	Licensing fees; service and transaction fees; maintenance and update fees; hosting fees	Advertising, marketing, and sales; content/information asset management; R&D; IT infrastructure

Infrastructure portal business model trends

- Horizontal infrastructure portals (ISPs, network service providers, and Web hosting providers) are merging or partnering with horizontal content portals to increase value created through intangible assets such as information, community, and brand.

- Horizontal content portals such as AOL are vertically integrating with horizontal infrastructure providers such as Time Warner Cable. (*Note:* Before the AOL and Time Warner merger, AOL was both a horizontal portal and a horizontal infrastructure portal.) As Internet advertising revenues fall, horizontal portals such as Yahoo! that do not provide other sources of revenue are evolving their business models to include transaction-oriented services and revenue-sharing partnerships with infrastructure portals.

- Convergence of voice, data, and video channels and global industry convergence at the content and infrastructure levels.

- Convergence of voice, data, and video channels and global acceptance of a common set of standards are leading to global industry convergence at the content and infrastructure levels.

- Aggressive pursuit of a growing market for hosted application services is leading to confusion as players with markedly different business models converge on a common competitive space.

- Two competing vertical infrastructure portal (ASP) models are emerging: Producer-ASPs (for example, Oracle, Siebel, SAP) provide online access to Internet-enabled versions of their brand-name software; distributor-ASPs (for example, US Internetworking and Jamcracker) offer application hosting of many software brands.

TABLE 2.6 Infrastructure Producer Business Models

Models and Examples	Model Differentiators				Likely Revenues	Likely Costs
	Manufacture Equipment	Develop Software	Services/ Consulting			
Equipment/ component manufacturers IBM Sony Lucent Intel	Yes	Possibly	Possibly		Product license or sales; installation and integration fees; maintenance, update, and service fees	R&D; advertising, marketing, and sales; production; physical facilities and infra-structure; specialized equipment, materials, and supplies; IT infrastructure
Software firms SAP Siebel Oracle Microsoft	Rarely	Yes	Possibly		Product license or sales; installation and integration fees; maintenance, update, and service fees	R&D; advertising, marketing, and sales; production; physical facilities and infrastructure; specialized equipment, materials and supplies; IT infrastructure
Custom software and integration service providers Accenture Scient Value-added resellers	Possibly	Possibly	Yes		Commission, service, or transaction fee	Access to specialized talent; professional development and training; travel
Infrastructure services Agency.com Federal Express	Rarely	Possibly	Yes		Commission, service, or transaction fee; hosting fee	Content/information asset management; R&D; IT infrastructure

Infrastructure producer business model trends

• Many hardware and software producers were early adopters of online commerce, selling directly to Internet-savvy customers and through online distributors. For example, in 1999, over 80 percent of Cisco's sales were through online channels, most of which was through online distribution partners.

Software firms such as SAP, Siebel, Oracle, and Microsoft design, produce, and distribute operating system and packaged software. Operating system software, which provides the instructions that power computers and networks, often is sold with a computer system or network. Software applications sold by firms such as SAP, Siebel, and Oracle often include both transaction systems that automate a set of activities or processes (for example, inventory management, accounting, and order fulfillment) and database systems that enable access, storage, and packaging of information and reports. Traditionally, software was sold through direct and indirect channels and revenues came primarily from product sales. Over time, firms selling enterprise and database software developed their own consulting and integration services businesses to enable them to capture the value of the service fees associated with customizing and installing complex packages. These service fees were often at least double the cost of the software package. More recently, software firms have shifted toward a hosted ASP business model (discussed above).

Custom software and integration service providers such as Accenture and Scient provide consulting and custom system development and integration services, primarily for large firms undertaking large projects. VARs provide similar services for small to medium-size firms. Revenues come primarily from consulting and service fees. Recruiting, training, providing incentives for, and retaining highly skilled professionals represent the largest cost categories.

Infrastructure Service Providers

Infrastructure service providers such as Agency.com and Federal Express provide online/offline services to support logistics, marketing, and other shared services. Revenues are often generated through a combination of subscription fees, service fees, and transaction fees. Costs are based on the level of physical infrastructure and skilled professionals required.

The business model classification presented above provides a standard language for describing the various roles that an organization may play within increasingly networked worlds. It is important to note that there is no universally accepted standard classification. As a result, executives must clarify the key features of the business model or models that their organization has adopted or is adopting. It is also important to recognize that businesses are built and evolve over time. The next section discusses approaches to business model evolution.

Evolving Business Models

Networked businesses are built by artfully combining a variety of business models. These businesses are then linked with others across multiple value chain networks to create what Frank Getman, chief executive officer (CEO) and president of HoustonStreet Exchange, refers to as a "web for the Web."[19] By incorporating multiple

[19]"HoustonStreet Exchange Weaves New Round of Investments and Strategic Partnerships into Its 'Web for the Web.' HoustonStreet press release, March 23, 2000.

FIGURE 2.4
Approaches to Business Model Evolution

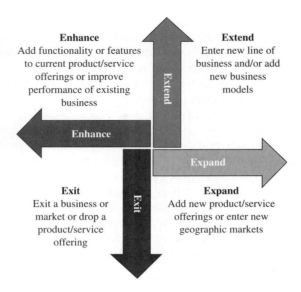

Enhance
Add functionality or features to current product/service offerings or improve performance of existing business

Extend
Enter new line of business and/or add new business models

Exit
Exit a business or market or drop a product/service offering

Expand
Add new product/service offerings or enter new geographic markets

business models that generate separate revenue streams from the same infrastructure, a network of businesses can more efficiently use resources, more effectively meet customer needs for integrated solutions, and drive additional value from the same level of investment. When the network of businesses inside a firm is linked with a business network composed of a much larger network of businesses, an organization can leverage the resources of the community to further enhance the value delivered to all the members.

The four approaches to evolving a business model that are shown in Figure 2.4 serve as a road map for evolving networked businesses. The evolution of the American Express and Amazon.com business models provides an excellent example of these four mechanisms in action.

Evolving the American Express Interactive Business Model

American Express had its roots in the "Wild West" of the 1850s.[20] The company started as the Wells Fargo Stagecoach Company and then evolved into the Pony Express. Over the next 150 years, American Express continued its pioneering spirit, inventing Travelers Cheques for the business traveler and the corporate card and the purchase card to help corporate customers manage and control travel and other expenses. In 1995, the company set out to use the Internet and associated networked technologies to transform its business yet again (see Figure 2.5).

American Express (AXI) recognized the potential of the Internet and started to explore the launch of an online travel service that would complement its face-to-face

[20]L. M. Applegate, *American Express Interactive* (HBS Publishing) (No. 802-022).

FIGURE 2.5
Evolving American Express Interactive: Timeline of Events

The Idea Takes Shape	AXI Travel Launched	Expense Management Launched	AXI Purchasing Solutions Launched	American Express@Work Launched	MarketMile Launched
1995	1997	1998	1999	1999	2000

services as early as 1995. Internal research at that time indicated that the profitability of AXI's traditional business would continue to erode because of decreased commissions from airlines and the increased cost of recruiting, training, and retaining the company's 12,000 travel counselors located in offices around the world. It was expected that an online travel service would reduce—but not replace—the cost of human travel counselors and physical brick and mortar and administrative infrastructure. It also would help solve the problem of industrywide shortages of travel counselors.

In addition, while it was impossible to quantify the value of the "strategic options" that could be pursued once an online channel to corporate customers was in place, all agreed that the follow-on business opportunities would be a significant component of the company's strategy in the years to come. In a stirring 1997 speech, an AXI senior executive called on corporate customers to work with the company to transform corporate travel:

> Some people think that the new Internet technologies will be harmful to the industry. Some of you have raised the question that, given our investment in the current way of doing business, why do we want to change? Well, the answer is simple. When change is inevitable, you have a choice: you can either follow or lead. And we all know that 9 times out of 10, the leader will get a disproportionate share of the gains. So we intend to lead. We know that we are better off working with you [our customers] to define the game rather than respond to someone else's standards.

Product/Service Enhancement

Planning for AXI Travel—the name of the online travel service—started in summer 1996. AXI Travel Version 1.0 was officially launched in November 1997. By February 1998, 50,000 business travelers in 225 corporations were using the online service to book $4.8 billion in travel. Enhancements were launched in March 1998 and June 1998 to respond to customers' and travel counselors' requests. This marked the beginning of a period of *continuous enhancements* that continued to February 2001. (See Figure 2.6 for a summary of the business model and evolutionary

FIGURE 2.6

Evolving
American
Express
Interactive:
Product/Service
Enhancements

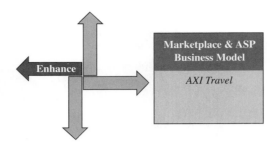

approach followed during late 1997 and early 1998.) An AXI executive explained the benefits:

> We found that AXI Travel decreased the cost of booking a travel reservation by over 50 percent. Thirty percent of the savings come from streamlining the process before adding the Internet reservation system, and the additional 20 percent come directly from AXI Travel. To realize the savings, we need to encourage our customers to shift at least 30 percent of their travel arrangements to AXI Travel.

Product/Service Category Expansion

The success of AXI Travel convinced executives that they could leverage the infrastructure and capabilities built for the online travel service and *expand* into new product categories (see Figure 2.7). An executive explained:

> AXI Travel was the perfect lead product because it was built from the beginning to be a hybrid product. Customers could still call up on the phone to make a travel reservation or they could use the computer. We've tried to make the barriers to using and adopting AXI Travel very low, because we think the leverage is in getting AXI Travel on as many desktops as possible and then launching additional products and services.

In 1998, AXI launched Expense Management, which enabled AXI corporate card users to integrate online expense data with internal expense management and general ledger systems. Because the expense management process was automated, corporate clients could further reduce their administrative costs. Expense Management also encouraged greater use of the AXI corporate card.

In May 1999, the company launched an enhanced Purchasing Solution to facilitate corporate procurement. A 1999 AXI/Ernst and Young study found that on average, firms that used manual purchasing processes spent approximately $90 to process a routine purchasing transaction, with some firms spending as much as $200 on certain transactions. In comparison, companies that used Internet-based and other electronic procurement systems to buy supplies, combined with a purchasing card for payment, spent from $4.44 to $15 per purchase. AXI Purchasing Solutions enabled AXI's corporate customers to capture those savings while also reducing AXI's costs for process transactions. At the same time, use of the new online service increased adoption and use of the AXI purchasing card.

FIGURE 2.7
Evolving
American
Express
Interactive:
Product/Service
Category
Expansion

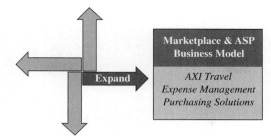

**Marketplace & ASP
Business Model**

*AXI Travel
Expense Management
Purchasing Solutions*

FIGURE 2.8
Evolving
American
Express
Interactive:
Business Model
Extension

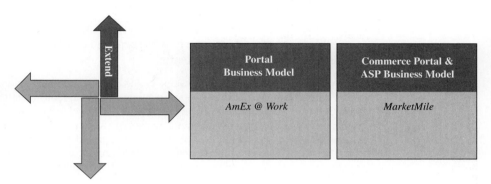

**Portal
Business Model**

AmEx @ Work

**Commerce Portal &
ASP Business Model**

MarketMile

Business Model Extension

As corporate customers gained experience using AXI's online services, they asked for a "gateway" through which they could access travel, expense, and purchasing services and reports. The fall 1999 launch of American Express @Work, an administrative services vertical portal, *extended* AXI's business model and provided the integrated view customers demanded. Word of its availability spread quickly through the travel agent network, and within the first quarter after launch, several hundred corporate customers had asked to gain access to the portal. (This is an excellent example of "viral marketing" within a B2B e-commerce network.)

By mid-1999, customers once again were encouraging AXI to offer new online services. This time they requested a robust, vendor-neutral one-stop shop through which buyers and sellers could conduct business. After attempting to launch a full-service B2B commerce portal inside AXI, the company determined that the scope of the new business justified the launch of a new company. MarketMile, a joint venture with Ventro Corporation, was announced in August 2000 to provide companies online procurement solutions. In addition to equity, Ventro brought several years of experience running multiple online vertical marketplaces[21] (see Figure 2.8).

[21]On January 15, 2002, Ventro changed its name to NexPrise, Inc. See M. Collura and L. Applegate, *Ventro: Builder of B2B Businesses* (HBS Publishing) (No. 801-042).

FIGURE 2.9
Evolving
American
Express
Interactive:
An Integrated
View

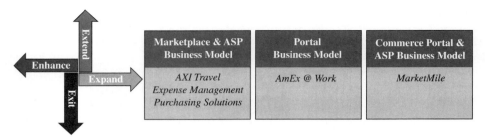

Summarizing AXI Evolution

In late 1997, even before American Express began to evolve AXI, a senior executive commented on its evolutionary potential:

> Once we have an electronic relationship, we have a great communication channel with a corporate customer. It allows us to create additional icons on our website through which we can present driving directions and travel information. We can enable business travelers to make hotel, restaurant, and car service reservations, and we can even help them obtain passports. More importantly, it also allows us to offer other American Express products and services to provide a one-stop shop for expense management, purchasing, and a wide variety of other business services. The possibilities are limitless.

Between 1997 and 2001, as AXI gained experience in running an online business and listened to the marketplace—especially its customers—new opportunities emerged, and the company capitalized on those opportunities (see Figure 2.9).[22] Early in 2002, it was clear that the opportunities would continue. For example, on February 18, 2002, IBM and MarketMile announced an alliance— E-Business on Demand—designed to help customers quickly reap the benefits of e-procurement and manage indirect expense spending via the Internet.[23] Under the terms of the agreement, MarketMile would provide new applications and a network of over 60 small to midsize suppliers for use on IBM's Leveraged Procurement Service.

Evolving the Amazon.com Business Model

The American Express story shows how an established company launched its first online product and then evolved it and its business model over time. Amazon.com

---

[22]At the time of the writing of this book, American Express Interactive had made no public announcements of exits from a product/service category or business.
[23]On February 25, 2002, American Express and IBM announced a technology services seven-year alliance worth more than $4 billion. Under the terms of the agreement, IBM would provide American Express with "utility-like" access to its vast computing resources. At the time of the agreement, IBM's computing operations were available in over 200 countries around the world and processed over 1 billion transactions daily (see American Express press release, February 25, 2002).

FIGURE 2.10
Evolving
Amazon.com

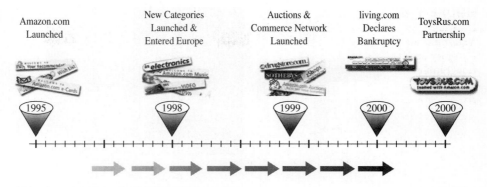

| Amazon.com Launched | New Categories Launched & Entered Europe | Auctions & Commerce Network Launched | living.com Declares Bankruptcy | ToysRus.com Partnership |

1995   1998   1999   2000   2000

FIGURE 2.11
Evolving
Amazon.com:
Product/Service
Enhancements

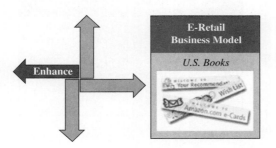

followed a similar pattern, launching its initial online bookstore in 1995, which then evolved to a full-service, horizontal portal and ASP (see Figure 2.10).

Product/Service Enhancement

From the moment it launched its online bookstore, Amazon.com immediately began *enhancing* its product/service offering and e-retailing capabilities (see Figure 2.11). It added new features, such as 1-Click shopping (which was later patented), sophisticated personalization, wish lists, and greeting cards. In 1999, it was one of the first online retailers to enable shopping through wireless devices.

Product/Service Category Expansion

Beginning in 1998, Amazon.com began aggressively *expanding* into new product categories (see Figure 2.12). It launched music and DVD/video in mid-1998, becoming the number one online music store within the first quarter of the launch and the number one DVD/video store within six weeks. Amazon.com also expanded internationally, acquiring British and German online bookstores to enter Europe in fall 1998. By early 2000, the company was not just an online bookstore but an online superstore, selling seven categories of products, from books, music, and videos to home furnishing, in over 160 countries.

FIGURE 2.12
Evolving
Amazon.com:
Category and
Geographic
Expansion

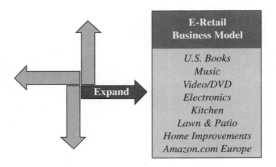

**E-Retail
Business Model**

*U.S. Books
Music
Video/DVD
Electronics
Kitchen
Lawn & Patio
Home Improvements
Amazon.com Europe*

Expand

FIGURE 2.13
Evolving
Amazon.com:
Business Model
Extension

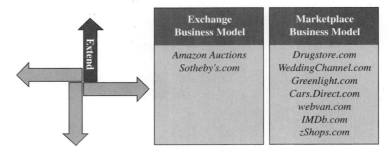

Extend

**Exchange
Business Model**

*Amazon Auctions
Sotheby's.com*

**Marketplace
Business Model**

*Drugstore.com
WeddingChannel.com
Greenlight.com
Cars.Direct.com
webvan.com
IMDb.com
zShops.com*

Business Model Extension

In 1998, Amazon.com extended its business model by launching two online auction stores—one low-end and one high-end—and an online marketplace for small merchants (called zShops)[24] (see Figure 2.13). In early 2000, Amazon.com extended its model once again, entering into a number of equity partnerships with brand-name online retailers such as Drugstore.com (health and beauty), Della.com (wedding and gift registry), Ashford.com (jewelry, watches, and gifts), furniture (living.com), and automobiles (Greenlight.com). It was estimated that these equity partnerships, which Amazon.com executives called its Commerce Network, would generate $1 billion in co-marketing revenues by 2005.[25]

Exit

Before summer 2000, the majority of Amazon.com's partnerships were with newly launched dot-coms that had yet to generate earnings.[26] With the bursting of the

---

[24]Over 100 small merchants could "rent" space in Amazon.com zShops. As of late 1999, zShop merchants paid the company $9.99 a month to open a web store, selling up to 3,000 items, or $.10 per individual item. In addition, the merchants paid Amazon a transaction fee of 5 percent for items priced less than $25, 2.5 percent for items worth $29 to $999, and 1.25 percent for items over $1,000.

[25]H. Becker, "Amazon.com," *Salomon Smith Barney Research,* December 8, 1999.

[26]Friday, April 14, 2000, ended a week of major downslides for both technology and blue-chip stocks. The Nasdaq Composite tumbled 355.46 points (9.7 percent) and closed at 3321.32 (its largest one-day point decline and second-largest percentage drop since

dot-com bubble in spring 2000, the alliances faltered. On August 30, 2000, Amazon.com partner living.com filed for Chapter 11 bankruptcy. Shortly thereafter, living.com executives announced their intention to seek an outright liquidation. Rather than find another partner, Amazon.com shut the doors of its Home Living online store and exited the product category. The company immediately informed its customers that their orders would be honored by other online retailers and redesigned its website to remove the "Home Living" tab. Anticipating the need for flexibility in the future, the new Amazon.com look downplayed the product categories offered on the site.

Evolution Continues

In August 2000, Amazon.com *extended* its model again with the announcement of a strategic alliance with ToysRus.com to create and operate a co-branded toy and video game store, which was launched in fall 2000.[27] With this move, Amazon.com adopted both marketplace and ASP business models. Under the terms of the 10-year agreement, ToysRus.com, in collaboration with its majority shareholder, Toys "R" Us, Inc., agreed to identify, buy, and manage inventory; Amazon.com handled site development, order fulfillment, and customer service. Adopting a business model similar to that of Federal Express, Amazon also managed ToysRus.com's inventory in its U.S. distribution centers. The agreement allowed for global expansion of the arrangement. Amazon.com was compensated through a combination of periodic fixed payments, per-unit transaction fees, and a "single-digit" percentage of revenue. Amazon.com also received warrants entitling it to acquire 5 percent of ToysRus.com. All the parties, including Toys "R" Us, Inc., marketed the co-branded store to their respective customers (see Figure 2.14).

FIGURE 2.14   **Evolving Amazon.com: An Integrated View**

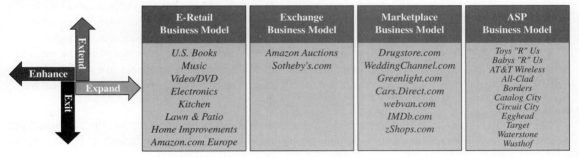

its inception in 1971). Amazon.com (stock symbol AMZN) was listed on Nasdaq. The Dow Jones Industrial Average slipped 616.23 points (5.6 percent) to 10,307.32, its worst ever one-day point loss. Amazon's stock price closed at $46.875 per share, down from its 52-week high of $113.00 on December 9, 1999. A. Task, "Ruthless Selloff Hits All Sectors: This Was One for the Record Books," www.theStreet.com (April 14, 2000). Declines continued throughout 2000, and by year end Amazon.com's stock price had sunk to less than $10 per share.
[27]T. Albright and L. Baker "Amazon.com," *Salomon Smith Barney Research*, February 5, 2001.

The economics of its ASP/marketplace business model were so favorable that many analysts expected that Amazon.com would continue to expand this model into new categories. Indeed, during 2001, Amazon.com signed partnership agreements with other established retailers and catalog merchants of physical products, adding new ASP/marketplace alliances[28] with All-Clad Metalcrafters, AT&T Wireless, Borders, Catalog City, Circuit City, Egghead.com, Target, Waterstone, and Wusthof. Amazon.com also extended its model to include the sale of digitally downloadable products, including a document delivery service, an e-books service, a magazine subscription service, a music download service, an online travel service (in partnership with Expedia), and a software download service. The flexibility of its platform enabled Amazon.com to respond to local trends quickly. For example, with the increasing popularity of the Seattle Mariners baseball stars Ichiro Suzuki and Kazuhiro Sasaki, Major League Baseball and Amazon.com teamed up in fall 2001 to sell Mariners team products in Japan. Seeking to capitalize on the powerful retailing franchise that Amazon.com had built, AOL Time Warner invested $100 million in Amazon.com to co-develop a powerful new shopping portal for its AOL.com and emerging broadband and wireless portals.[29]

During the first six years of its existence, Amazon.com evolved rapidly from an online bookstore to a multicategory/multimodel horizontal portal that offered a wide variety of niche businesses built using a variety of business models. By early 2001, its domestic books, music, and video stores were profitable on a pro forma basis.[30] During the fourth quarter of 2001, despite the economic downturn, Amazon.com announced its first quarter with over $1 billion in revenues and posted its first company profit of $5 million (in accordance with Generally Accepted Accounting Practices, or GAAP).[31]

Summary

It is just an incredible time to be in business and have the rules of business changing . . . For many years we operated under a pretty consistent set of rules. They evolved maybe . . . but now they're morphing and that presents a situation that challenges entrepreneurs to figure out: Are these rules real, or are they temporary? Should we respond to them? Do we create new rules? How do we run a company in a world like this when we have 13,000 employees trying to figure out where we are going and what we should do?[32]

If you think about it, we spent most of the 20th century creating the business rules that were used to build and run a successful company in the Industrial Economy and

---

[28]Many of these alliance partners allowed online customers to pick up and return physical products at the store.
[29]AOL Time Warner press release, July 23, 2001.
[30]In its annual report and SEC reporting, Amazon.com states that its pro forma accounting excludes stock-based compensation, amortization of goodwill, and certain other intangibles, restructuring charges, and other noncash costs.
[31]Amazon.com press release, January 22, 2002.
[32]David Pottruck, president and co-CEO of Charles Schwab, address to executives at the Harvard Business School, October 1999.

spent the last two decades breaking those rules. As we stand at the threshold of the 21st century, we are searching for new business models that enable a company to achieve the efficiency, power, resources, and reach of being big and the speed, agility, and responsiveness that come from being small.

As executives attempt to sort through the options available for building firms that can compete and succeed in the 21st century, they are finding that it is becoming less important to watch the actions of competitors and more important then ever to make decisions based on a deep understanding of the "business fundamentals" that define the structure and dynamics of markets, industries, and the organizations that compete within them. The following steps can be used to help guide business model analysis.

A Step-by-Step Approach to Analyzing Business Models

Step 1: *Profile your current business models.* Identify the generic models being used today. Analyze revenue and cost models. Determine strengths, weaknesses, and opportunities for improvement.

Step 2: *Determine how you might evolve your current model and/or identify new models to pursue.* Check out the business models used by your suppliers, customers, partners, and competitors. Check out business models of other companies outside your industry. Talk with customers, suppliers, partners, and industry experts.

Step 3: *Use the business model analysis framework to prioritize new models and initiatives.*

Evaluate the concept (opportunity): Assess market opportunity and dynamics, industry and competitive dynamics, business context and risk, product/service positioning, basis of differentiation, and evolutionary potential (strategic options). The analysis of the concept provides the foundation for developing a pricing model and a revenue forecast.

Evaluate the capabilities and resources required: Assess your ability to attract, engage and retain customers, suppliers, partners, and employees. Do you have the expertise and leadership needed to execute your short-term strategy and long-term strategy? Assess the appropriateness of operating and marketing plans and the infrastructure requirements. The capability and resource analysis provides the foundation for developing cost forecasts. Do you have the capabilities and resources that you need today and in the future? How will you build capabilities and acquire the resources required to reduce gaps?

Evaluate the value proposition (returns to all stakeholders): Evaluate benefits to all stakeholders; revenue, cost, and asset models; a profit model; cash flow projections; break-even timing; and financing needs. Check the consistency of the assumptions used to build the financial model with the opportunity and resource analysis.

Step 4: *Use the analysis in Step 3 as a benchmark to develop real-time performance monitoring systems.*

Step 5: *Revise your strategy, implementation plan, and performance measurement systems on an ongoing basis.*

The following questions can be used by executives to evaluate current and evolving business models.

1. What business model/models is your organization using today?

2. Does your business infrastructure enable you to evolve your business model to increase revenues generated per customer and to respond quickly to opportunities and threats?

3. Do you have the capabilities and resources that you need today and in the future? How will you build capabilities and acquire resources to reduce gaps?

4. Are you delivering benefits to all stakeholders? Can you demonstrate and communicate those benefits in ways that are objective and easy to evaluate and measure?

Appendix 2A

Business Model Revenue, Cost, and Asset Options

Sample Revenue Options

Commerce Revenues	
Revenue Category	**Description**
Product sales	Sell or license physical or information-based products
Commission, service, or transaction fees	Charge a fee for services provided; can be a set fee or a percentage of the cost of a product or service
Content Revenues	
Revenue Category	**Description**
Subscription fees	Charge for receipt of updated information on a particular topic or a broad range of topics for a specified period of time (e.g., annual)
Registration or event fees	Charge a fee for attendance at an online event, workshop, or course
Community Revenues	
Revenue Category	**Description**
Advertising, slotting, affiliate, and referral fees	Collect a fee for hosting a banner advertisement or special promotion Collect a fee for an exclusive or nonexclusive partnership relationship Collect a fee each time a visitor clicks through from your site to another company's site
Membership fees	Charge a fee to belong to a private group or service

Infrastructure Revenues	
Revenue Category	**Description**
Software/hardware sales	Sell or license a technology product
Installation and integration fees	Charge either a set or a variable fee for services provided; large-scale fixed-price projects are often broken into a series of discrete projects with well-defined time frames and deliverables; variable fees are often based on time, materials, and expenses incurred while working on a project
Maintenance and update fees	Charge a fee for software/hardware maintenance and updates
Hosting fees	Charge a fee for hosting a software application, website, data center, or network
Access fees	Charge a fee for providing access to a network and/or an Internet service

Sample Cost Categories

Cost Category	**Description**
People & partners	Cost to acquire, develop and retain skills and expertise needed to execute strategy; includes employees and partnerships
Advertising, marketing, sales	Cost of offline and online advertising, marketing, and sales
Business development	Cost of designing and launching new businesses, developing alliances, and acquiring partners
Materials & supplies	Cost of physical materials used in production of products and delivery of services; includes general purpose and specialized supplies and components
Specialized equipment (does not include IT)	Cost of equipment—especially capital equipment—used in design, production, delivery, and distribution
Research & development	Cost of designing and developing products and services; may overlap with IT infrastructure costs
Physical facilities and infrastructure	Cost of corporate and regional headquarters, sales offices, factories, warehouses, distribution centers, retail stores, service centers etc.
Information technology (IT) infrastructure	Cost of computers and equipment (e.g., printers, data storage devices) Cost to operate and maintain data centers Cost to design, develop, implement, and maintain software Cost of voice, data and video network equipment (e.g., physical cables, routers) Cost to design, operate, and maintain networks

(continued)

Sample Asset Categories

Current Assets	
Asset Category	**Description**
Financial assets	Accounts receivable Cash and convertible notes
Marketable securities	Investments made as part of a cash management program

Tangible Assets	
Asset Category	**Description**
Property, plant and equipment	Physical facilities Fixed assets required to produce goods and services
Inventory	Assets held for sale

Investments	
Asset Category	**Description**
Securities	Stock held by one firm to enable joint control over shared business activities Stock held by one firm in anticipation of a return at some time in the future
Real Estate	Investment in property in anticipation of a future return

Intangible Assets	
Asset Category	**Description**
Relationships	Breadth and depth of relationships with customers and the business community Loyalty and commitment of customers and business community members
Strength of online and offline brand	Strong brand recognition among business and consumer communities (includes corporate brand, business unit brands, product brands, and global brand) Ability to generate strong personal identification with brand Ability to leverage "Internet" brand image Reputation and image
Knowledge and expertise	Experience, skills, and intellectual capabilities of employees and partners Understanding of market and business dynamics Scope and granularity of stored information Flexibility and ease of accessing, customizing, and distributing information Information literacy Understanding of technical and business evolution and ability to identify opportunities and threats
Agility and responsiveness	Ability to quickly recognize and act on new opportunities and threats Ability to access and efficiently utilize resources required to execute strategy Ability to capture the attention and mobilize the commitment of customers and members of the business community to implement new strategies
Intellectual property	Patents, copyrights, etc., for which an objective measure of value can be assessed
Goodwill	Value of an acquired company over and above current and tangible assets The value of an acquired company's "franchise"—e.g., loyalty of its customers, expertise of its employees—that can be objectively measured at the time of a sale or change of control

Building the Network Economy: Capabilities and Organization

by Lynda M. Applegate

Few would dispute that the 1990s was a period of dramatic change. That decade dawned as a time of retrenchment as large, established firms struggled to shed the static, rigid structures, processes, and technologies that remained as a legacy of the Industrial Economy. As the decade drew to a close, we found ourselves in a period of unparalleled business innovation led by bold entrepreneurs with a vision of a global Networked Economy. While the early days of the Internet revolution were characterized by what many have called "irrational exuberance," the year 2000 marked a shift to a search for analytics and frameworks that could be used to build successful—and profitable—businesses.

The two chapters in this module discuss the design principles required to build successful 21st-century networked organizations. The module provides frameworks to guide executives in analyzing opportunities and in the design, launch, and growth of new ventures inside established firms or as independent, venture-funded start-ups.

3

Building Networked Businesses[1]

> Our dream and our plan well over a decade ago was simple. We set out to shape a global enterprise that preserved the classic big company advantages while eliminating the big company drawbacks. What we wanted to build was a hybrid enterprise with the . . . body of a big company and . . . the soul of a small company.[2]

Today's executives are both fascinated by and often skeptical of the new organizational models that they read about in the business press. But no matter what their position on any given model, most agree that traditional Industrial Economy designs will not work in a networked world. Large, established firms are trying to "act small" while not losing the advantages of "being big," and start-ups must act big to survive in a fast-paced, global Internet economy. As a result, all organizations must be designed to be big and small simultaneously. To accomplish this, new capabilities must be developed and new approaches to building and growing a company must be implemented.

This chapter examines the hybrid "big-small" organization design that is emerging as entrepreneurs and executives in established firms attempt to build businesses that can survive and prosper in today's fast-paced and uncertain environment. As the quote that starts this chapter implies, the challenges of building a big-small company are not new. Indeed, the insights presented in this chapter have emerged from over 15 years of research within hundreds of large firms that struggled throughout the 1980s and 1990s to transform their organizations to cope with

---

[1] This chapter is adapted from papers and materials published in L. M. Applegate, "Building Networked Organizations," in *Building Businesses in a Networked Economy* (Harvard Business School Publishing No. 802-063). Clipart used in the figures is reprinted with permission of Art Today (www.arttoday.com).
[2] J. Welch, "Letter to Shareholders," General Electric Annual Report, 1995.

the demands of a rapidly changing global economy.[3] The research insights from this study suggest that the new models that are emerging draw on many of the fundamental design principles that guided the way we built successful businesses in the past. (See appendix 3A for organization design characteristics.)

The Need for New Capabilities

If you think about it, we spent most of the 20th century building and perfecting Industrial Economy organization designs and the last two decades tearing them down. During the 1980s and 1990s, executives in large companies were obsessed with downsizing, delayering, and reengineering. Rigid organizational boundaries were shattered to enable firms to focus on core competencies while expanding into global markets. Strategic partnerships and alliances were formed to ensure access to capabilities and expertise that could not be built and managed inside.

The vision of eliminating hierarchy was compelling, and the change initiatives—many of them enabled by emerging information technologies—shook established organizations to their foundations. But if you took a walk around most firms in the mid-1990s, it was clear that the hierarchy was far from dead. Yet when asked what their companies should look like, most executives continued to express the need for a new design that would enable an organization to function as if it were both big and small.[4] The problem confronting these managers was that they could not sacrifice efficiency for speed and could not abandon the need for control as they empowered employees to make decisions addressing real-time customer needs.

Jack Welch, former chief executive officer (CEO) of General Electric, summed up this dilemma when discussing the challenges that his company faced when he assumed control in the early 1980s[5] (see Figure 3.1). "[When we entered the 1980s], we saw two challenges ahead of us, one external and one internal," he said. "Externally, we faced a world economy that would be characterized by slower growth, with stronger global competitors going after a smaller piece of the pie. Internally, our challenge was even bigger. We had to find a way to combine the power, resources, and reach of a large company with the hunger, agility, spirit, and fire of a small one."

In the early 1990s, Percy Barnevik, CEO of Asea Brown Boveri (ABB), echoed Welch's comments: "ABB is an organization with three internal contradictions. We want to be global and local, big and small, and radically decentralized with centralized reporting and control. If we resolve those contradictions, we create real competitive advantage."[6]

[3]L. M. Applegate, "In Search of a New Organization," in *Shaping Organization Form: Communication, Connection and Community,* eds. G. DeSanctis and J. Fulk (Newbury Park, CA: Sage, 1999); L. M. Applegate, "Time for the Big-Small Company," *Financial Times Mastering Information Management,* April 1999.
[4]L. M. Applegate, *Business Transformation Self-Assessment—1992–1993* (Harvard Business School Publishing, No. 194-013).
[5]J. Welch, "Managing in the 90s," GE Report to Shareholders, 1988.
[6]R. Simons and C. Bartlett, *Asea Brown Boveri* (Harvard Business School Publishing No. 192-139).

FIGURE 3.1
**The
Organization
Design
Challenge**

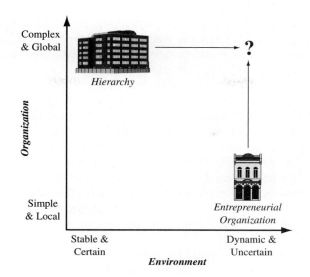

In the age of the Internet and associated networked technologies it is not just large established companies that are coping with the challenge of being big and small simultaneously. Entrepreneurial start-ups are also struggling with the problems that come from getting very big very fast. Consider the success—and challenges—experienced by Yahoo! and eBay. Those two Internet powerhouses grew from a handful of entrepreneurs in 1995 to multibusiness global companies in a few short years. While the pace of growth for entrepreneurial start-ups slowed during 2000 and 2001, executives leading small firms must still expand product lines and geographic reach quickly if they hope to keep pace and do business with the large firms that dominate most markets.

Is History Repeating Itself?

As timely as it seems, the management dilemma depicted above is not new. In fact, descriptions of "hybrid" organizations designed to enable companies to act big and small simultaneously were common in the 1950s and 1960s.[7] (Interestingly, these new organizational models were pioneered by rapidly growing technology start-ups in the aerospace and computer industries.) One of these hybrid designs—the matrix—was originally billed as the "obvious organizational solution" to the

[7]T. Burns and G. M. Stalker, *The Management of Innovation* (London: Tavistock, 1961); J. Woodward, *Industrial Organization, Theory and Practice* (London: Oxford University Press, 1965); J. D. Thompson, *Organizations in Action* (New York: McGraw-Hill, 1967; P. Lawrence and J. Lorsch, *Organization and Environment* (Boston: Harvard Business School Press, 1967, 1986); L. Greiner, "Evolution and Revolution as Organizations Grow," *Harvard Business Review* 50(4):37–46, 1972; J. Galbraith, *Designing Complex Organizations* (Reading, MA: Addison-Wesley, 1973).

need for control and efficiency while simultaneously enabling flexibility and speed of response.[8] Decades ago, proponents of the matrix argued for an "adaptive, information-intensive, team-based, collaborative, and empowered" organization—all characteristics of today's 21st-century organizations.

But companies that adopted the hybrid designs of the 1960s and 1970s soon learned that the new structures and systems bred conflict, confusion, information overload, and costly duplication of resources. Bartlett and Ghoshal discuss why many firms adopted the matrix only to abandon it several years later: "Top-level managers are losing control of their companies. The problem is not that they have misjudged the demands created by an increasingly complex environment and an accelerating rate of environmental change, nor that they have failed to develop strategies appropriate to the new challenges. The problem is that their companies are organizationally incapable of carrying out the sophisticated strategies they have developed. Over the past 20 years, strategic thinking has outdistanced organizational capabilities."[9]

Given such problems, one might legitimately ask, "If these hybrid organizations failed in the past, why are we trying them again?" Interestingly, one of the major sources of difficulty with the matrix was the dramatic increase in the need for timely information to manage it successfully.[10] While the hierarchy managed complexity by minimizing it, the matrix demanded that managers deal with complexity directly. Product managers had to coordinate their plans and operations with functional managers. Country managers had to coordinate activities with headquarters. And senior managers, attempting to reconcile overall organization performance and plan corporate strategy, were faced with a dizzying array of conflicting information.

In the large hierarchical companies of the 1960s and 1970s, paper-based and word-of-mouth information moved slowly and channels of communication were limited. While the mainframe computer systems of the day helped process some of that information, they were designed, like the hierarchy itself, to support centralized decision making and hierarchical communication. The microcomputer revolution of the 1980s provided tools to decentralize information processing, which helped improve local decision making, but the technology to support both local and enterprisewide information sharing and communication was inadequate.

Only recently has information technology (IT) become capable of meeting this challenge (see Figure 3.2). The "networked IT revolution" of the late 1990s—reflected in the emergence of the Internet, electronic commerce, and increasingly integrated, powerful, and flexible databases and business systems—has made possible information processing and communication infrastructures that match the needs of companies that wish to operate as if they were both big and small.

---

[8]C. Bartlett and S. Ghoshal, *Managing across Borders: The Transnational Solution* (Boston: Harvard Business School Press, 1991).
[9]Ibid.
[10]Research in the mid-1960s suggested that successful firms operating in uncertain and complex environments developed systems to improve vertical and lateral information processing in the firm. See Galbraith, op. cit., and Lawrence and Lorsch, op. cit.

FIGURE 3.2
Networked
Organizational
Models Are
Enabled by
Networked
Technologies

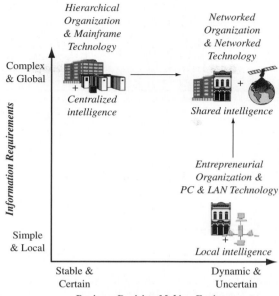

Business Decision Making Environment

But improved technology is not the complete answer. Although the networked IT infrastructure can provide important tools, it cannot define the information that needs to be in the system. In addition, while the networked infrastructure can *enable* new organizational structures and systems, it cannot motivate people to use the information to make decisions and take actions on behalf of the organization. New organizational capabilities are required to execute the sophisticated network strategies and business models.

Blueprint for a Networked Organization

Designing, implementing, and constantly evolving the structures and systems that enable an organization to execute its strategies and accomplish its goals is one of the most formidable tasks facing 21st-century business executives. Architects understand that a poor building design leads to inefficiencies, cost overruns, and construction delays. A well-conceived architectural blueprint, by contrast, helps prevent such problems. Likewise, executives must have a well-conceived "business blueprint" to design a successful company. Each floor in the business blueprint depicted in Figure 3.3 represents a category of business design. The three categories—operating and innovating, managing and learning, and leading and engaging—build upon one another to provide the organization and technological infrastructure required to build a networked organization for the 21st century.

FIGURE 3.3
Blueprint for a "Big-Small" Business

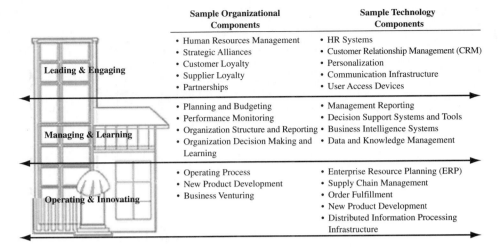

	Sample Organizational Components	Sample Technology Components
Leading & Engaging	• Human Resources Management • Strategic Alliances • Customer Loyalty • Supplier Loyalty • Partnerships	• HR Systems • Customer Relationship Management (CRM) • Personalization • Communication Infrastructure • User Access Devices
Managing & Learning	• Planning and Budgeting • Performance Monitoring • Organization Structure and Reporting • Organization Decision Making and Learning	• Management Reporting • Decision Support Systems and Tools • Business Intelligence Systems • Data and Knowledge Management
Operating & Innovating	• Operating Process • New Product Development • Business Venturing	• Enterprise Resource Planning (ERP) • Supply Chain Management • Order Fulfillment • New Product Development • Distributed Information Processing Infrastructure

In the past, managers learned to create and use business blueprints as they progressed up the management ladder. In the Network Economy, old blueprints are not adequate and new ones are only beginning to be developed. The business design represented in the business blueprint must unite organizational and technological capabilities to enable a network of organizations and individuals to accomplish shared goals. To simplify our discussion, we begin by defining new management principles from the perspective of a single organizational entity. Later sections of this chapter expand the discussion to examine emerging networked models of organization.

Operating and Innovating

The operating processes of a firm include all the activities a firm and its suppliers and partners undertake to design, build, market, sell, and deliver products and services as well as serve and "care for" customers, suppliers, and business partners. The key to success for companies operating in turbulent, rapidly changing environments is the ability to flexibly adapt these operating activities to address customer, market, competitive, regulatory, or environmental requirements or to adapt to business innovations or changes in strategy.

Hierarchical Operations

Traditional hierarchical firms define rigid procedures that structure how operating activities must be performed and then group them within the functional units that will be responsible for them. Strategy and performance goals are set at the top and cascade down to all employees. At lower levels in the organization, detailed policies, procedures, and job descriptions ensure that everyone has the skills needed and knows exactly what needs to be done to ensure smooth, efficient operations.

Entrepreneurial Operations

Entrepreneurial companies do not depend on well-defined policies and procedures or structured jobs. Entrepreneurial work is defined, coordinated, and performed in real time by founders and employees who are in constant contact with each other and the marketplace. Employees may be chosen on the basis of specific skills and experience, but once hired, they are expected to play multiple, changing roles as the company grows and evolves. While hierarchical firms use structure, systems, and the scale that comes from being big to ensure efficiency and precision execution, entrepreneurial firms use their small size, ready access to information, and capability for direct and continuous interactions to operate in real time, responding quickly to customer needs, opportunities, and competitive threats.

Networked Operations

Big-small companies must ensure both precision execution and fast-cycled innovation. This requires that operating processes be designed to fully exploit the power of both people and technology—whether these assets are in your firm or in someone else's. When embedded within a digital operating infrastructure, technology can be used to ensure precision execution and coordination of routine tasks while people use real-time information generated by technology-enabled *transaction systems* to deal with unforeseen problems or opportunities and to personalize and continuously improve operations.[11]

To prevent digital operations from being encased in rigid technology, executives must ensure that systems and the processes they support are designed from the beginning with change in mind. This requires careful attention to modular design with standardized interfaces between modules.[12] In addition, information required to coordinate activities and improve them continuously must be siphoned into flexible, powerful, and robust enterprise information management systems (often called data warehouses). Finally, easy-to-use information access and analysis tools can be used to put executives, employees, and partners directly in touch with the real-time information and expertise needed to manage the business. This flexible, robust, fully networked digital operating infrastructure—combined with big-small company structures, processes, and incentives—is a key tool for building the networked business capabilities summarized in Figure 3.4.

---

[11]In computer programming, a transaction refers to a sequence of computer code that is used to perform a specific task. In business, the exchange of information, goods, and/or services is also called a transaction. Uniting these technical and business definitions, a transaction system is one that enables one or more individuals or organizational entities to perform a task or exchange information, goods, and/or services. The "transaction layer" of an IT architecture forms the core of an organization's IT infrastructure.

[12]C. Baldwin and K. Clark, *Design Rules: The Power of Modularity* (Cambridge, MA: MIT Press, 2000).

FIGURE 3.4 Operating and Innovating Capabilities

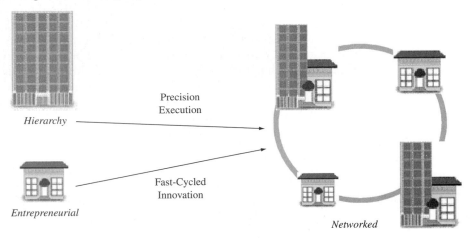

Capabilities	Business Design Requirements
Precision execution	• Streamlined, integrated, and efficient operations seamlessly link activities performed inside the firm with those performed by customers, partners, and suppliers. • Cost, cycle time, and quality levels are benchmarks within the industry and exceed customer-stakeholder requirements.
Fast-cycled innovation	• Flexible, modular designs enable customization, personalization, and continuous improvement. • Change processes are embedded within the company's day-to-day operations. • Employees are rewarded for devising new, innovative ways to serve customers. • Resources for change are available. • There is a standardized and widely accepted process used to develop and present the "business case" and implementation plan for a potential idea.
Customer and community connected (All key stakeholders, including suppliers and partners, are considered "customers" of an e-business.)	• Executives and employees in all parts of the organization have the information required to understand the lifetime value of customers, suppliers, and partners and have the ability and authority to make decisions and take actions to improve satisfaction and loyalty. • Incentive systems reward success in attracting and retaining profitable customers, suppliers, and partners and in increasing the frequency and level of engagement.

PSA is an excellent example of a company that has exploited the power of digital technologies to build the operating and innovating capabilities required to succeed in the Network Economy.[13] The company, which calls itself "The World's Port of Call," operates and manages transshipment ports for the country of Singapore and 10 other ports in eight countries around the world, including China, Italy, India, Yemen, Brunei, and Portugal. PSA began building its digital operating capabilities in the mid-1980s with the automation of both its internal port operations and routine transactions with external stakeholders, including freight forwarders, shipping companies, and government agencies. By 2000 the company had launched a fully integrated and streamlined Internet-based networked operating infrastructure that provided the small country of Singapore with the distinction of being the number one transshipment port in the world.

Between 1993 and 1999 the company exploited the operating capabilities it had built to (1) increase the total transshipment volume handled in PSA's ports in Singapore from 9 million to over 17 million 20-foot equivalent units (TEUs),[14] (2) increase the number of ships able to unload over 100 containers per hour from 59 to almost 800, (3) increase the number of ports connected from 374 to over 509, and (4) increase the number of airport passengers from 2.4 million to over 6.2 million. In addition, productivity increased from 1,200 TEUs per employee in 1993 to over 2,300 TEUs per employee in 1999.

PSA not only increased the precision with which it executed port operations, it also dramatically increased the pace of innovation, launching two new product/service offerings and two new businesses in the late 1990s. Each new venture leveraged the infrastructure and capabilities PSA had built for use inside its organization to enter new markets and generate new sources of revenue. In the early 1990s, PSA launched a consulting service to assist ports around the world in streamlining and automating operations. The second venture enabled distant ports to outsource port operations to PSA. The third, a wholly owned subsidiary called Portnet.com (www.portnet.com), was a software company that licensed PSA's software to ports, shippers, and other members of the shipping community. Alternatively, the software could be hosted by Portnet.com and delivered as a service. The fourth new venture, Port Care Services, provided distribution, logistics, inventory management, and asset management services for members of the shipping community.

In 2001, in recognition of the precision execution, quality, and innovation of its operations, the Asian Freight Industry voted PSA as the "Best Container Terminal Operator (Asia)" for the 11th consecutive time, and Singapore was voted "Best Seaport (Asia)" for the 12th consecutive time. PSA's subsidiary, Changi International Airport Services Pte Ltd., was voted the "Best Air Cargo Terminal Operator" for the second time. In addition, PSA Corporation scored a "Double First" at the prestigious

---

[13]Privatized in 1997, PSA originally operated as a unit within the government of Singapore. See L. M. Applegate, Neo Boon Siong, Nancy Bartlett, et al., *PSA: The World's Port of Call* (Harvard Business School Publishing No. 802-003). Visit PSA at www.psa.com.
[14]The shipping industry measures the volume of work performed by a port in terms of 20-foot equivalent units. Each unit represents one 20-foot container ship.

Lloyd's List Maritime Asia Awards organized by *Lloyd's List,* an international shipping daily. In the same competition, PSA Corporation won the "Best Container Terminal Award," while its flagship project in China, Dalian Container Terminal, won the "Best Emerging Container Terminal Award."

Managing and Learning

The management processes and structures of a firm include all the activities that a firm and its business community (including customers, suppliers, and partners) undertake to

- Plan strategy and how it will be executed

- Allocate resources

- Organize people into groups and coordinate work

- Monitor and measure performance

- Adjust strategies, plans, budgets, and organizations based on learning

Traditional Management Process

In traditional hierarchies, planning, budgeting, and performance monitoring are often driven from the top of the firm. Given that fact, until recently, major strategic initiatives usually were planned well in advance of execution (before the 1990s, 10-year strategic plans were typical), policies, procedures, and organization design changed slowly. As a result, most planning and budgeting processes focused primarily on setting incremental goals and allocating the resources required to carry them out. These formal planning and budgeting systems have formed the basis for routine performance monitoring and reporting systems that in public firms often are tied to quarterly reporting requirements.

Accompanying this routine reporting process is daily monitoring and control of local operations. At the most fundamental level, hierarchies control operations through detailed policies and procedures that tell employees inside and outside the firm exactly what needs to be done to perform routine operations.[15] Once everyone knows what to do, local on-site supervisors are placed in the hierarchy to watch and make sure everyone performs efficiently and effectively. When something unexpected happens or a problem occurs (and the solution to the problem is within a local supervisor's accountability and authority), a decision can be made on the spot. If the decision requires coordination with others at a higher level or in other parts of the organization, the problem or opportunity is passed up the line until someone (or a group of people) is willing and able to make a decision. These decisions must unite the vision and goals of senior executives with the reality of the business environment. Without a clear understanding of strategic direction *and* detailed and timely information from the field, these decisions take time. Thus, hierarchical manage-

---

[15]It is important to note that structured outsourcing contracts enable an organization to extend hierarchical control across organizational boundaries.

ment is effective only in relatively stable business environments where change happens slowly and there is sufficient time to gather information, analyze and make sense of it, define what needs to be done, and then hire, train or redeploy the people required to implement the necessary solutions.

Entrepreneurial Management Process

In traditional entrepreneurial organizations information and management decision making are timed to the rapidly changing business environment. This enables founders and employees to keep in close touch with each other and the market. As a result, planning, decision making, action, and performance management are informal and ad hoc. Real-time sharing of information and perspective and the ability to respond quickly on the basis of what is being learned are fundamental to effective entrepreneurial management. As an entrepreneurial firm grows larger and more complex, this learning model of management breaks down and more structured operating and management processes are required. Therefore, the evolution of a successful entrepreneurial firm often results in its passage through a series of stages, during which the organization evolves divisionally from a team to a simple functional structure to a multitiered hierarchy.[16]

Networked Management Process

"Big-small" companies must unite the high levels of control and integration achieved through hierarchical planning, monitoring, and performance measurement systems with the fast-cycled "learning by doing" approach that is characteristic of an entrepreneurial organization. Twenty-first-century IT enables this vision by providing access to a shared source of real-time information on market dynamics, operations, and performance that enables real-time planning and performance monitoring. Tools to support analysis, interaction, and collaboration enable perspectives to be shared and decisions to be made by people who work in distant locations and even different companies. Broadband communication systems can be used to help share the "vision" of senior management with employees in the parts of an organization. When flexible Internet technologies are embedded within a company's day-to-day operations *and its organization design and management process,* a firm's routine activities can operate smoothly and efficiently. At the same time, improved access to information enables employees, customers, and partners to invent new ways of working and to respond quickly.

But technology is not sufficient. In a constantly changing and complex global firm, information comes from many sources. Learning requires that people get together to debate the meaning of the information and its implications for decisions and actions. Even when insights have been translated into actionable plans, no single individual can make change happen. As a result, the ability to learn while we execute today's business and invent tomorrow's also requires that people be organized and motivated to take what they learn and share those insights with others. These capabilities are summarized in Figure 3.5.

[16]Greiner, op. cit.

FIGURE 3.5 **Managing and Learning Capabilities**

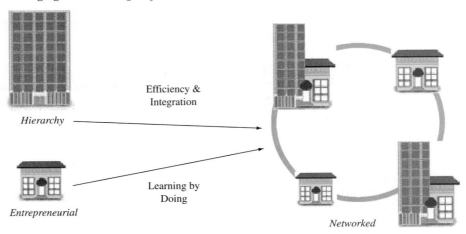

Capabilities	Business Design Requirements
Control and integration	• Coordination and control of routine operations are embedded within the digital operating infrastructure. • Early-warning systems enable close monitoring and immediate response to threats and opportunities. • "Critical failure factors" have been identified, and "disaster recovery" procedures are in place.
Learning by doing	• Real-time information and interactive management systems—a mix of face-to-face decision making supplemented by high-bandwidth communication systems—enable large dispersed teams of people (not all of whom may work in the same company) to make informed decisions, take action, and receive immediate feedback. • Key operating metrics are directly linked to financial and market results to provide real-time feedback. • Shared, actionable goals provide direction and the framework within which decisions can be made and evaluated.
Flexible and well-managed boundaries	• Employees and partners have a clear understanding of the role they play and how to work with others to get things done. But these clearly defined roles must not limit people's ability to work across boundaries—inside the firm and with suppliers, partners, and customers. • In a networked organization, companies are highly skilled at forming and successfully managing strategic alliances and partnerships. • If a company is growing by acquisition, companies must be highly skilled at identifying and effectively integrating the people, processes, and systems that unite acquired companies.

FIGURE 3.5 Managing and Learning Capabilities *(continued)*

Capabilities	Business Design Requirements
Flexible and well-managed boundaries *(continued)*	• Formal and informal communication systems support frequent two-way interactions inside and outside the firm. • Coordinating mechanisms (for example, advisory councils, governing boards, liaison roles, and information systems) enable effective coordination and control of activities that cross internal and external boundaries.
Accessible knowledge assets	• The information needed to make decisions and take actions is relevant, timely, and readily available to those who need it. It is presented in a form that is immediately actionable. • People are information-literate and have the skills and incentives needed to turn information into action that is consistent with the best interests of the organization and its stakeholders. • Information and best practices are openly shared. • Politics, bureaucracy, and poorly aligned incentives do not get in the way of sharing and learning from information. • Processes are in place to ensure that information is accurate and reliable and that employees, partners, customers, and suppliers trust the information they receive. • Privacy and confidentiality are safeguarded, and security procedures are strictly enforced.

Founded in 1994, Internet Securities, Inc., provided business professionals with reliable, timely financial, business, and political information on emerging markets. Its information service was launched on the Internet in 1995, and it was one of many entrepreneurial firms in the late 1990s that faced the challenge of building the management systems and organization required to succeed in the Network Economy.[17] By the time of its sale to Euromoney PLC in 1999, Internet Securities was providing information on 26 emerging markets as widely dispersed as Bulgaria, Croatia, Hungary, Poland, Romania, Russia, Argentina, Chile, Colombia, Ecuador, China, Malaysia, and Vietnam.[18] The company connected over 650 information suppliers to thousands of business professionals in over 600 global firms, including General Electric, JP Morgan, Deutsche Morgan Grenfell, KPMG, and ING Barings. CEO and founder Gary Mueller explained: "[In a few short years] we built this company from a few people working together out of a third-floor walk-up apartment to over 250 people with highly specialized expertise located in 18 country offices around the world."

During the early days, the company was structured as a single, self-managing team. But as the company began to sell its service and collect revenues, functional

---

[17]L. M. Applegate, *Internet Securities Inc.: Building a Business in Internet Time* (Harvard Business School Publishing No. 398-007).
[18]The data in this case example were collected in late 1999. In April 2002, Internet Securities provided information from over 4,400 local information sources on 35 emerging markets. Visit the company website at www.securities.com for up-to-date information.

specialists such as accountants, salespeople, and operations professionals were hired. As the company added country offices, regional headquarters offices were opened and experienced executives were hired. Along with the structure came formal management processes, but the cycle time of those processes was much faster than would be expected in a hierarchical firm. For example, senior management met (either face to face or through teleconferencing) weekly rather than quarterly to plan and review performance, and everyone received daily information on critical business measures. Formal budgeting systems were implemented. Chief Financial Officer (CFO) Jack Hanna explained:

> We roll up the entire company's books within ten days of month-end and then formally close the books. Considering that we are in 18 different emerging markets, each of which has its own currency, this requires a significant amount of staff time as well as integrated and reliable information systems. Most entrepreneurial firms do not have strong systems and processes until much later in their development. We put these systems in ahead of the curve. We believe that it provides a tremendous level of discipline in the firm and also enables us to better understand our business. We catch problems much earlier and can take actions to solve them before they escalate. We can also spot opportunities much faster. A well-designed budgeting system is the most basic form of control in companies; it's the blueprint that outlines the strategy and business plan, and it gives everyone a way to measure progress toward business goals.

But Mueller and Hanna recognized that formal systems could not replace the real-time learning and interactions that had enabled the company to respond quickly when the firm was small:

> We report sales and detailed information on operations on a weekly basis. Everyone in the firm can review online sales charts and drill down so we know exactly which of our information products is selling to individual users within each customer site. We know who is using our service and how they are using it. We also have very detailed information on all of our information providers. We know exactly what type of information they provide and how well, and where, it is selling. A country manager and local salespeople can tell exactly how well our information products are selling and can work with information providers to help them target and deliver the most valuable information. They can see what local customers are viewing and can use this information to help increase subscription revenues. They can also see what information is selling in distant markets and can coordinate with salespeople in nearby country offices to identify changes that might be needed to meet a specific customer's requirement. For example, if certain types of information on Russia or Brazil are not selling well in Poland, the information analysts in Russia or Brazil will know immediately. They can talk to local salespeople in Poland, who in turn can talk with customers to find out why. The information analysts in Russia and Brazil can then talk with their local information providers to create new information or to package existing information to meet the needs of distant customers. Access to this detailed, timely operating data provides direct benefits to local employees. Their bonuses are tied to increasing revenues from customers and information providers in their market. It also benefits senior management since it helps us understand the dynamics of the business and enables us to participate as full partners in making business decisions.

Leading and Engaging

Leadership is a buzzword, like *empowerment,* that everyone uses yet most people still struggle to define. Many believe that leadership is just a matter of charisma and vision—either you have it or you don't. Nothing is further from the truth. Leadership skills, like the management skills discussed above, can be acquired and honed. While management is all about coping with complexity, leadership is all about attracting and mobilizing the resources for change.[19] As can be seen below, both involve complementary activities:

- While management involves planning and budgeting, leadership involves defining a clear, compelling vision and ensuring that it is translated into a set of actionable strategies and initiatives.

- While management involves organizing and staffing, leadership involves attracting, motivating, energizing, and retaining top talent inside an organization and within partner, supplier, and customer networks.

- While management involves control and problem solving, leadership creates a culture and ensures that values, beliefs, and behaviors are deeply ingrained and reflected in the decisions made and the actions taken.

Hierarchical Leadership

In traditional hierarchical firms, the emphasis at most levels was on *managing complexity by minimizing it.* Thus, management process overshadowed leadership. Much of the problem was due to the fact that information moved slowly and inefficiently. Thus, the cost of coordinating activities and decisions across organization boundaries increased significantly. Risks were minimized by centralizing decision making, segregating activities, and structuring work rigidly. Deep hierarchical chains of command enabled direct monitoring and supervision of work. Segmentation of work and authority, together with direct supervision, ensured that, short of sabotage, no one had the authority—or opportunity—to perform an action that would threaten the entire company. But this consistency and control came at a cost.

In large, established companies, employee self-interest (usually motivated by pay for performance) and compliance replaced the commitment and engagement found in entrepreneurial firms. Real-time understanding of business and market dynamics and the ability to respond quickly to change were also lost. But as long as the business environment remained stable, there was time for scores of analysts and controllers in corporate headquarters to provide senior executives with the information needed to set the direction, attract and train employees, and implement performance management systems and incentives to ensure that the strategy was executed efficiently and effectively.

---

[19]See J. Kotter, "What Leaders Really Do," *Harvard Business Review,* 2001 (HBR On Point No. 3820).

Entrepreneurial Leadership

Howard Stevenson, professor of business administration and longtime head of the entrepreneurial management unit at Harvard Business School, defined entrepreneurship as the ability to "create or seize an opportunity and pursue it *regardless of the resources currently controlled.*"[20] Thus, entrepreneurial leadership requires that founders be able to attract, motivate, and engage people, partners, and investors in the task of working together to create a new venture. To accomplish this, entrepreneurs must be able to create a clear and compelling vision that excites and deeply engages all involved. While the vision may include a monetary incentive, often it is so vague and far off in the future that it cannot serve as a primary motivator.[21] Thus, entrepreneurial leadership must be capable of energizing and inspiring others, and entrepreneurial cultures drive this engagement and motivation toward a common vision throughout an organization and into its dealings with customers, suppliers, and partners. Shared goals, beliefs, and values provide the guiding principles that enable people to make decisions and take actions to execute strategy and meet shared objectives.

Networked Leadership

In the Network Economy, the free flow of information throughout the company (and with customers, suppliers, and business partners) enhances the ability of employees, customers, partners, and executives to share in defining both a clear and compelling vision for change and the necessary tactical initiatives required to achieve business goals. When this is aligned with incentives and motivations that foster commitment rather than simply compliance, large companies can adopt entrepreneurial-style decision-making structures and entrepreneurial leadership can be infused throughout the organization.

What keeps entrepreneurial, self-managing teams from doing things that will harm the company? In entrepreneurial organizations, the close proximity and shared perspective among founders, employees, customers, and partners enables everyone to be involved in key decisions and actions and to monitor results closely. Small size also enables a fast response when problems occur.

In complex global organizations senior executives cannot oversee every decision or action taken by empowered teams. As a result, it is more important for them to identify key strategic risks—which we call *critical failure factors*—and ensure that they have effective control systems in place. The availability of real-time information can assist with risk management, but senior managers should not delude themselves that online monitoring is all that is required. Direct supervision and segregation of authority may be required to manage areas of extreme vulnerability. Figure 3.6 illustrates the capabilities required to effectively engage employees, partners, customers, and suppliers in achieving shared goals.

---

[20]H. Stevenson, "A New Paradigm for Entrepreneurial Management," *Proceedings of the 7th Anniversary Symposium on Entrepreneurship,* July 1983 (Boston: Harvard Business School, 1984).
[21]It is important to note that in the late 1990s, the promise of quick returns on investment distorted the entrepreneurial leadership process.

FIGURE 3.6   Leading and Engaging Capabilities

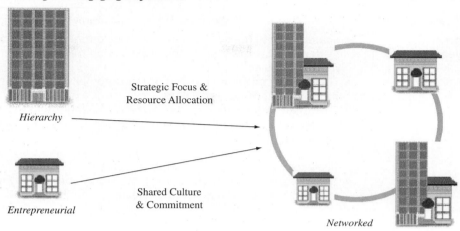

Capabilities	Business Design Requirements
Visionary yet pragmatic leadership	• Credible leaders at all levels of the organization are able to articulate clear direction. • Leadership is trusted and well respected and, as a result, is able to attract and retain high-quality partners and talented employees. • "Visions" are translated into actionable strategies that can be executed and deliver results while the window of opportunity is still open. • Leaders are able to set tangible goals and make focused decisions. • Executives are directly involved in the business; they ensure that barriers are removed, resources are available, and employees have the skills and motivation to accomplish growth.
Energized participation	• Culture and incentives foster innovation while ensuring a strong commitment to delivering results. This requires that large projects be broken into smaller, more focused deliverables and that senior management break down barriers and realign goals. • Employees, customers, suppliers, and partners believe that managers and other leaders possess the knowledge, skills, and experience needed to run the business. • "Stretch targets" energize action and motivate everyone to achieve peak performance. • Leaders display a strong commitment to career development and learning for all.
Skilled in conflict resolution, negotiation, and consensus	• Processes are in place to ensure that conflicting opinions are discussed openly without becoming destructive. • Employees and partners are skilled at negotiating "win-win" agreements. • Despite conflicting opinions, consensus decisions can be reached and implemented quickly.

(continued)

FIGURE 3.6 **Leading and Engaging Capabilities** *(continued)*

Capabilities	Business Design Requirements
Ingrained values	• Shared values are widely communicated, routinely reevaluated, and evident in how everyone in the organization treats customers, suppliers, partners, and each other. • The strategy of the firm and its organization design are consistent with its espoused mission and values. • The organization considers the interests of—and fulfills its obligations to—all of its stakeholders, including customers, suppliers, partners, employees, and investors. • The organization fulfills its obligations to society and contributes positively to the communities in which it operates. • The company is consistently ranked as "highly admired" by industry analysts, business and government leaders, and the general public.

PepsiCo is a firm that built a big-small company long before it became fashionable.[22] As early as the 1960s PepsiCo executives had emphasized divisional autonomy and decentralization. During the 1980s, the newly appointed CEO, Wayne Calloway, pushed the concept further as he embraced the idea that success would come only if all employees experienced the same sense of ownership and excitement in growing the business that senior executives had always felt. In his words, "all 450,000 employees must be chief executive of their corner of our world."

The organization Calloway created combined (1) a shared and highly compelling vision for the future of the company, (2) a culture that stressed entrepreneurial decision making and action, and (3) incentives that rewarded aggressive growth. As PepsiCo's spans of control increased to provide the desired organizational agility, younger, "empowered" employees were pressured to deliver on grueling growth goals with low levels of supervision. The potential for problems was exacerbated by PepsiCo's global expansion.

As the organization grew and changed during the late 1980s and early 1990s, Calloway relied increasingly on leadership and shared values to hold the company together. "All the changes, the empowerment, and the growth . . . employees hear a lot about that," he stated. "But it's all pulled together by leadership and integrity."

> What we mean by integrity is not just honesty; it's openness, trust, sharing rewards, and sharing responsibility . . . We spend a lot of time taking out layers, taking out reporting structure, and talking about empowerment . . . As we do, the traditional structures and systems for holding our company together are gone. With 450,000 employees located all over the world and our spans of control and commitment to decentralization, you need [something to hold the company together]. All the auditors in the world can't ensure control—and even if they could, you'd never be

[22]See L. Applegate and L. Schlesinger, *PepsiCo: A View from the Corporate Office* (Harvard Business School Publishing No. 694-078).

able to afford them. With empowerment you need shared values, integrity, and trust. I consider leadership of [PepsiCo's] value and integrity systems to be my most important role. This is not soft stuff—it's hard stuff; it will determine our future survival.

The blueprint for a big-small business discussed in this section describes the organizational capabilities required to build and grow successful 21st-century organizations. In the Network Economy, this blueprint often extends across organizational boundaries to enable a network of organizations and individuals who work together to accomplish shared goals and create value for all the participants. The next section describes emerging models for building and running value networks.

Building Value Networks

As was mentioned in Chapter 1, most organizations operate within a network of suppliers, producers, distributors, and retailers that work together to design, make, market, sell, and deliver products and services. These activities often are referred to as a *value chain* since they describe the steps through which the inputs from suppliers are transformed into outputs for customers that have an intrinsic market value.[23] Accompanying the physical value chain is a related information value chain through which the involved parties coordinate and control activities and an infrastructure on which firms do business.

As executives build the business blueprint for an organization, they must also consider the business blueprint for the value network within which they will operate. As they do, they are confronted with two fundamental questions:

1. Which activities should we perform ourselves and which should we source from the outside?

2. How should we relate to outside parties, including customers, suppliers, distributors, business partners, and others?

Where Should Activities Be Performed?

Value chain activities can be organized in three basic ways[24] (see Table 3.1). First, all but the most routine value chain activities can be incorporated within a single "vertically integrated" firm. Second, one or more selective activities can be sourced from an external party. Finally, a collection of highly specialized independent firms can work together to perform, coordinate, and control value chain activities. This option is often called *virtual integration.*

[23]M. Porter, *Competitive Strategy* (New York: Free Press, 1995).
[24]O. Williamson, *Markets and Hierarchies* (New York: Free Press, 1975); O. Williamson, "Comparative Economic Organization: The Analysis of Discrete Structural Alternatives," *Administrative Sciences Quarterly* 36: 269–296, 1991; W. Powell, "Neither Market nor Hierarchy: Network Forms of Organization," *Research in Organizational Behavior,* 12:295–336, 1990.

TABLE 3.1 Options for Structuring Market Activities

Options	Description
Vertical integration	Locate all but the most routine, transaction-oriented activities inside the firm.
Selective sourcing	Source selected activities from the outside. Traditionally, sourced activities were controlled through short-term contracts.
Virtual integration	Become part of a network of highly specialized, independent parties that work together to perform, coordinate, and control value chain activities.

Traditionally, managers chose to locate an activity within organizational boundaries (i.e., vertically integrate) when a significant cost (or risk) was involved in managing it on the outside.[25] Costs and risks increased when (1) a firm was required to make a significant investment in physical facilities, people, or management systems to integrate operations and coordinate and control activities with customers, suppliers, or partners, (2) the services or activities were critical to the effective and efficient delivery of the firm's products and services, or (3) a high degree of uncertainty surrounded the ongoing nature of the relationship with outside parties, which in turn made it difficult to develop a comprehensive, structured contract to govern the partnership.

Eastman Kodak, for example, was highly vertically integrated well into the 1980s.[26] The company was founded in the 1800s on the principle of "commitment to quality," and its executives believed that the costs and risks associated with managing activities on the outside were greater than the benefits that would be achieved through sourcing. General Motors followed a similar strategy throughout the first half of the 1990s; many recall its familiar slogan: "Genuine GM Parts."

During the 1970s and 1980s visionary firms within a number of industries found that they could use IT to help manage the risks and cost of performing interorganizational transactions and ensuring interorganizational coordination and control of those transactions.[27] By establishing electronic linkages with suppliers, distributors, customers, and even competitors, electronic commerce pioneers were able to integrate and coordinate cross-boundary activities much more efficiently, monitor operations more closely, and communicate with external organizations more interactively.

[25]O. E. Williamson and S. G. Winter, *The Nature of the Firm* (New York: Oxford University Press, 1993).
[26]L. M. Applegate and R. Montealegre, *Eastman Kodak Co.: Managing Information Systems through Strategic Alliances* (Harvard Business School Publishing No. 192-030).
[27]T. Malone, J. Yates, and R. Benjamin, "Electronic Markets and Electronic Hierarchies," *Communications of the ACM* 484–497, vol. 6, 1987; J. L. McKenney and D. O. Copeland, *Waves of Change: Business Evolution through Information Technology* (Boston: HBS Press, 1995).

TABLE 3.2   Relationship Options

	Transaction	Contract	Partnership
Basis of interaction	Discrete exchange of goods, services, and payments (simple buyer/seller exchange)	Prior agreement governs exchange (e.g., service contract, lease, purchase agreement)	Shared goals and processes for achieving them (e.g., collaborative product development)
Duration of interaction	Immediate	Usually short-term and defined by the contract	Usually long-term and defined by the relationship
Level of business integration	Low	Low to moderate	High
Coordination and control	Supply and demand (market)	Terms of contract define procedures, monitoring, and reporting	Interorganizational structures, processes, and systems; mutual adjustment
Information flow	Primarily one-way; limited in scope and amount; low level of customization	One- or two-way; scope and amount usually defined in the contract	Two-way (interactive); extensive exchange of rich, detailed information; dynamically changing; customizable

How Should We Relate to Market Participants?

All firms also make choices about the nature of the relationships that they develop with customers, suppliers, and other external industry participants. These choices fall along a continuum from transactions to contracts to partnerships[28] (see Table 3.2).

Transactions involve the simple exchange of goods, services, and payments, usually during a specific time period and with limited interaction or information sharing between the parties involved. The act of purchasing a brand-name item from a grocery store or retail outlet is an example of a transaction relationship.

In contractual relationships, the products or services to be provided by each party and the length of the relationship are well defined and clearly documented at the time the relationship is struck. The formal "terms of the contract" become the basis for coordinating and controlling the exchange of goods, services, payments, and information throughout the length of the contract.

Partnerships are required when the activities that are to be jointly managed are complex, uncertain, and critical to the success of the firms involved. Partnerships require

[28]M. Granovetter, "Economic Action and Social Structure: The Problem of Embeddedness," *American Journal of Sociology* 1:481–510, 1985; A. Stinchcombe, "Contracts as Hierarchical Documents," in *Organizational Theory and Project Management,* ed. A. Stinchcombe and C. Heimer (Bergen, Norwegian University Press, 121–171, 1985; J. Bradach and R. Eccles, "Price, Authority and Trust," *Annual Review of Sociology* 15:97–118, 1989.

FIGURE 3.7
Impact of Information Technology on Market Evolution

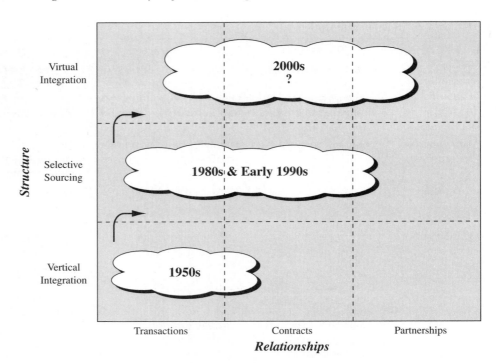

shared goals, complementary expertise and skills, and integration of processes and work across organizational boundaries. The exchange of goods and services is ongoing, and the interactions and relationships must adapt to the changing priorities of the parties involved. Partnerships often require significant investments in interorganizational governance and management systems for carrying out, coordinating, and controlling shared activities. An example of an interorganizational governance system is the establishment of an advisory board or joint equity board of directors. An example of an interorganizational management system is the joint development of service-level agreements (SLAs) and ongoing performance monitoring and management.

The framework depicted in Figure 3.7 integrates this analysis of market structure and market relationships into a single framework.[29] Trends in market evolution over the second half of the 20th century are highlighted. These trends are discussed in the next section.

Evolving Market Structure and Relationships

In the Industrial Economy organizations were built on proprietary capabilities and infrastructure. This made it difficult to integrate operations, share information, and coordinate and control activities across organizational boundaries, whether those

[29]See L. M. Applegate, "Electronic Commerce," in *The Technology Management Handbook,* ed. Richard C. Dorf, (New York: CRC Press, 1999), for a more in-depth discussion of this framework.

FIGURE 3.8   **Proprietary Capabilities and Infrastructure Create Walls inside an Organization and among the Members of a Value Chain Network**

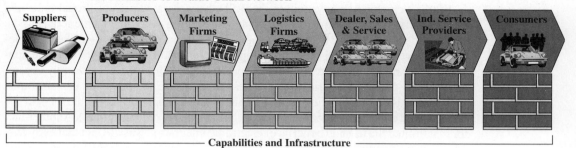

| Suppliers | Producers | Marketing Firms | Logistics Firms | Dealer, Sales & Service | Ind. Service Providers | Consumers |

Capabilities and Infrastructure

boundaries were between units within a firm or between market participants in a value chain network. In effect, the specialized "brick and mortar" infrastructure created "walls" that isolated groups within organizations and market participants within an industry (see Figure 3.8).

As firms grew and became more complex, it became harder and harder to coordinate and control multiple market relationships. Over time, many large, growing firms *vertically integrated:* They bought or built the capabilities and infrastructure required to perform all but the most routine market transactions and structured contractual relationships.

But specialized infrastructures and capabilities continued to isolate functional units within organizations as activities were brought inside. Corporate headquarters expanded dramatically during the mid-1900s as information analysts, controllers, and staff attempted to coordinate and control the increasingly complex set of value chain activities performed inside the organization. So too did hierarchical reporting structures as deep layers of middle managers were added to ensure that strategic objectives, plans, and work procedures were passed down the organization and performance information was passed up.

By the late 1970s the giants of the Industrial Economy had grown to become multinational conglomerates, which were plagued with deep management hierarchies, bloated corporate headquarters, and costly duplication of resources. During the 1980s, leveraged buyout firms stepped in to break apart these sluggish industrial giants and release the value trapped within them. To prevent breakup by an outside party, many companies hastened to shed noncore assets. This enabled an increased focus on, and improved productivity of, the "core competencies" that remained inside. Over time, *selective sourcing* replaced vertical integration.

As organizational assets and businesses were spun out, companies sought better ways to improve the ability to do business with outside parties. Proprietary information and communication systems were often built to coordinate and control transactions and the flow of information among market participants. Enterprise resource planning (ERP) systems and related enterprise integration software packages were implemented to coordinate and control transactions and the flow of information within organizational boundaries. As they automated internal and external operating and management processes, large companies began to evolve the capabilities associated with a big-small organization.[30]

While it created windows within the walls that separated organizational units and market participants, the impact of IT-enabled operations and management during the 1980s and early 1990s was limited. The technology infrastructure was costly to develop, took years to build, and, most important, was built on a proprietary and specialized technology infrastructure. Therefore, organizations were able to apply this approach only to the most critical processes and strategic relationships (for example, Wal-Mart's use of information technology to link key suppliers and enable them to coordinate and control inventory ordering, fulfillment, and replenishment). Another factor that limited the use and benefits of electronic integration was the fact that early systems achieved virtual business integration by "hard-coding" operating procedures and rules into the technology. This made the resultant systems and IT-enabled processes exceedingly difficult and costly to operate, maintain, and change. Finally, the specialized nature of the systems limited the ability to reuse technology and capabilities built for one process when redesigning and virtually integrating another process.

As we enter the 21st century, networked technologies, including the Internet, the World Wide Web, intelligent agents, and modular system designs, are providing a densely connected, flexible, yet robust infrastructure for sharing information and coordinating work. The shift to an all-digital standard for creating, packaging, storing, and sharing voice, video, and data and the accompanying shift to mobile communications are enabling people to connect to this infrastructure any way, any place, and any time. This *nonproprietary and shared* internetworked infrastructure dramatically decreases the cost and time needed to connect, transact business, share real-time information, and, when necessary, disconnect. It also increases the range of activities and transactions that can be performed online and the ease with which those activities are managed and maintained across organizational boundaries.

Until recently, most people believed that these new capabilities and infrastructures would cause consolidated industries to fragment as neutral third-party players entered the market to provide the platform on which participants within an industry and across industries would do business. It was believed that the dominant impact of the Internet would be to create a shift toward *virtually integrated* market structures within which many small, specialized participants would relate through a series of market transactions and short-term contracts. Indeed, during the late 1990s, new entrants such as eBay and Amazon.com quickly assumed positions of power as channel facilitators, connecting sellers and buyers within disaggregated, virtually integrated consumer-to-consumer (C2C) Internet markets.

In the late 1990s, new entrants such as CommerceOne (www.commerceone.com) and Ventro, now called NexPrise (www.nexprise.com),[31] announced their intent to become channel facilitators within disaggregated business-to-business (B2B) markets. But the dot-com demise of 2000 and 2001 caused these independent players to

[30]L. M. Applegate, *Emerging Network Business Models: Lessons from the Field* (Harvard Business School Publishing No. 801-172); L. M. Applegate, "Time for the Big Small Company," *Financial Times: Mastering Information Management,* March 29, 1999.
[31]See L. M. Applegate and M. Collura, *Ventro: Builder of B2B Businesses* (Harvard Business School Publishing No. 801-042).

lose power. By 2002, established players had stepped in to fill the void, launching jointly owned industry coalitions to coordinate global, industrywide supply and/or distribution channel activities. In many industries, these coalitions coordinated with e-commerce network infrastructure providers, but ultimate power usually rested with the established industry players rather than the infrastructure providers.

Global Healthcare Exchange (GHX) and Healthcare Purchasing Partners International (HPPI), which were discussed in Chapter 1, are examples of B2B Internet market facilitators that use a combination of transactions, short-term contracts, and partnerships to coordinate and control operations within a virtually integrated market structure. Covisint, formed in February 2000 through a joint venture between Ford Motor Company, General Motors, DaimlerChrysler, Oracle, and CommerceOne, is an example of a channel facilitator within a virtual supply chain market for the global automobile industry. By January 2002, 11 automobile manufacturers and over 5,000 suppliers from around the world were participating in the Covisint network.[32] During 2001, over $50 billion worth of online bids flowed through Covisint's Online Auction service and over $100 billion in future program contracts flowed through its Quote Manager service.[33] The potential scope of these virtual B2B marketplaces is staggering when one considers that in May 2002, Covisint managed a four-day auction during which DaimlerChrysler purchased approximately $2.6 billion worth of auto parts.[34] By comparison, eBay reported gross merchandise sales of $2.7 billion during the entire fourth quarter of 2001.[35]

While we are seeing increasing virtual integration in the global automobile industry, we are not seeing a corresponding shift to a more egalitarian power base. Thus, it is unclear at this time whether B2B automobile markets will experience increasing consolidation or increasing fragmentation over time. Over the last year we have seen market structures emerge to link networks of industry players. But unlike the health-care original equipment manufacturer (OEM) networks that link to supplier networks, the automobile industry continues to maintain its "tiered" industry structure. For example, in 2001 Covisint launched the Ford Supplier Network (an automobile manufacturer portal), which connected Ford Motor Company to its large and midsize suppliers. In 2002 Covisint announced that it would build similar portals for two top-tier suppliers, Delphi and Johnson Controls. These supplier portals eventually would connect thousands of "Tier 2 and 3" suppliers. These coalition-based B2B markets differ from the C2C (peer-to-peer) markets, yet all are examples of the increasing trend toward virtually integrated markets. Figure 3.9 depicts the Covisint network.

While we see a shift toward increasing virtual integration in some industries, we also see examples of increasing vertical integration, especially in industries where there is a need for the deployment of a new capital-intensive platform upon which the industry will conduct business (for example, the cable industry and mobile

[32]Speech made by Covisint CEO, Kevin English, at the Automotive News Congress, January 16, 2002.
[33]P. Loftus, "Making it Work," *Wall Street Journal Online,* February 12, 2002.
[34]Ibid.
[35]eBay press release, January 15, 2002 (www.ebay.com).

FIGURE 3.9 Covisint's Role in the Virtually Integrated Global Automobile Market

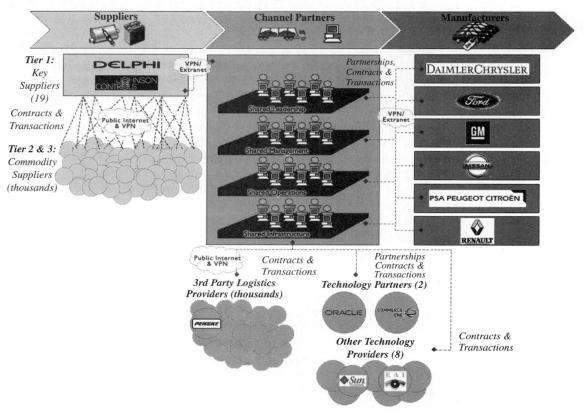

telecommunications). The historic AOL Time Warner merger provides a glimpse of the extent of vertical integration that can occur within and across previously distinct market segments.

With the completion of the merger in January 2001, the new AOL Time Warner represented a vertically integrated megacorporation that owned content, packaging, and distribution businesses within the publishing, filmed entertainment, music, sports, and news industries, to name just a few. While expansion of its cable franchise required significant capital, its Internet network infrastructure required little change to enable it to support the packaging and distribution needs of its content businesses. As a result, rather than vertically integrate its businesses *inside* the corporation, AOL Time Warner was able to leave them separate.

Each AOL Time Warner business was able to focus its resources and energy toward building best-in-class products and services for customers in its distinct in-

FIGURE 3.10   AOL Time Warner's Virtually Integrated Organization within a Vertically Integrated Market

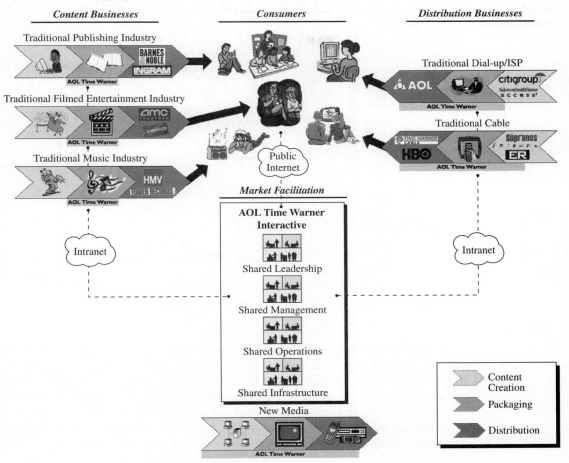

dustry segment. In addition, each unit of the merged company continued to distribute its products and services across traditional channels. If the company had stopped there, it would have resembled one of the large conglomerates of the 1980s within which synergies (if they were achieved) came from traditional market mechanisms (e.g., transactions—supported by complex transfer pricing—and structured contracts). But AOL Time Warner executives developed a new unit—AOL Time Warner Interactive—that was charged with integrating the media channels and content that would *transform the industry*. This new unit mirrored the role and actions of independent channel facilitators such as eBay and Yahoo! and coalition channel facilitators such as Covisint and GHX. The result was a *virtually integrated market within a vertically integrated industry* (see Figure 3.10).

FIGURE 3.11
Four
Networked
Market Models

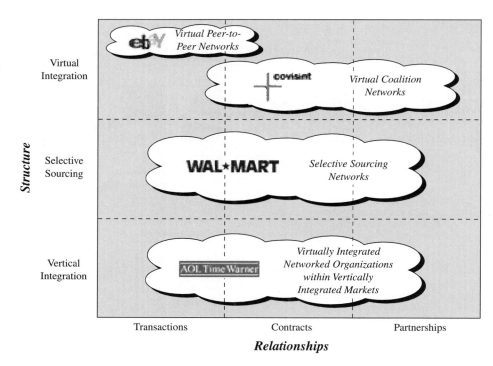

In summary, in 2002 we are seeing the emergence of four network market models (see Figure 3.11). *Virtual peer-to-peer networks* are composed of individuals, teams, and small businesses that relate to one another primarily through market-driven transactions on publicly owned networks operated by neutral third-party channel facilitators (e.g., eBay and Yahoo). *Virtual coalition networks* are composed of businesses of varying size that relate to one another through a combination of market-driven transactions, short- and long-term contracts, and partnerships across a combination of public and privately owned networks operated by joint equity coalitions (e.g., Covisint and GHX). *Virtually integrated organizations within vertically integrated markets* are composed of independent, focused businesses and units within an organization that relate to one another through a combination of internal market-driven transactions, contracts, and partnerships across privately owned networks operated by corporate headquarters or one of the units. Finally, many companies continue to do business within *selective sourcing networks* composed of a company's key suppliers, customers, or partners that relate to one another through a combination of internal and external market-driven transactions, contracts, and partnerships across privately owned networks that often are maintained by one of the parties. All four of these value network models develop shared infrastructure and capabilities that unite the three levels of a business blueprint—operating and innovating, managing and learning, and leading and engaging—across a network of entrepreneurial units inside and outside a firm.

Summary   Executives made significant efforts during the last decade to reorganize to meet the challenges of operating in a more dynamic, hypercompetitive world. But as we entered the 21st century, it became clear that even more radical change is required. As the Internet transforms markets, industries, and the organizations that compete within them, executives are being forced to respond even more quickly, deliver higher-quality and more customized products and services, and cut costs even more deeply. In large companies during the 1980s and 1990s, layers of management were cut and spans of authority were increased to the point where many worried that their organizations would spin out of control. Entrepreneurial start-ups of the middle to late 1990s were required to "get big fast" without losing their agility, speed, and responsiveness to local needs. In short, the assumptions behind traditional organizational models, such as the hierarchy and the entrepreneurial model, were pushed to the limit and were found lacking.

It has been shown time and time again in history that crisis is a precondition for the emergence of a new theory or model.[36] But when presented with crisis, most people do not immediately reject existing models. Instead, they attempt incremental adjustments that over time begin to blur the fundamental structure and assumptions on which the old models were based. Practitioners are often the first to lose sight of old models as the familiar rules for solving problems become ineffective. At some point, total reconstruction is required. During the transition, however, there is frequently an overlap between the problems that can be solved by the old and new models. But no matter which is used, there is a decisive difference in the modes of solution.

This appears to be the point at which we now find ourselves. A crisis, largely driven by a fundamental mismatch between environmental demands and organizational capabilities, has called into question many of the assumptions of traditional organizational models. Academic thinking in this area is being led by practice. The lessons from managers in the field suggest that a new organizational model is emerging that puts the power of today's technologies in the hands of a more knowledgeable workforce to create networks of organizations that can act big and small at the same time. But these new models and capabilities are built on design principles we already know. The steps listed below can be used to guide you as you build successful big-small businesses.[37]

A Step-by-Step Approach to Analyzing Markets and Capabilities

Step 1: Define the stream of value-creating activities required to execute strategy. Determine which activities you will perform inside your organization and which can be performed by outside parties.

Step 2: Determine the nature of the relationship you will have with customers, suppliers, partners, and other external market participants.

---

[36]T. Kuhn, *The Structure of Scientific Revolution* (Chicago: University of Chicago Press, 1970).
[37]See M. Collura and L. M. Applegate, "Capability Assessment Tool," in *Building E-Businesses Online* (Harvard Business School Publishing, No. 801-232).

Step 3: Define the network market model that is most appropriate for your business and industry.

Step 4: Conduct a high-level audit of the capabilities required at the three levels specified in your business blueprint.

- *Operating and innovating capabilities:* Assess your ability to operate with precision while innovating and personalizing to ensure a best-in-class experience for customers, suppliers, partners, and other members of the markets within which you do business.

- *Managing and learning capabilities:* Assess your ability to manage routine operations with control and efficiency while enabling individuals and teams inside your firm and across firm boundaries to "learn by doing."

- *Leading and engaging capabilities:* Assess your ability to develop visionary yet pragmatic leaders and to fully engage individuals, teams, partners, customers, and suppliers to participate energetically in defining direction and accomplishing goals.

Step 5: Review findings and identify strengths and weaknesses. Discuss the findings with employees, customers, suppliers, partners, and industry experts.

Step 6: Develop a set of initiatives and prioritize. Define an agenda for change.

The following questions can be used by executives to evaluate an organization's capabilities.

1. What are your organization's core capabilities? In general, do your colleagues, customers, business partners, and other interested parties share your beliefs about your core capabilities, strengths, and weaknesses?

2. What operating processes, policies, structures, and systems must be changed to enable you to operate efficiently while also improving your ability to innovate quickly and successfully?

3. What management systems (e.g., planning and budgeting, performance management, human resource management, business development, and alliance management) must be changed to enable you to ensure that the company is in control yet is able to "learn by doing"?

4. Is leadership stressed throughout the company? What organizational structures, incentives, and cultural changes need to be made to enable the company to act both big and small simultaneously?

5. Within which market or markets do you currently participate? Are you participating in the right markets? What is the structure of the markets within which you currently do business? How do market participants relate? How have these markets evolved over time? How do you expect them to evolve in the future?

6. Given your current and future strategy, what is the stream of activities that must be accomplished to develop products and services that create value for all stakeholders? Which of these activities should you perform and which should you source from the outside?

7. How should you relate to outside parties, including customers, suppliers, distributors, business partners, and others?

8. Are you and your customers, suppliers, and partners capturing the full value that can be achieved by streamlining and integrating value chain activities inside and outside your respective organizations? Are there opportunities to eliminate intermediaries, simplify and streamline product or service delivery, dramatically improve quality, or decrease costs?

9. Is there an opportunity for you to become a channel facilitator, coordinating and controlling the flow of transactions, information, and interactions among market participants? Should you own the infrastructure upon which market participants do business?

10. Are you at risk for disintermediation? Are your products and services at risk for potential commoditization and/or obsolescence? What actions should you take to prevent these risks and protect market share and price?

11. Is your firm's technical infrastructure appropriate for the new types of e-commerce you are considering? Do you maintain an appropriate balance between experimentation and control? Have you instituted appropriate levels of security and reliability? Are your systems flexible enough to respond to dramatic changes in capacity requirements and service offerings?

12. What are key areas of improvement that must be addressed *immediately*? Who needs to address these problems? What additional weaknesses or gaps should be improved in the *longer term?*

Characteristics of the Hierarchy, Entrepreneurial and Networked Organization

Characteristic	Hierarchy	Entrepreneurial	Networked
Process integration and synchronization	• Process activities segregated into distinct tasks managed by functions. • Activities are synchronized during yearly planning sessions.	• Process activities defined on an ongoing basis by the people doing the work. • Activities synchronized through ad hoc discussion (face-to-face, e-mail, phone).	• Process activities integrated and synchronized through the flow of information in IT systems. • Changes discussed and planned through frequent interactions among those doing the work (face-to-face, e-mail, phone). • In the case of unstructured and uncertain activities, teams may meet daily or weekly to plan activities.
Process cycle time	• Operating cycle time based on organization's management cycle time. • For highly structured, routine, automated processes (e.g., factory operations), cycle time can be shortened. • In unstructured situations, time and inventory buffers used to manage uncertainty.	• The operating cycle time based on the cycle time of changes in the business environment. • Operating activities not structured; as a result, all activities managed in the same, unstructured way.	• Information on the market, industry, and operations available and acted on in real time. • The cycle time of operating activities approaches the cycle time of changes in the business environment.

Characteristic	Hierarchy	Entrepreneurial	Networked
Process complexity	• The inherent complexity of the business environment minimized through structure and slow response to change. • Standard products and services mass-produced for mass markets to reduce business complexity. • Processes structured to reduce operating complexity.	• Start-up firms offer a limited product set to a limited market. • Within this simple business environment, significant customization provided to ensure that products meet the requirements of individual customers.	• Despite significant business complexity, real-time information and sophisticated analytical tools enable products and services to be customized for increasingly smaller customer segments. • At the limit, a company can personalize for a "market of one." • Real-time information and sophisticated analytics enable a large firm to manage complexity directly rather than managing through complexity reduction.
Management cycle time	• Defined around yearly planning and budgeting systems. • Yearly and quarterly performance monitoring and reporting dictated by country-level regulations for public and private firms.	• Management processes defined by the founder, often ad hoc. • Direct involvement of the founder in most decisions and activities causes the management cycle time to be timed directly to the business cycle.	• Real-time information and reporting enables the management cycle time to be tied directly to the operating cycle, which in turn has been timed to the inherent cycle time of the business environment.
Scope and granularity of business understanding	• Understanding of business limited to specific job an employee is hired to do. At operating levels, scope is limited to a specific task. Only top management team understands business dynamics across scope of enterprise, but depth of understanding of any one portion of the business is limited. • Employees at all levels unable to link specific decisions and actions to the firm's overall performance. • Planning targets and goals set on a yearly basis and monitored and adjusted quarterly. This results in quarterly cycles of feedback/feedforward. • Understanding of business dynamics predicated on the organization operating as originally structured.	• Because of their direct involvement in all activities and decisions, founders and employees have an in-depth understanding of the business. • Business performance monitored and communicated in real time, enabling founders and employees to link actions to performance in a real-time cycle of feedback/feedforward. • Operations continually adjusted and refined in an ad hoc manner.	• Detailed information on the market, industry and business performance, and operations enables operating teams (which may include customers, suppliers, and business partners) to refine and adjust goals and activities *within the scope of their authority*, based on changes in the business environment. • Operating teams rather than individuals have authority over a broader set of business activities (processes), and senior management, like the founders in an entrepreneurial venture, takes a more active role in monitoring business operations and participating in high-risk decisions.

(continued)

Characteristic	Hierarchy	Entrepreneurial	Networked
Information and business literacy	• Employee understanding of business dynamics and information limited to specific assigned tasks.	• Employees and founders have access to all information required to run the company and are expected to use that information to solve problems, make decisions, and take actions to accomplish firm's goals.	• Employees at all levels have access to information on business goals and operations across a wide range of activities and, working in teams within the scope of their collective authority, are expected to use that information to make decisions and take actions to accomplish firm's goals.
Boundaries and values	• Activities and authority segmented so that no one individual has the power or authority (short of sabotage) to cause irreparable harm to company (even the CEO reports to a board of directors). • In areas of high risk, special security precautions (e.g., restricted access, direct supervision) prevent sabotage. • Since broad decision-making authority is limited to upper levels of management, company-wide value systems are not crucial.	• Boundaries and values created in real time and transmitted directly by founders. • Founders directly involved in most decisions and actions. • The size of the company limits risk to the founders and a small number of investors.	• As decision authority is pushed down, shared values become an important component of strategic control.
Units of work and chain of command	• Work highly segregated by function with duplication of resources within each operating unit. • Deep chain of command with functional supervisors reporting to several layers of functional managers, who report through business unit heads to corporate headquarters.	• Simple, functional chain of command. • Flat chain of command (three or less) with functional managers reporting directly to the founder.	• Flat, team-based chains of command. • Market-focused operating teams composed of functional managers report to business unit managers, who report to corporate headquarters. • Broad chains of authority with work teams reporting to operating management teams.
Span of management	• Each manager supervises five to seven direct reports.	• Varies with the size and stage of development. Spans of more than 10 are common.	• Spans of 30 or more are common.

Characteristic	Hierarchy	Entrepreneurial	Networked
Corporate headquarters	• Large corporate headquarters staff assumes major responsibility for planning, budgeting, and performance management. • Large staff of analysts required to plan, monitor, and coordinate work.	• Single site for headquarters and operations. • Little formal planning, budgeting, and performance monitoring. • Operations planned, coordinated, and managed by those who do the work.	• Small corporate headquarters with minimal responsibility for planning, performance monitoring, and organizationwide resource management. • While formal planning, budgeting, and performance monitoring still take place, planning, coordinating, and managing operating activities take place in operating units.
Coordinating mechanisms	• Work is coordinated primarily through direct supervision and the chain of command.	• Work is coordinated through ad hoc adjustments by those directly involved in the work.	• Work coordinated through the integrated flow of information. • Routine work coordinated through real-time feedback and adjustment. • Important decisions and actions coordinated through meetings of operating managers and employees who analyze real-time operating information to adjust and refine goals and their execution continually.
Roles	• Except at top levels of firm, roles and accountability defined in formal job descriptions. • Roles based on functional expertise and skills.	• Minimal to no formal specification of roles. • Emphasis on hiring innovators ("pioneers").	• All organizations, regardless of size, require innovators ("pioneers") and operators ("settlers"). • Senior executives must be skilled at leading and engaging. • Self-managing work teams define work and how it gets done.
Career progression	• Employees advance through functional hierarchical progression. • Seniority is as important as (and in some organizations more important than) expertise and performance as a criterion for advancement.	• Career progression is often lateral. • In a rapidly growing firm, employees may move down in rank as senior managers are hired to ensure the leadership required by the more complex organization. Original employees may leave at this point.	• Minimal opportunities for advancement within flat hierarchical chains of command. • Innovators may have an opportunity to launch and grow new businesses. • Expanded jobs, increased lateral movement, and ownership incentives make work environment more challenging and rewarding.

Chapter

4

Making the Case for Networked Business[1]

The valuation of New Economy players represents a bet by the world's financial markets that a few companies will leverage the Internet to fundamentally change the competitive game in their industries. It is a gamble that powerful, low-cost business models will emerge, that new businesses will rise from disintermediated value chains, and that some companies will exert such influence that they will generate extraordinary long-term shareholder returns. [While] we cannot predict the winners of the e-races . . . we can be sure that the winners will be few and the losers will be many.[2]

Have you found it difficult to separate fact from hype when attempting to assess the value of networked business opportunities? Rest assured that you are not alone.

It's tough to make decisions and take actions when the world is changing at warp speed. We knew how to build a company and create value in the Industrial Economy, but we are just beginning to define what makes a successful business in the Network Economy. This chapter examines how the Internet is redefining the fundamental economics on which successful businesses are built. New approaches and metrics for measuring value are required to take advantage of the new opportunities.

---

[1]This chapter is adapted from papers and materials published in L. M. Applegate, "Analyzing Business Value," in *Building Businesses in a Networked Economy* (Harvard Business School Publishing No. 802–101).
[2]C. Lucier and J. Torsilieri, "The Trillion-Dollar Race to E," *Business & Strategy* 18:6–8 and 13–14, first quarter 2000.

The chapter begins with a discussion of the changing economics that drive business value. It then presents a framework for linking strategy to execution to results and ends with a discussion of how to develop the business case for evaluating and prioritizing digital business opportunities.

Changing Economics

Industrial Economy businesses were built on internal economies of scale and scope. In contrast, Network Economy businesses are built on network economies of scale and scope. This shift from internal, specialized, and proprietary to external, networked, and shared economies of scale and scope has driven a very different approach to building businesses and creating value.

Comparing Industrial and Network Economics

Successful Industrial Economy firms created *economies of scale*—the ability to produce and distribute products and services faster, better, and cheaper than competitors can—by building specialized plants, creating specialized jobs, and hiring specialized workers.[3] Yet the launch of a new product category or business often meant building *new* plants, training *new* workers, and hiring *new* salespeople. As a result, *economies of scope*—the ability to leverage an existing business infrastructure to produce and distribute new products or launch new businesses—were limited to enhancements in product design or features (see Figure 4.1). Because success was tied to proprietary and highly specialized brick and mortar infrastructures and face-to-face interactions, the capabilities that enabled economies of scale and scope were built and closely guarded within a company's walls.

As we saw in earlier chapters, the key technological innovations of the Industrial Economy were *production technologies* such as the assembly line and mechanically operated machines. As firms grew, new management innovations such as job specialization, hierarchical supervision, and pay-for-performance incentive systems were developed to exploit those technologies. The 20th century entrepreneurs who successfully created businesses around those innovations flourished, and over time a dominant business model—the hierarchy—emerged.

The companies that were able to use those innovations to achieve economies of scale and scope the fastest created significant value and assumed a position of power in an industry. Over time, industries consolidated and several large firms came to dominate, erecting powerful barriers to entry. Lacking the ability to share information with others, small suppliers, distributors, and consumers were disconnected, doing business on the margins in industries dominated by large players. Economists called these unconnected spaces in an organization, market, or

---

[3]A more comprehensive discussion of Industrial Age economies of scale and scope can be found in A. D. Chandler, *Scale and Scope: The Dynamics of Industrial Capitalism* (Cambridge, MA: Harvard University Press, 1990).

FIGURE 4.1
Industrial Economies of Scale and Scope

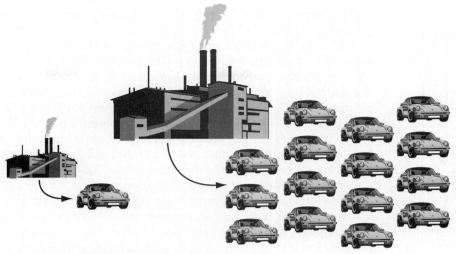

Example of Industrial Economies of Scale:
In the early 1900s, Ford Motor Company executives demonstrated that industrial technologies and management principles could enable the company to dramatically lower the cost and increase the output of cars in its assembly plants.

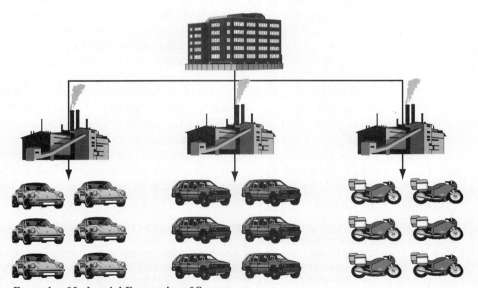

Example of Industrial Economies of Scope:
Because of the specialized nature of the technology and processes used, Ford Motor Company executives found that economies of scope were limited. The decision to introduce new products, such as trucks, required that new plants be built. In fact, assembly plants were closed for several weeks each summer to enable new models of cars or trucks to be built in existing plants.

industry *network holes.*[4] Those "holes" became a prime target for Internet entrepreneurs in the late 1990s.

While the key technological innovations of the Industrial Economy enabled economies of scale and scope in production, the technological innovations of the Network Economy are improving economics of *distribution,* especially in relation to coordination, communication, and information sharing. Successful entrepreneurial organizations of the late 1990s such as America Online and eBay built businesses that leveraged a *nonproprietary, shared* Internet infrastructure to unite buyers and sellers in fragmented markets. By offering a compelling value proposition and a low-cost way to connect, transact business, and share information, these Internet pioneers were able to create network economies of scale and scope.

Network economies of scale are achieved when a "community" of firms uses a common infrastructure and capabilities to produce and distribute products and services faster, better, and cheaper. *Network economies of scope* are achieved when a community of firms uses a common infrastructure and capabilities to launch new products and services, enter new markets, or build new businesses. For example, we saw in Chapter 3 that as a network market facilitator, Covisint provides a nonproprietary, shared infrastructure for the global automobile industry.

In early 2002, Covisint united its eight equity partners (the auto manufacturers DaimlerChrysler, Ford Motor Company, General Motors, Nissan, Renault, and PSA Peugeot Citroen and the technology firms CommerceOne and Oracle) with over 19 "Tier 1" suppliers (including Arvin Meritor, Delphi, Faurecia, Johnson Controls, and Siemens) and thousands of smaller (e.g., "Tier 2" and "Tier 3") suppliers. This "network of networks" all shared access to Covisint's Internet-enabled infrastructure and capabilities.[5] Community members used this infrastructure to conduct routine business and *develop and execute proprietary strategies and capabilities.*

Demonstrating its ability to dramatically increase network economies of scale, in spring 2001, Covisint hosted a four-day auction at which DaimlerChrysler purchased $2.6 billion worth of parts and components from suppliers located around the world[6] (see Figure 4.2). Before Covisint, auto-supply auctions could take several days or weeks. Purchasing managers would invite a few suppliers to bid for a contract or order and suppliers would mail or fax bids without knowing which other suppliers were bidding. The process was costly, paper-intensive, and biased.

---

[4]R. Burt, *Structural Holes: The Social Structure of Competition* (Cambridge, MA: Harvard University Press, 1992).

[5]While it was built on the Internet's open standards, it is important to recognize that Covisint created *proprietary* technologies and organizational capabilities that were then shared by all the members of the Covisint networked community. As we will see, the members of the community were then able to use the shared infrastructure to develop and execute proprietary strategies for their firms. Understanding this important distinction between what is proprietary to one member of the network and what is shared among all network members is critical to identifying and prioritizing opportunities and executing strategy in the Network Economy.

[6]P. Loftus, "Making It Work," *Wall Street Journal Online,* February 11, 2002 (www.wsj.com).

FIGURE 4.2   Network Economies of Scale and Scope

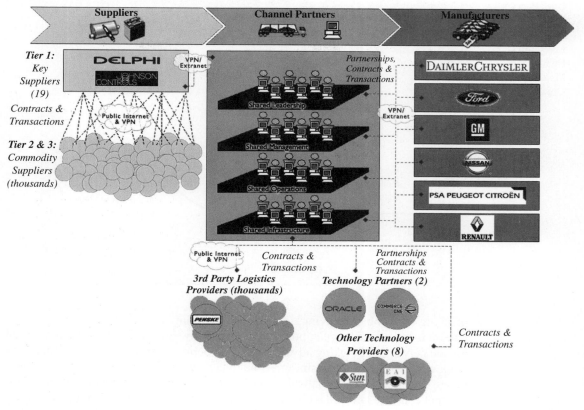

Example of Network Economies of Scale:
Using Covisint's networked auction services, DaimlerChrysler dramatically lowered the cost and decreased the time for purchasing supplies.

Example of Network Economies of Scope:
Covisint leveraged the infrastructure, capabilities, and community that it built for its first two network services (auctions and catalogs) to launch eight new services in less than one year.

Demonstrating its ability to dramatically increase network economies of scope, Covisint leveraged the infrastructure, capabilities, and community membership that it built for its initial online auction and catalog Web services to launch asset control services, collaboration services (including shared design collaboration and quote management), supply chain services (including fulfillment, supplier connections, and document exchange services), and quality services (including advanced quality

FIGURE 4.3
Dave Perry's
View of How
Network
Economics
Enable Market
Makers to
Create Value

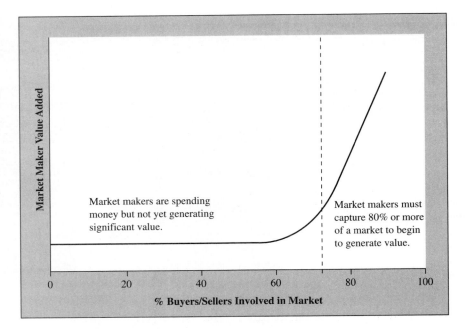

Market makers are spending money but not yet generating significant value.

Market makers must capture 80% or more of a market to begin to generate value.

Y-axis: Market Maker Value Added

X-axis: % Buyers/Sellers Involved in Market (0, 20, 40, 60, 80, 100)

planning and problem solving). In addition, Covisint developed and hosted private-label automaker and supplier portals that operated within closed membership virtual private networks. By taking advantage of the nonproprietary, modular Internet technology infrastructure, Covisint was able to launch these new products and services in less than one year, dramatically increasing the range of new business opportunities that could be pursued while dramatically decreasing the cost and time to pursue them. In addition, Covisint provided its community members with a shared infrastructure on which each member of the community could dramatically increase network economies of scale and scope for its firm.

As we enter the 21st century, the Internet's flexible, robust, and ubiquitous platform for conducting business, sharing information, and coordinating work is opening windows in the brick and mortar walls that separated people and work inside and outside a firm. By taking advantage of the shared platform, multiple firms can work together to produce and distribute products within markets that transcend geography and time.

In the Industrial Economy, the evolutionary process through which successful firms built new industries took decades to play out. In the Network Economy, we see new industries being created and established industries being transformed within a few years. Dave Perry, chief executive officer (CEO) and founder of Chemdex and Ventro (the latter is now called Nexprise), explained the challenges that he faced in building businesses that would leverage network economies of scale and scope to transform markets and industries (see Figure 4.3):

> Business-to-business e-commerce is about taking all the existing buyers and all the existing sellers who are already doing business together and putting yourself in

between them and creating an Internet solution that allows them to do business together more effectively. The nice thing about it is that you don't have to get rid of the players in the market. You can go from 0 percent market share to, theoretically, 100 percent market share.

The hard thing about it is that you haven't done anything worthwhile until you have a critical mass of both buyers and sellers. You have no value whatsoever to a buyer until you have most of the sellers they need. Unfortunately, you're of no value to the sellers until you have the buyers they need . . . It quickly becomes obvious to most people that the more buyers and sellers you have, the more useful you are to both sides. Unfortunately, the path doesn't progress linearly. It's in fact very exponential. If you have 10 percent of the suppliers a buyer needs, you've created no value whatsoever. The same is true at 20 percent, the same is true at 30 percent, the same is true at 40 percent, and so on. You have to have the vast majority of what somebody needs as a buyer before they're going to find you useful, 80-plus percent in most markets. This is fundamental economies of scale—network economies of scale. The really powerful thing about it is that once you've created that critical mass of buyers and sellers [and the platform upon which they can do business], you have a very valuable entity and a very valuable asset, but until you get there, you've created nothing worthwhile and you can go out of business tomorrow and nobody cares.

As 21st-century organizations such as Covisint and Ventro begin to test the full potential of network economies of scale and scope, the business logic that framed investment decision making in the Industrial Economy is being radically redefined. New approaches to measuring performance and analyzing business value are required.

Linking Strategy to Execution to Results

For decades we have known that a single set of performance measures will not suffice when industries, markets, and the companies that compete within them are undergoing massive upheaval and change. In fact, decades ago the management guru Peter Drucker spoke of the need for a deep understanding of *business fundamentals* when one is managing in a turbulent environment.[7] "In turbulent times," he said, "an organization has to be managed to withstand sudden blows and avail itself of sudden unexpected opportunities. This means that, in turbulent times, the fundamentals have to be managed—and managed well."

Today even the most seasoned managers reel at the rate of disruptive change. In today's turbulent environment, everyone involved in making decisions and taking actions must have access to a common set of performance measures that link strategy to execution and results. When linked together, these measures enable executives to define a unique value proposition and manage for superior performance.

In Chapter 2 we presented a framework for building businesses and analyzing business models. That framework highlighted the fact that a business model consists of three key components: (1) a concept that defines the opportunity and *strategy,* (2) capabilities that identify the resources required to exploit the opportunity and *execute* the

[7]P. Drucker, *Managing in Turbulent Times* (New York: Harper & Row, 1980).

FIGURE 4.4   Linking Strategy to Execution to Results

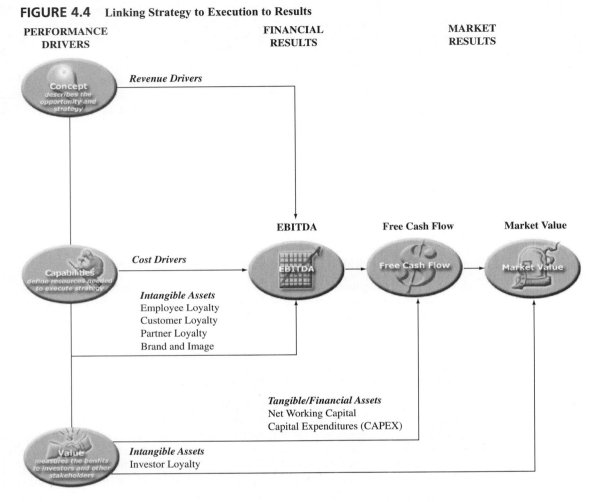

strategy, and (3) a value proposition that identifies the benefits returned to all stakeholders and the *results* executives have achieved or expect to achieve. This business
model framework provides the foundation for linking strategy to execution to results
(see Figure 4.4).

Analyzing Performance Drivers

As shown in Figure 4.4, the three components of a business model enable a broad-
based approach to measuring the drivers of business performance that begins with
analysis of the market opportunities, business capabilities, and value created. These
three categories of measures link directly to revenues, costs, and assets, which in turn

drive financial performance and, in the case of publicly held companies, capital market valuation. Executives in public sector agencies and nonprofit companies can use the framework by limiting measurement to the performance driver portion of the framework. Best practices and sample measures are summarized in Appendix 4A.

A firm's *business concept* defines the opportunities a firm will pursue and its strategy for capturing a dominant position in its industry and markets. Opportunity analysis includes a market assessment, analysis of product/service offerings and pricing, assessment of competitive and industry dynamics, and plans for evolution and growth of the business. *The business concept frames the assumptions used to forecast revenues.*

Jeff Timmons, a leading expert on entrepreneurship and an investor and board member in many new ventures, explained that an attractive opportunity is the foundation of successful entrepreneurship.[8]

> An opportunity [should be] attractive, durable, and timely . . . For an opportunity to have these qualities, the "window of opportunity" must be opening and remain open long enough . . . An attractive new venture [must] sell to a market that is large and growing . . . [and should be] anchored in a product or service that creates or adds value for the buyer or the end user.

Paul Maeder, founder and managing general partner of Highland Capital Partners, explained the evaluation criteria that his venture capital firm uses to screen opportunities.[9]

> When we invest in [early-stage] businesses, [we always ask]: Is this a unique [opportunity]? Do we have a real shot at being first in the market? Is it a compelling enough proposition that people are going to be drawn to it, initially employees and managers, and ultimately customers? Are there barriers to entry that we can erect so that when other people see our good ideas they don't pile in? Can we build it with a reasonable amount of capital in a reasonable period of time? If the answers to those questions are satisfactory, we'll typically fund it.

Once the business concept has been defined and a strategy is in place to provide direction and focus, *capabilities* must be built to execute the strategy. Capability analysis begins with an assessment of resource requirements and availability (including leadership, people, partners, expertise, time, and money). It also includes an assessment of the organization and infrastructure that have been (or will be) created to enable efficient and effective use of those resources to enable the organization to accomplish its goals and execute its strategy. *Analysis of an organization's capabilities frames the assumptions used to forecast costs.*

As was discussed in Chapter 3, three levels of organizational capabilities and infrastructure must be built. As will be seen in the next section, these three levels of capability provide the foundation for the development of an information technology

[8]J. Timmons, *New Venture Creation* (New York: McGraw-Hill/Irwin, 1999), Part 1, pp. 3–211.
[9]Author interview with Paul Maeder, March 14, 2000.

(IT) business value scorecard that can be used to forecast the benefits from investments in building digital business capabilities.

Operating and innovating capabilities include: (1) the core processes through which an organization converts inputs to outputs that create value for customers, suppliers, and partners (e.g., procurement, product development, service delivery, order fulfillment, marketing, and brand management), (2) the processes through which an organization continuously improves existing operations and launches new products, services, and businesses (e.g., new product development, business development, continuous improvement, and quality management), and (3) the IT infrastructure that supports these processes (e.g., distributed information processing and transaction systems).

Managing and learning capabilities include: (1) the processes through which a firm plans, budgets, and monitors performance, (2) the organization design (e.g., units and divisions, reporting structure, authority structure, and governance), (3) information, knowledge management, and decision-making processes, and (4) the IT infrastructure that supports these processes (e.g., management reporting and business intelligence systems, decision support systems and tools, and database/data warehouse management).

Leading and engaging capabilities include: (1) human resource management systems, (2) alliance and partnership management, (3) customer and supplier relationship management systems, and (4) the IT infrastructure that supports these processes (e.g., communication infrastructure and tools such as e-mail and voice mail, wireline and wireless communication systems, human resource management and customer relationship management software, personalization systems, and services).

In the Network Economy, capability analysis extends across boundaries inside and outside the organization to include shared resources, infrastructure, and capabilities made available by partners, suppliers, customers, and even competitors.

Value refers to the benefits delivered to investors and other stakeholders in an organization. Value analysis begins with an assessment of the subjective and objective benefits delivered to customers, suppliers, partners, and employees. *These benefits, in combination with an organization's concept and capabilities, create the assets that drive financial and market performance.*

The framework for linking strategy to execution to results that is discussed in this section enables a broad-based approach to measuring performance that unites performance drivers with traditional financial measures and market value. (See Appendix 4B for a discussion of traditional financial performance measures.) Performance drivers form the foundation for the assumptions used to forecast the impact of strategy and its execution on short-term and long-term earnings and market value. Table 4.1 presents an approach that executives can use to implement this approach to forecasting firm value.

When industries and organizations are stable and predictable, performance drivers and assumptions can be based on historical performance and comparisons with

---

[10]T. Copeland, T. Koller, and J. Murrin, *Valuation: Measuring and Managing the Value of Companies* (New York: Wiley, 2000); R. Brealy and S. Myers, *Principles of Corporate Finance* (New York: McGraw-Hill, 1984).

TABLE 4.1   A Scenario-Based Approach to Valuation

Step 1:	Define the purpose for the value assessment (e.g., seeking funding, buying a company, investing in an established business).
Step 2:	Pick a point in the future when you expect your business strategy to deliver value (most venture capitalists choose three to five years, but you may wish to shorten the time frame).
Step 3:	Analyze the business concept and strategy and forecast market size, your share, and revenues. Identify yearly changes that reflect how your firm and the market would reach this future state. List key assumptions used in constructing revenue forecasts. Talk with others and adjust assumptions.
Step 4:	Analyze the capabilities and resources required to reach the future state and forecast the cost of building those capabilities and those acquiring resources. Identify yearly costs and the resources that will be required by you and your partners, suppliers, and customers. List key assumptions used in constructing cost forecasts. Talk with others and adjust assumptions.
Step 5:	Based on this analysis, construct estimates of financial performance and market value that reflect the "most likely" assumptions. Clearly state the performance drivers that form the foundation for the assumptions in your model.
Step 6:	Factor in the uncertainty in your assumptions by developing several scenarios that represent upper and lower bounds on key variables in your forecasts. Most plans include scenarios that reflect the "most realistic case," "best case," and "worst case." However, additional scenarios may be needed. Test the sensitivity of your forecasts based on changes in key assumptions.
Step 7:	When appropriate, validate your model by using alternative approaches such as discounted cash flow and comparable company analysis.
Step 8:	Discuss the value analysis scenarios you have constructed with others and critique the findings and assumptions not just once but on a regular basis. Keep in mind that this analysis is based on highly uncertain business judgments. As a result, it is important to stay informed about what is happening in the market and industry, your company, and your community. Use the analysis as a baseline and update it often based on what you learn as you execute strategy and conduct business. Finally, be sure to set up a dynamic and broad-based measurement system that collects real-time metrics of company and industry performance.

"comparable companies."[10] (See Appendix 4C for a discussion of commonly used valuation approaches.) Yet even in the most stable of times, the assumptions used to forecast organizational performance and value creation are, by their very nature, uncertain. The more volatile the business context, the more uncertain the assumptions. In the presence of disruptive technologies or rapidly changing business models, valuations become highly suspect and must be evaluated and adjusted frequently.

Needless to say, traditional financial measures have been highly unreliable over the last few years. The difficulty that executives at AOL Time Warner and the analysts that follow the company have had in providing realistic estimates of business performance highlights the need for a more comprehensive approach to measuring business value.

Developing the Business Case for IT

While the framework in Figure 4.4 has been shown to be useful for analyzing a business model and the links to shareholder value, it also can serve as the foundation for analyzing and prioritizing IT investments. Table 4.2 presents an IT business value scorecard that can be used to forecast benefits or conduct a postimplementation audit of IT projects. The scorecard distinguishes between two major categories of benefits. Type I benefits are delivered through investments in a networked IT infrastructure. Type II benefits are delivered through investments in digital business opportunities that lower cost, increase revenues, or increase on-balance-sheet or off-balance-sheet assets.

Benefits from Investments in Infrastructure

Type I benefits arise from improvements in IT infrastructure, including computers, databases, data centers, Web hosting services, networks, and IT professionals. Most large, established companies assembled their IT infrastructure in a piecemeal fashion over the last 20 to 30 years. They adopted new technologies as they became available and added them to the existing IT infrastructure without considering how the different technologies might have to work together in the future.

By the early 1990s, most companies' IT infrastructures had become a hodgepodge of incompatible and inefficient technologies that were costly and difficult to manage and maintain. At the same time, executives recognized that the ability to integrate those technologies had become a competitive necessity. These trends converged and stimulated the transition to the Network Era of technology. (See Table 4.3 for an overview of the three eras of technology evolution.)

The transition to the Network Era began not with the Internet but with the early "client-server" technologies of the late 1980s (examples include systems from SAP and PeopleSoft). While this new approach promised network connectivity, it did so at a tremendous cost. In fact, by 1997, a Gartner Group survey estimated that the cost of maintaining a client-server system was over $10,000 per workstation per year.[11]

The increase in the cost and complexity of IT infrastructure came at a time when senior managers were ruthlessly eliminating costs. Business managers complained loudly that they were paying too much for IT with too little business benefit. It took too long, they said, to realize new IT-enabled business opportunities, and systems were out of date before the projects had been fully implemented. Few non-IT professionals understood that the cost of maintaining and managing the IT infrastructure often represented 80 percent or more of the yearly IT budget, leaving few resources to be directed toward creating business value.

By the mid-1990s the IT infrastructure in most companies had become an "underperforming asset" that needed to be cut with surgical precision and then made

---

[11]W. Kerwin, "TOC: New Technologies, New Benchmarks," *Gartner Group Research Note* (No. K-TOC-252), December 5, 1997.

TABLE 4.2 The IT Business Value Scorecard

Categories of Benefits	Goals and Measures	
	Internal	**External**
Type I: Benefits from Investments in a Networked IT Infrastructure		
Functionality and flexibility	Improve infrastructure performance; increase the functionality and range of strategic options that can be pursued	Create an efficient, flexible online/offline platform for doing business with customers, suppliers, and partners
	Sample measures: Decrease the cost and/or improve the performance of internal IT operations; enable new IT applications to be created at lower cost, in less time, and with less risk; expand the range of internal IT initiatives	*Sample measures:* Decrease the cost and/or improve the performance of doing business online; decrease the time, cost, and risk of launching new online business initiatives; expand the reach of existing IT-enabled businesses and the range of business opportunities that can be pursued.
Type II: Benefits from Doing Business on a Networked IT Infrastructure		
Commerce	Improve internal operating efficiency and quality	Streamline and integrate channels to market, create new channels, and integrate multiple online/offline channels
	Sample measures: Internal process performance and work flow improvements; cost savings or cost avoidance; increased quality; decreased cycle time	*Sample measures:* Supply chain or distribution channel performance improvements; cost savings or cost avoidance for the organization and its customers, suppliers, or partners; decreased time to market or just-in-time order replenishment; enabling of new channels to market and/or extending the reach and range of existing channels
Content / knowledge	Improve the performance of knowledge workers and enhance organizational learning	Improve the performance of knowledge workers in customer, supplier, and partner organizations; add "information value" to existing products and services; create new information-based products and services
	Sample measures: Enable individuals to achieve and exceed personal performance goals; increase the speed and effectiveness of decision making; increase the ability of the organization to respond quickly and effectively to threats and opportunities	*Sample measures:* Provide information to customers, suppliers, and partners that enables better decision making; charge a price premium for products and services based on information value added; launch new information-based products and services; increase revenue per user and add new revenue streams
Community	Attract and retain top talent; increase satisfaction, engagement, and loyalty; create a culture of involvement, motivation, trust, and shared purpose	Attract and retain high-quality customers, suppliers, partners, and investors; increase external stakeholders' satisfaction, engagement, and loyalty
	Sample measures: Length of time to fill key positions; attrition rate; trends in hiring and retaining top talent (over time, by industry, by region)	*Sample measures:* Customer, supplier, and partner satisfaction and lifetime value; average revenues per customer and trend over time; level of personalization available and percent that use it; churn rate

TABLE 4.3   **Comparing the Three Eras of IT Evolution**

Time Frame	Mainframe Era 1950s to 1970s	Microcomputer Era 1980s to Early 1990s	Network Era 1990s to Present
Dominant technology	Mainframe, stand-alone applications, databases	Stand-alone microcomputer and end-user tools (e.g., word processing, spreadsheets)	Client-server, Internet, browser, and hypertext
Organization metaphor	"Data management" Hierarchy	"Information management" Entrepreneurial organization	"Knowledge management" Networked business community
Primary IT role	"Centralized intelligence"	"Decentralized intelligence"	"Shared intelligence"
	Automate back-office activities	Provide information and tools to improve decision making and knowledge worker performance	Transform organizations and markets to create business value
Typical users	IT specialists	IT-literate business analysts	Everyone
Location of use	Computer room	Desktop	Everywhere
Planning process	Yearly budgeting	Individual expense	Business development and strategic planning
Justification	Cost savings	Increased decision quality and personal performance	Business value
Implementation	Independent projects	Ad hoc	Strategic initiatives (See Appendix A4)

capable of greater flexibility and performance. Infrastructure benefits are designed to achieve this goal. The shift to networked IT infrastructure dramatically reduces the cost of maintaining and running the IT infrastructure of a company or industry while simultaneously improving the functionality needed to support critical business operations.

In many cases, moving to a new networked IT infrastructure makes it possible to pursue new IT-enabled business opportunities more quickly than was possible with the old platform and at less cost. And if industry-standard Internet technologies are used, managers can extend the scope of the business opportunities that can be pursued to reach new markets and launch new digital businesses without having to in-

FIGURE 4.5   **Benefits of Investments in Infrastructure**

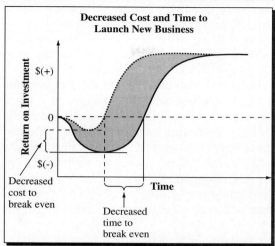

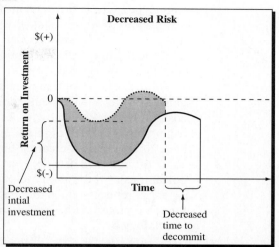

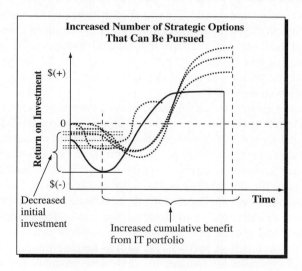

vest in a new platform. Thus, the financial risk of pursuing new business-building opportunities can be minimized. The increased flexibility and speed with which such opportunities can be pursued expand the "options value" of investments in infrastructure and enable a networked organization such as AOL Time Warner or a network of organizations such as Covisint to achieve network economies of scale and scope (see Figure 4.5).

Thinking of IT investments as growth options challenges conventional wisdom about IT budgeting. In financial terms, a securities option gives the owner the right (as distinct from the obligation) to buy a security at a fixed, predetermined price (called the exercise price) on or before some fixed date (the maturity date). Important features of securities options that determine value include: (1) the nature of future benefits (risky projects often generate the highest returns), and (2) the length of time one has to exercise the option (the longer the time frame, the greater the present value of the option).

Similarly, an IT option provides managers with the right (as distinct from the obligation) to pursue value-added IT-enabled business opportunities at a lower cost, more quickly, and with less inherent risk throughout the useful life of the technology. Features of an IT option that determine value include: (1) potential benefits from value-creating business opportunities that could be pursued (the value of these benefits depends on the number, type, and range of business opportunities), (2) the ability to pursue riskier opportunities where there is a higher potential return, and (3) the length of time for capturing value (keeping in mind that IT options can be exercised over and over throughout the useful life of the technology).

Benefits from Doing Business on a Networked Infrastructure

With a flexible and robust IT networked infrastructure in place, a company is poised to pursue the Type II benefits that accrue when an organization exploits new IT-enabled business opportunities that take advantage of the infrastructure. There are three categories of Type II benefits, which can be further subdivided based on whether the primary target of the benefit will be delivered inside or outside the organization (refer to Table 4.2).

Commerce benefits are created when a company uses IT to improve its internal and external operations. Internally, a company can use IT to streamline, integrate, and synchronize key operating processes such as procurement, order fulfillment, and customer service. Then it can extend these IT-enabled processes to improve the efficiency and effectiveness of supply or distribution channels.

Content (or knowledge) benefits are created when a company harnesses information and knowledge located inside or outside an organization to improve the performance of individuals and groups as they make decisions and take actions. The individuals and groups may belong to the same organization or may be customers, suppliers, or business partners. As well as helping people "work smarter," information and expertise can be used to create new products and services or to add value to existing ones, thus increasing the flow of revenues and improving a company's competitive position.

Community benefits are created when a company uses networked technologies to increase the commitment and loyalty of internal and external stakeholders. Inside the organization, e-mail, groupware, and Intranets can be used to link employees around the world to information resources and expertise, improve the performance of virtual work teams, and create communities of interest. Outside the company, the same technologies can be used to establish a position at the center of an electronic market around which a "virtual community" of customers, suppliers, and business partners can grow.

The ideal IT project, at least to begin with, often streamlines highly leveraged, resource-intensive processes while layering in important components of reusable infrastructure to produce measurable results in a short period of time. These projects often have a clearly defined scope.

As the project unfolds, however, astute managers must be on the lookout for follow-on projects that leverage reusable components of the infrastructure (e.g., databases, networks, processing power, user access devices) to increase the value of IT assets and enable a steady flow of value-creating IT-enabled business opportunities.

A *Fortune 100* global manufacturing company which we call "BigCo" provides an excellent example of the IT business value scorecard in action.

Improve Infrastructure

Like most companies, BigCo's IT infrastructure had been assembled in a piecemeal fashion over the last 20 to 30 years. Responding to a serious decline in market share, in 1993 a new CEO initiated a massive restructuring and cost-cutting initiative. As part of that project, the chief information officer (CIO) launched a two-year project to consolidate the company's 155 stand-alone data centers into 18 regional data centers that would feed three global megacenters. At the same time, the CIO embarked on a project to consolidate BigCo's network infrastructure from numerous incompatible country-based and local networks to a single global Internet-based network.

Launch a New IT Services Business

The state-of-the-art infrastructure quickly became a benchmark in the industry. BigCo used the internal infrastructure as the foundation to launch a new IT services business that would host and maintain e-business infrastructure and applications for large, medium, and small businesses.

Business Case for Improving Infrastructure	
Additional Cost	$100 million over 5 years
Benefits	50% reduction in the cost of running and maintaining the information and communication infrastructure during the first year after the launch
	60% reduction in IT professional headcount
	Payback = 1 year (based on cost savings alone)
	Time to implement e-business initiatives decreased by 70%
	Network reach increased by over 25%
	Between 1998 and 2000, cost savings from e-business represented over $4 billion

Business Case for Launching a New IT Services Business	
Additional Cost	Approximately $36 million per year
Benefits	By 2000, e-services revenues were $5 billion, up 70% from 1999
	E-services business was fastest-growing unit in the company
	Total IT services market size was estimated at $470 billion in 2003, growing at a 14% per year rate over next 5 years

Launch and Continually Enhance Internal Web Services

Building on the new Internet-based global information processing and communication platform, BigCo launched an Intranet that gave employees access to company, industry, and market information and collaboration and workflow tools (e.g., e-mail, project management tools, online travel and benefits systems). Employees and teams used this internal portal to customize a personal work environment that would enable them to make better decisions and improve productivity and performance. In addition, an innovative program that combined 75 percent e-learning with 25 percent face-to-face learning was used to improve the performance of all employees at BigCo.

Improve Knowledge Worker Performance

Using the information and personalization tools available on the Intranet, a key account consultant in the IT services business unit developed a customized portal to manage his key accounts. Interest spread among other key account consultants, and a portal was developed to enable all consultants to access information available on the public Internet, in company databases, and in files located throughout the company. Using the portal, consultants shared consulting methodologies and frameworks, engagement summaries, expertise, and best practices.

Business Case for Launching and Continually Enhancing Internal Web Services	
Additional Cost	N/A
Benefits	In a 2000 survey, employees ranked the Intranet the preferred channel for doing business with the company and the most credible, useful source for company information
	Over 2.5 million employees visited the Intranet every week
	During 2000, over 200,000 employees around the world participated in e-learning programs offered on the Intranet
	E-learning enabled the company to save $350 million in education and training costs

Business Case for Improving Knowledge Worker Performance	
Additional Cost	$50,000 over 6 months
Benefits	Decreased engagement time by 40% to 80%
	Expanded customer base and number of engagements without additional staff
	Increased revenues per consultant by 20%
	Improved consulting margins by 400%

Launch E-Procurement

In 1997, the U.S. procurement group began a project to implement e-procurement. By 2000, the entire global buying process, including the ability to select suppliers, negotiate contracts, place orders, and handle payments, took place online.

Launch Customer-Focused E-Commerce

As BigCo streamlined and integrated supply chains, the company also deployed an integrated web-and-call center distribution channel that enabled customers and distribution partners to buy and receive ongoing support for over 14,000 products and services.

Generate Increasing Returns

Like all public companies, BigCo's success or failure ultimately will be measured by the firm's ability to generate increasing returns to shareholders and earn their trust and confidence in the company's future success. As can be seen in the table on page 134, financial performance increased significantly during the period covered in the study. Driven by strong revenue growth and improved operating margins, earnings per share (EPS) rose from $0.91 in 1994 to $4.22 in 2000, and the stock price rose from $18.37 per share at year end 1994 to $85 in 2000. (In 2001, EPS increased to $4.42 and stock price rose to $120.96 per share.)

Business Case for Launching E-Procurement	
Additional Cost	N/A
Benefits	One year after implementation of phase 1, costs were down 20% and the time needed to order supplies had decreased from an average of 48 to 2.5 hours
	By 2000, 94% of goods and services, representing over $4.3 billion, were purchased online from 24,000 worldwide suppliers
	Year-over-year growth in purchases increased 60% from 1999 to 2000 without addition of staff
	Cost savings through e-procurement were $370 million in 2000

Business Case for Launching Customer-Focused E-Commerce	
Additional Cost	N/A
Benefits	During 2000, e-commerce revenues from customers grew 143% to $23.3 billion
	Distribution channel partner revenues grew 50%

Generating Increasing Returns							
	1994	**1995**	**1996**	**1997**	**1998**	**1999**	**2000**
Revenue (mm$s)	64,052	71,940	75,947	78,508	81,677	87,548	88,396
Cost (mm$s)	38,767	41,573	45,407	47,899	50,795	55,620	55,971
Gross margin	39.5%	42.2%	40.2%	39.0%	37.8%	36.5%	36.7%
Operating margin	7.8	13.1	11.9	11.6	11.2	13.6	13.2
Net income (mm$s)	3,022	6,018	5,430	6,093	6,329	6,954	8,093
Return to assets	3.7%	7.5%	6.7%	7.5%	7.4%	7.9%	9.2%
Return to equity	12.9	26.8	25.1	30.7	32.6	33.9	39.2
Current ratio	1.4	1.3	1.2	1.2	1.2	1.1	1.2
Earnings per share	0.91	2.39	2.70	2.98	3.18	4.36	4.22
Stock price (on 12/31)	18.37	22.84	37.87	52.31	92.19	107.88	85.00
Avg no. outstanding shares	2,350.840	2,191.096	2,031.924	1,916.182	1,831.814	1,784.216	1,742.900
Market capitalization (mm$s)	43,157.13	51,016.00	78,408.13	101,713.31	170,150.81	194,455.88	149,122.25

The CEO of BigCo attributed a major portion of the company's success to the series of digital business initiatives that the company implemented during the 1990s:

> If there is a lesson to be extracted from the dot-com crash, it may be this: There is no shortcut to e-business. And if 2000 comes to be seen as a watershed, it will be because this was the year the world's established enterprises awoke to the true possibilities of e-business. I believe a broad consensus has emerged that e-business is just . . . real business. And real business is serious work.

Summary

As we enter the 21st century, excitement concerning the potential of IT to transform business and drive improved performance has never been higher. But the fascination with IT business innovation comes at a time of significant uncertainty and change in the industry as both entrenched players and new entrants struggle to position themselves for success in the emerging global Network Economy. While most agree that Internet-based technologies have progressed at lightning speed since they were introduced to the business world in the early to middle 1990s, developing common standards and robust commercial technologies takes time.

The challenge of integrating new technologies into the "legacy" of computers, networks, and systems already in place within companies adds to the problem. To achieve the grand vision of the Network Economy, a new approach to building businesses and measuring performance is needed.

This chapter explored the challenges that executives face as they attempt to develop the business case for digital business in the context of increasing volatility and uncertainty. Executives should consider the following questions as they attempt to forecast the value of digital business strategies and the ability of their organizations to execute them.

1. How well do you understand the link between your strategies, the capabilities and infrastructure built to execute those strategies, and the value created for all stakeholders (e.g., customers, suppliers, partners, employees, investors)?

2. What are the key performance drivers for your business, including revenue and cost drivers? How do the benefits delivered to stakeholders create financial, physical, and intangible assets?

3. What are the key areas where a change in strategy or an improvement in infrastructure and organizational performance could create significant short-term and long-term value?

4. Conduct an audit of your digital business infrastructure. How much are you spending to operate computing and network operations? On average, how long does it take and how much does it cost to implement a new digital business initiative? What are the key bottlenecks that slow the process and the key activities that increase the cost?

5. How could a shift to an open standard, global networked infrastructure improve network economies of scale and scope by lowering operating cost, increasing functionality, and increasing the range of digital business solutions (strategic options) that can be pursued?

6. Create a list of digital business strategies and solutions that could be developed to leverage an open standard networked infrastructure. Are there opportunities to
   a. Improve internal operating efficiency and quality?
   b. Streamline and integrate channels to market, create new channels, and integrate multiple online/offline channels?
   c. Improve knowledge worker performance and enhance organizational learning?
   d. Add "information value" to existing products and services or create new information-based products and services?
   e. Attract and retain top talent?
   f. Increase employee satisfaction, engagement, and loyalty while creating a culture of motivation, commitment, and trust?
   g. Attract and retain high-value-added customers, suppliers, and partners?
   h. Increase customer/supplier satisfaction, engagement, and loyalty?
   i. Increase investor satisfaction and loyalty?

7. From the above list, identify one or more simple yet powerful "big wins" where a digital business solution could significantly improve business performance. What are the realistic business goals you expect to achieve? Define measurable performance improvements that can be achieved quickly (usually within one year) and the follow-on benefits that will accrue as you pursue strategic options. How will these performance drivers link to financial and capital market performance? Validate your analysis by talking with others who have implemented

similar systems. Ask for lessons learned and areas of high risk that must be managed closely. Collect benchmark data on the benefits that can be expected.

8. Do you have the resources, expertise, and skills required to complete these projects successfully? Can outside partners be identified when the organization's resources are not sufficient?

9. Do you have the political support required to ensure that the project can be completed quickly and effectively? Do project leaders have the resources, authority, and accountability required to get the job done?

10. Have you considered ways to limit the scope of the project? Keep in mind the "80/20 rule": You can often achieve 80 percent of the benefit with 20 percent of the effort. Don't push to include hard-to-implement features and functions that are not critical to overall project success.

11. Has an effective change control process been implemented? Can you ruthlessly manage "project creep" while not losing sight of the good ideas that emerge during implementation? To assist with this task, create two task forces to search for follow-on "options" benefits. One task force can be charged with identifying new IT-enabled business building opportunities to improve operating and channel performance, build and leverage knowledge assets, strengthen and leverage the community, and launch new ventures. The second task force can be charged with searching for ways to enhance infrastructure performance continuously.

Appendix 4A

Analyzing Business Models

Analyzing the Business Concept

Categories of Analysis and Best Practices	Sample Measures
Market opportunity Large and growing market High levels of demand and market readiness Opportunity is large enough to enable evolution of the business model and generation of multiple revenue streams Window of opportunity is long enough to support time required for development and growth of business but short enough to build barriers to entry	Size of markets served today and in the future (number of customers, units sold, revenues, etc.) Anticipated rate of market growth by product category and customer segment Total size and length of the "window of opportunity" Current and forecasted market share and "share of wallet" (total spending across categories) Current revenue (and revenue projections) by product category and customer segment Committed revenues for future business

Analyzing the Business Concept

Categories of Analysis and Best Practices	Sample Measures
Product/service offerings Solves a very real problem for a large customer base Compelling benefits for all members of the community Short, straightforward purchase decision and ease of adoption Personalized products and services Product/service offerings satisfy an unmet need	Subjective and objective benefits for channel customers and end consumers Importance of product/service features to the buyer and the user (if different from the buyer) Differentiation from alternatives Price position vis-à-vis alternatives Price premium related to product/service features and attributes Adoption cycle time and decision-making process
Competitive dynamics and strategy Opportunity to be number one or number two in a structurally attractive industry No one player or group of players exerts significant influence and power Defensible position vis-à-vis competitors and substitutes Ease of entry, but barriers can then be erected	Key competitors and substitutes today and in the future Number, concentration, and power of competitors Amount of excess versus scarce capacity today and in the future Basis for competition and differentiation Propensity to collaborate and compete Entry and exit barriers today and in the future
Business context and risk Favorable business context Manageable risks	Nature and magnitude of risks and strategies for managing them Presence or absence of "fatal flaws" in the business model
Strategic options Leader in leveraging business infrastructure to expand the customer base and increase revenues from existing customers Leader in increasing the range of products and services offered and in decreasing the cost and time of launching new products and services Leader in ability to modularize business initiatives, projects, and investments Leader in the ability to decrease the cost and time required to stop a project or exit a business that does not meet profitability expectations and return hurdles	Profile of business initiatives, project activities, and investments Revenue growth from new and existing customer base Number of new products, services, and businesses introduced versus industry average Cost and time to develop and launch new products and services and to enter new business or geographic markets versus industry average Average time to achieve profitability in a new product, service, or businesses Length of time and cost to stop a project and exit a business Dollar savings from delaying an investment and/or exiting a business

(continued)

Analyzing Capabilities

Categories of Analysis and Best Practices	Sample Measures
Operating Capabilities	
Operating performance Streamlined, integrated processes and channels Efficient operations Recognized leader in asset utilization	Cycle time of key processes and activities Operating cost by activity, product, customer segment Sales per employee Savings from headcount reduction Costs of supplies, parts, and service and yearly savings from improved management and operations Cost of inventory, frequency of inventory turns, and estimated savings
Customer and community-focused quality Recognized quality leader Ability to charge a price differential and/or attract customers and community members based on reputation for high quality	Quality measures (e.g., defect levels, rework, returns, compliance with standards, waste) Cost of poor quality Administrative costs for managing quality Price differential and community penetration/loyalty based on quality
Cost savings and improved asset utilization Best-in-class operating costs Recognized leader in efficient and effective capital asset utilization	Sales per employee vis-à-vis previous performance and competitor performance Yearly savings from headcount reductions Cost of paper-based processes and communications and yearly savings from the shift to electronic distribution Cost of supplies, parts, and service and yearly savings from improved supply chain management and operations Cost of inventory, frequency of inventory turns, and estimated savings Current asset utilization and estimated improvements
Fast-cycled innovation Cost and time to pursue follow-on initiatives is lower than industry average Cost and time to stop a project or exit a business are lower than industry average	Increased range of new opportunities that can be pursued Cost and time to develop and launch new products and services and to enter new business or geographic markets versus industry average Average time to achieve profitability in a new product, service, or business Length of time and cost to stop a project and/or exit a business

Analyzing Capabilities

Categories of Analysis and Best Practices	Sample Measures
Information and Knowledge Capabilities	
Knowledge capital Recognized leader in managing knowledge assets and intellectual capital Effective and efficient processes for acquiring, creating, packaging, and distributing data, information, and knowledge	Market value/book value Number of and value of patents Percent of earnings related to knowledge capital* Ratio of knowledge capital earnings to sales Ratio of knowledge capital earnings to operating income
Strong leadership Experienced and committed leaders with a demonstrated track record of success in the industry and business Leaders are well connected within the industry and business community	Executive, director, and adviser profiles and qualifications Executive achievements and performance in current firm and previous positions Ability to create a compelling vision for the business that attracts top talent (employees, partners, and investors) and high-value customers and suppliers
Expertise and skills Recognized leader in attracting and retaining top talent Ability to attract and retain key people at a rate that exceeds industry and geography average	Partner and key employee profiles Number of offers made and accepted Average number of positions open Average length of time and cost to fill a key position or sign a key partnership deal
Development and retention of employees and partners Recognized leader in providing high-quality career development, expertise, and motivation Recognized leader in creating a culture that rewards career development of employees and partners	Development resources available and percent utilization Ratio of development resources used to employee/partner performance Career trajectory for key employees Attrition rate versus historical, geographic, and industry averages
Informed decision making and action Readily available, easily accessible, and relevant information High levels of information literacy throughout the firm and within customer, supplier, and partner communities Recognized leader in fostering a culture of information sharing and knowledge building	Relevance and currency of information and expertise delivered face-to-face and through online channels Employee computer and information literacy Ease of use and functionality of technical systems Patterns of information sharing and use of information stored on Intranets (for internal employees) and Extranets (for partners, suppliers, and customers)

(continued)

Analyzing Capabilities

Categories of Analysis and Best Practices	Sample Measures
Information and Knowledge Capabilities (continued)	
Information-based products and services Price premium due to information value added	Number and profile of information-based products and services Revenues/earnings generated through information-based products and services Price comparison and market share
Community Penetration, Loyalty, and Value	
Community penetration Dense, well-connected network of customers, suppliers, employees, and business partners	Number of customers, suppliers, and partners Profile of key customers, suppliers, and partners Profile of interactions among community members
Personalization Multiple opportunities for personalization are available, and community members take advantage of them to improve experience of doing business with you	Level of personalization available Percentage of community members that choose to use personalization features
Engagement and loyalty Highly engaged community members interact and do business on a regular basis Community members choose to do business with you despite readily accessible alternatives	Frequency of interactions among customers, suppliers, and partners Average amount of money generated per transaction, per month, etc. Frequency of return visits and repeat interactions Percentage of first-time versus repeat customers (or other community members) Satisfaction with products, services, and "experience" while doing business Conversion rate: percentage first-time versus repeat visitors over time
Lifetime value Recognized leader in the cost of acquiring and serving community members Recognized leader in maximizing lifetime value of a community member (The calculations presented at the right are specific to customers but also can be used to calculate the value of suppliers or other community members)	Cost to serve = (operating expenses + cost of sales)/number of customers Expenses related to acquiring and retaining an individual customer or group of customers Customer value = (number of customers attracted to your business through all channels) × (average monetary value of each visit) − (costs to acquire, retain, and serve) Lifetime value = (current value of a community member) × (estimated length of relationship) × (expected percent change in value over time)

Analyzing Capabilities

Categories of Analysis and Best Practices	Sample Measures
Infrastructure Capabilities	
Infrastructure functionality and flexibility Cost advantage due to infrastructure efficiency Recognized leader in introducing successful new products, entering new markets, and launching new businesses	Administrative costs (total dollar amount as a percentage of total expenses versus competitors) Average time to launch new products or business or enter a new market Average time to achieve profitability, scale, and market dominance Number of successful new products, market entries, or businesses during a given period (over time and versus competitors)

Analyzing Value

Categories of Analysis and Best Practices	Sample Measures
Benefits to community members Unique value proposition attracts loyal customers, suppliers, and partners	Subjective and objective benefits for customers, suppliers, and partners Market share and "share of wallet" Pricing benchmarks and comparisons Current revenue (and revenue projections) by product category and customer segment Committed revenues for future business
Brand equity Leader in brand awareness High levels of loyalty and trust High brand value	Advertising dollar to sales ratio Level of brand awareness inside and outside your business community Strength of brand relative to competitors Overall brand perception (positive, negative, neutral) Price premium and/or community loyalty related to knowledge of and trust in brand
Investor loyalty and trust Investors exhibit confidence and trust in the business and its management Increasing stock price and market value despite minor fluctuations in business performance	Stock price Market value = (stock price) $\times$ (number of equity shares outstanding) Price/earnings ratio (P/E)

(continued)

Analyzing Value

Categories of Analysis and Best Practices	Sample Measures
Returns to company and investors Increasing returns to investors while maintaining long-term viability of the business	Net income (or profits) Earnings before interest, taxes, depreciation, amortization (EBITDA) (reflects profitability of ongoing operations) Earnings/share ratio (EPS) Working capital = (current assets) − (current liabilities) Invested capital = working capital + capital expenses (reflects the money put into a company to build and maintain it) Free cash flow = EBIAT − (invested capital + depreciation) + (net change in working capital) + (net change in other long-term capital) Current ratio = current assets/current liabilities (reflects company's ability to pay current obligations from current assets) Investor dividends (if paid) Value of stock options to executives, employees, and partners
Profitability ratios Recognized leader in generating returns to investors (especially compared with investments in other companies or investment alternatives)	Return on sales (ROS) = net income/sales Return on equity (ROE) = net income/equity Return on assets (ROA) = net income/assets Return on investments (ROI) Return on invested capital (ROIC) = net income/invested capital Rate of return (ROR)
Performance ratios Recognized leader in converting revenues into earnings	Gross margin = gross profit/net sales Operating margin = earnings before interest and taxes/revenues Fixed asset turnover = revenues/(cost of property, plant, and equipment, or PPE) Capital turnover = revenues/invested capital

*This approach to measuring knowledge, capital earnings, and associated ratios is discussed in B. Lev, "Seeing Is Believing: A Better Approach to Estimating Knowledge Capital," *CFO,* February 1999; and A. Webber, "New Math for a New Economy," *Fast Company,* January–February 2000.

Appendix 4B

Analyzing Financial Performance

The financial performance of a public company is most commonly measured through an assessment of its earnings. These measures provide various views of the cash that "flows through" a company to investors. In growing firms, especially those that require a high level of capital investment, analysts commonly begin with an assessment of earnings before interest, taxes, depreciation, and amortization (EBITDA). In essence, EBITDA provides an assessment of operating performance minus nonoperating income and expenses (e.g., interest and taxes) and noncash charges (e.g., depreciation and amortization).

When evaluating a company's performance, it sometimes makes sense to ignore nonoperating cash flows and accounting conventions that could complicate an assessment of the efficiency and effectiveness of ongoing operations. However, there are problems with looking solely at EBITDA that must be kept in mind.[12] First, EBITDA leaves out many expenses and, as a result, cannot be used to measure profitability. Second, it cannot be considered a proxy for cash flow since it does not measure actual cash generated (or used) during a given period. Specifically, EBITDA neglects the following:

- Cash required for working capital[13]
- Debt payments and other fixed expenses
- Capital expenditures

Finally, aggressive accounting practices can make it difficult to calculate true revenues and expenses, which can invalidate EBITDA.

While EBITDA provides a measure of how much money a business generates when operating at its current scale, it does not measure the cash investments required to accomplish a specific strategy and grow the business. Better measures for cash flow are available by looking at the cash flow statement, which breaks out cash flow from operations (true cash profits from ongoing operations), from financing (dividend payments and stock repurchases), and from investing (capital expenses, purchase and sale of businesses, and equity investments). Alternatively, it is helpful to calculate free cash flow (FCF), a measure of the cash that a company makes (or uses) to support existing operations *and to fund growth*. FCF is calculated as follows:

Earnings before interest but after taxes (EBIAT)	Plus
(Depreciation + noncash expenses)	Minus
Total capital expenditures	Minus

[12]For more information on measuring financial performance, see Motley Fool (www.motleyfool.com). Articles of special interest include P. Weiss, "The Earnings Game," www.motleyfool.com, February 4, 1999; P. Weiss, "Tying It All Together with the Flow Ratio," www.motleyfool.com, Part 1, December 10, 1999, and Part 2, December 14, 1999; and M. Richey and P. Weiss, "Ignore EBITDA," www.motleyfool.com, September 6, 2001.

[13]Working capital is simply current assets minus current liabilities and can be positive or negative. Working capital defines the value of a company's liquid assets—those that can be readily converted into the cash needed to build the business, fund its growth, and produce shareholder value.

Change in net working capital	Plus/ minus
Change in other net long-term capital.[14]	

If FCF is positive, the extra cash flow can be used for other purposes (for example, payment of dividends to shareholders, payment of interest, repayment of debt, repurchase of stock, or other investments). If FCF is negative, the company must make up the difference by borrowing money (thus increasing debt) or issuing new equity. It is important to keep in mind that many terrific companies have been EBITDA-positive and cash-flow-negative in their formative stages. In fact, Wal-Mart reported negative FCF for years while it built its retail empire. Thus, focusing on FCF alone can lead investors to miss opportunities.

Another useful measure of financial performance is return on equity (ROE). ROE measures the efficiency and effectiveness of management in controlling the three main levers of business performance: profitability, asset management, and financial leverage. It is calculated by dividing earnings by shareholders' equity (liabilities minus assets). To better highlight the three management levers, a more expanded calculation can be performed:

$$\text{ROE} = (\text{earnings/sales}) \times (\text{sales/assets}) \times (\text{assets/shareholders' equity})$$

where

Earnings/sales = an organization's profit margin

[14]See C. Baldwin, *Fundamental Enterprise Valuation: Free Cash Flow* (Harvard Business School Publishing No. 801–126).

Sales/assets = asset turnover

Assets/shareholders' equity = financial leverage

These and other measures of financial performance can be used by investors, analysts, and executives to make decisions on whether and at what price to invest in a company. The cumulative result of these decisions is called the market value of a company. In publicly held companies,[15] the market value is determined as individual and institutional investors[16] buy and sell stock. The price of a publicly traded stock is influenced by a company's current and historical financial performance, predictions of future financial performance (especially in relation to other types of investments), availability of equity for sale at any given time, and the confidence and trust of investors in the company's strategy, capabilities, and management. The price of a privately held stock is based on similar decisions made by private investors: high-wealth individuals (often called angels), banks, venture capitalists, and companies (often called strategic investors). The market value of a firm is calculated by multiplying the stock price at any given time by the number of equity shares outstanding.

[15]Publicly held firms offer stock for sale to the public, usually on a stock exchange such as the New York Stock Exchange, the London Stock Exchange, or the Nasdaq Stock Exchange.
[16]Institutional investors are organizations (for example, banks, insurance companies, pension funds) that invest in a company's stock.

Appendix 4C

Approaches to Valuing Public Companies

Formal valuation models provide a *disciplined approach* to thinking about performance and value that can help executives make decisions and take action based on "informed intuition." This intuition is dramatically improved when performance drivers are used to explicitly define the assumptions on which financial forecasts are based. When used to analyze a business operating in highly uncertain and rapidly changing markets, industries, and organizations, these assumptions must be tested continually against real-time data on strategic and operating performance. Scenarios and the ability to triangulate using multiple valuation approaches help account for uncertainty in assumptions and the lack of historical earnings data.

This appendix presents two commonly used valuation methods: discounted cash flow (DCF) and comparable company valuation. In addition, it shows how a "sum-of-parts" valuation approach can be used with either DCF or comparable company valuation to calculate the value of independent cash flow streams and then add the partial company valuations to determine total value.

Discounted Cash Flow

The value of a mature business in a stable industry is most often measured by using DCF methods. Typically, forward-looking financial projections drive the analysis. The analyst, investor, or executive identifies anticipated cash flows and then discounts them back to their net present value (NPV). The terminal value that best reflects the effects of future years is then calculated and added to the present value of the cash flows in the model. While details vary, the general approach to conducting a DCF analysis is presented below.

- Decide how far in the future to project performance drivers and financial performance.

- Analyze the assumptions that underlie projections of future revenues, costs, and working capital and construct a spreadsheet that projects free cash flow.

- Determine a discount rate that reflects the opportunity cost of the investment.

- Discount each year's free cash flow to the current year and add them together.

- Calculate the terminal value of free cash flow streams in future years and add this to the previous sum.

If a firm has multiple business units, each of which employs a different business model, a sum-of-parts analysis can be performed. Using this technique, DCF streams from the different business units are calculated. Different assumptions are used to forecast revenue growth, costs, and cash flow, and different discount rates may be used to determine present value. Then the DCF streams are added together to calculate total value. If desired, weightings can be applied to each of the DCF streams. For example, analysts used different assumptions to forecast revenue growth and EBITDA for AOL Time Warner's publishing, music, filmed entertainment, cable systems, cable networks, and AOL.com businesses.

Valuation purists often argue that the sole determinant of company value is the ability of the business to generate cash for investors. Thus, they often view DCF as the only acceptable method to determine the value of a business. While it is essentially true that all valuation techniques attempt to capture future cash flow either explicitly or implicitly, there are problems with applying the DCF approach indiscriminately. First, estimating the cash flow rate for high-growth companies operating in a highly unstable industry is a somewhat speculative process. This is illustrated by comparing the DCF valuations of the AOL Time Warner merger that were performed by the same Salomon Smith Barney (SSB) analysts in 2000 and 2001. The earnings calculated by the SSB analysts were based on assumptions for future revenues, costs, and working capital. Given the rapid fall in investor confidence in Internet stocks, coupled with a significant decline in the economy and an associated decline in advertising revenues, predictions of revenue growth, costs, and market value in March 2000 proved highly unreliable when viewed in April 2001.

A second and equally important problem with DCF valuations is that the appropriate discount rate to use is not always immediately apparent. Traditionally, analysts might choose to use the capital asset pricing model[17] (CAPM) to estimate cost of capital. The CAPM equation is given below:[18]

$$\text{Cost of capital} = \beta \times \text{risk premium} + \text{risk-free rate}$$

where beta is a number derived from the price variations of the stock, the risk-free rate is typically the interest rate that could be earned by investment in a relatively low-risk government bond, and the risk premium is the difference between the expected return from the stock market and the risk-free rate. Once again, volatility of the stock market and the lack of certainty concerning the strength of the global economy in the future can lead to a significant margin of error in calculating the cost of capital.

A third problem with using the DCF approach is that it fails to directly measure the value of intangible assets such as brand, knowledge, and customer loyalty. At the time when the AOL Time Warner merger was announced, it was assumed that access to over 25 million unique customers and over 70 percent market share would enable AOL.com to continue to grow at rates much higher than those of other competitors. In the absence of reliable, objective performance measures, decisions to increase the market value of a firm to account for intangible assets involve even more risk than decisions made on the basis of historical financial performance. Once again, these risks are magnified during times of rapid change and high levels of uncertainty.

As a result of these and other difficulties, many analysts, executives, accountants, venture capitalists, and investment bankers turn to other valuation techniques to complement or substitute for DCF valuations.

Comparable Company Valuation

Another popular technique that is employed by many analysts is to examine key *multiples* for several companies in the same industry. The price/earnings ratio is perhaps the most prevalent of the multiples used. At times, analysts will compare companies across more than one set of criteria.

The comparable company valuation approach is different from DCF in that instead of asking, "What should the business be worth, based on its cash flows?" an investor, analyst, or executive asks, "What is the market willing to pay for a business like this?" There is some validity to this

---

[17]R. A. Brealey and S. C. Meyers, *Principles of Corporate Finance* (New York: McGraw-Hill, 2000).
[18]Strictly speaking, analysts should calculate a *weighted average cost of capital* that takes into account the different risks based on a company's financing strategy. For example, much of Amazon's financing comes from debt, which carries a lower cost of capital.

approach as long as the right set of companies is chosen and historical performance is a good indicator of future value. Using comparable valuations provides a fast, easy-to-understand valuation framework that does not require complex financial modeling. It can also, in theory, capture the effect of intangible assets and investor confidence by factoring in the premium or discount within an investment category or across categories. Unfortunately, there are also problems with this approach.

First, complex companies with multiple business models may not fit neatly into a single category. As we saw with DCF analysis, sum-of-parts valuations can help mitigate this problem. Second, the choice of comparable companies may not be clear when the company's products, services, and/or business model are innovative or unique. Third, even if a valid set of comparable companies can be identified, the range of values for multiples of companies within a given category or across different categories may be quite large. Fourth, an analyst must determine which multiple to use to calculate his or her estimates. This is often driven by the purpose of the valuation. For example, earnings multiples reflect the performance of the company during the time period under study and often are used to value a "going concern." Asset multiples capture the value of underlying assets and may be used alone or in conjunction with earnings multiples to analyze an acquisition. Finally, no matter which category of company or multiple is cho-

sen, an analyst who chooses to use a comparable company valuation approach must assume that investors have the information they need to make valid and rational investment decisions.

Dealing with Uncertainty

As has been clearly stated in this chapter, valuations are based on assumptions about the future performance of a business. Triangulation—the practice of using multiple different valuation techniques and multiple different measures—can help increase confidence but does not take the place of frequent comparisons between forecasted and actual performance. Finally, scenarios can be used to test the sensitivity of the valuation model to changes in key assumptions. At a minimum, most analysts routinely examine the best, worst, and most likely cases.

While all these approaches can help validate a financial model, the real test of the model comes only as executives implement strategies and operate their businesses. Access to detailed, timely, and accurate information enables them to measure the impact of business decisions and actions as they occur and to compare actual performance to forecasted performance. The ability to make sense of the information and implement correctional actions based on the insights gained is the essence of designing "learning" organizations that can link strategy, actions, and decisions to assessments of value.

Managing Networked Infrastructure and Operations

by Robert D. Austin

3

Over the last decade, a dramatic change in computing infrastructure has led to fundamental changes in how businesses operate. As a result, today's infrastructure managers must deal with new challenges and new threats. Fortunately, ever-improving technology offers a growing number of problem-solving options. Indeed, entirely new businesses and industries have emerged to help operational managers realize greater efficiencies and capabilities.

The chapters in this module provide a basis for discussing how changing information technology (IT) infrastructure affects business, how management priorities must shift, and how the risks that affect day-to-day operations can be reduced. The focus of the module is on frontline operational issues. Without management frameworks that deliver real operational results, the best-laid plans, the greatest ideas, and the shrewdest strategies cannot create value.

Chapter 5

Understanding Internetworking Infrastructure[1]

> Seventy-five percent of all IT dollars go to infrastructure. Isn't it time you learned what it is?[2]

Information technology (IT) infrastructure[3] lies at the heart of most companies' operating capabilities. For that reason, changes in information technologies lead to fundamental changes in how businesses operate. Because many companies in fact depend on these technologies, no longer is IT infrastructure just nice to have; no longer is it just value-adding. It is vital.

Recent technological advances have led to major changes in how IT services are delivered. For some time now, low-cost computing power has driven a shift toward more distributed processing. The rise of *Internetworking technologies,* which provide a low-cost way to connect virtually everyone on the same network, offers new possibilities for addressing business computing needs. As a result, the operational mechanisms at the heart of many businesses continue to evolve. New technologies add to, improve, and interconnect older systems to yield infrastructures with new and complex operational characteristics, which are discussed in detail in this chapter.

---

[1]This chapter is adapted from materials in Professor Robert D. Austin's *Managing Information Technology Infrastructure* course module, Harvard Business School Publishing No. 601–181.
[2]IBM advertisement in *The Wall Street Journal,* November 19, 2001.
[3]In this and the following chapters, we use the word *infrastructure* to refer to the entire layered fabric of hardware, software, systems, and media that collectively deliver IT-based services.

This infrastructure evolution brings with it many benefits. IT services few envisioned several years ago have become commonplace. Older services can be delivered in new, more customer-responsive ways, and the cost structures underlying new service delivery methods are superior to those of older methods. New business models enabled by the new service possibilities have emerged. Industries restructure to realize greater efficiencies and capabilities as part of a long-term trend that will continue and accelerate regardless of occasional technology market slumps.

Along with benefits, however, come challenges. In this chapter and the next two, we address the challenges associated with new service possibilities and consequent shifts in infrastructures. Our focus is on frontline issues of execution. Grand visions are of little use unless they can be translated into reality. New business models and systems cannot succeed unless they can be relied on to operate at key moments. New technologies provide less value if they cannot interoperate effectively with the older technologies in which most companies still have major investments. Most seriously, IT infrastructure greatly determines a company's differentiating capabilities; effective infrastructure enhances those capabilities, while ineffective infrastructure destroys them. In today's environment, a seemingly minor IT decision made two or three years ago by a low-level technical employee can turn out to be the decisive factor in defining a winning strategy, closing a sale or deal, or surviving a competitive challenge.

Consider the experiences of a U.S. consumer products company in the late 1990s. The company adopted a Web server technology that was highly regarded for its ability to support graphics. Developers built product websites by using this leading-edge technology. A few years later, early in the 21st century, the company performed an experiment to see how its products would show up if consumers performed Web searches on product categories such as "paper towels." The marketing staff hoped to see its products in those categories near the top of lists that resulted from consumer searches. Instead, the searches turned up little sign of the company's products. An investigation was launched to determine why. As it turned out, the leading-edge Web server technology chosen by this company did not lend itself readily to text-based searches because of its advanced graphics-based design. The IT and marketing staffs, working together, began an effort to remedy the situation, but their options were limited by the server technology selected a few years earlier that now supported almost all the firm's websites. The solution was more expensive and time-consuming than expected.

This example illustrates a critical point: Infrastructure decisions can come back to haunt companies. In this case, the problem was not serious and the company was able to remedy it. But the constraints of past IT infrastructure decisions can be much more severe, for example, when a company deploys a technology that proves to be a loser in the marketplace; such a company can be left with poor (or no) vendor support, inferior business capabilities, and costly-to-maintain infrastructure that cannot easily be shut down or replaced. Infrastructure decisions are difficult because they arise in a dimly illuminated realm halfway between business and technology. In this realm, technology issues are tightly interwoven with business issues, and it is unclear who should be making the decisions. Often general managers are tempted to leave it to the "techies," but that is a formula for disaster. Technology elements of decisions may seem alien to nontechnical managers, but technologists see some business issues in similar terms. The deepest challenges of infrastructure management, then, are in understanding and assigning responsibility for making these not just technical, not just business decisions, in bridging the gap between the business and technology domains. Only when we are successful in this will we see clearly how evolving technologies affect business, how management priorities should evolve, and how we can reduce the risks that affect day-to-day operations.

The Drivers of Change: Better Chips, Bigger Pipes

In 1965, Gordon Moore, who would later cofound Intel, noted that the performance of memory chips doubled every 18 to 24 months, whereas their size and cost remained roughly constant. He predicted that the trend would continue and that its impact on the world would be profound. Nearly four decades later, most people are familiar with changes wrought by the continuing downward slope in the cost of processing power predicted by Moore's "law." The computing power in a 21st-century desktop, laptop, or even handheld computing device far exceeds that of machines the size of large rooms at the time of Moore's observation (see Figure 5.1). Equally significant is the low cost of modern devices. Once scarce, expensive, and therefore centrally controlled computing power is now abundant, inexpensive, and widely distributed in everything from general-purpose computers to toaster ovens.

Centralized computing architecture prevailed during the 1960s and 1970s (see Figure 5.2). Specialized data processing staffs presided over large mainframe computers accessed via awkward punch card, Teletype, and terminal machines. Dealings

FIGURE 5.1
A Graphical Representation of Moore's Law

Source: Adapted by Mark Seager from *Microprocessor Report* 9(6), May 1995, and Aad Offerman, "ChipList 9.9.5," July 1998, *http://einstein.et.tudelft. nl/~offerman/chiplist. html.* See *http://www. physics.udel.edu/www users/watson/scen103/ intel.html,* April 20, 2000, George Watson, University of Delaware, 1998.

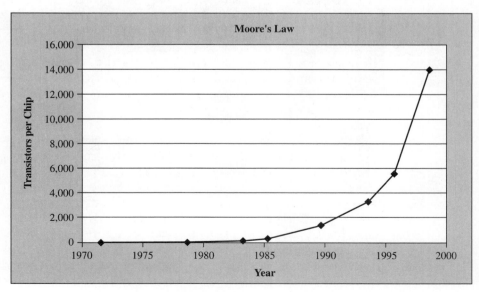

FIGURE 5.2 The Evolution of Corporate IT Infrastructure

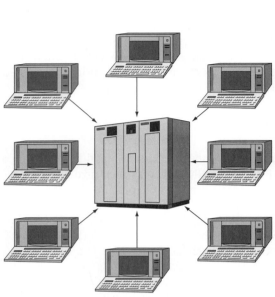

Mainframe-Based Centralized Computing (Pre-1980)

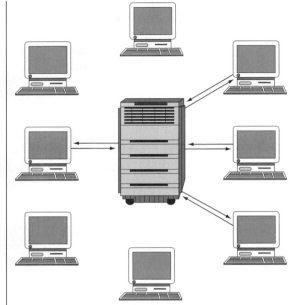

PC-Based Distributed Computing (1980s)

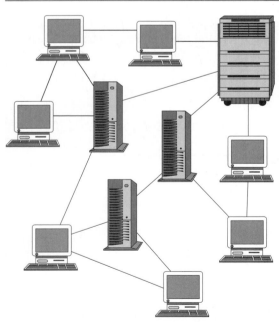

Client-Server Computing (Late 1980s, Early 1990s)

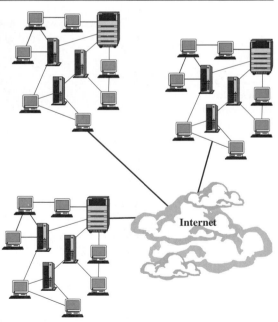

Internetwork-Based Computing (Mid-1990s to Present)

between humans and computers were not very interactive; programs ran infrequently, in batches, often only once each day, which made modifying and testing programs time-consuming and difficult. Access devices were "dumb"; they had little inherent capability but served merely as murky windows into complex mainframes. Mainframes provided all computational and storage capabilities. The occasional need to share information between mainframes led to the development of early networks. These early networks were simple because they only had to handle traffic between a few large mainframe computers.

The impacts of Moore's law disrupted the mainframe paradigm. An advertisement for the Intel 4004 in the fall 1971 issue of *Electronic News* exaggerated when it announced "a new era in integrated electronics," a "computer on a chip."[4] But this new era was not long in coming. The immediate successors of the programmable 4004 were the basis for the first general-purpose desktop computing machines capable of real business functionality: personal computers (PCs). When the IBM PC appeared in late 1981, few realized how radically it would change business computing.

With the emergence of PCs, computing that had resided in centralized enclaves staffed by data processing specialists spread throughout an organization and into the eager hands of business users. Financial analysts embraced spreadsheets. Marketers designed and analyzed their own databases. Engineers adopted computerized drawing packages and programmed their own PCs for more specialized purposes. For a growing number of computing tasks, response time delays and extensive reliance on techies became distant memories.

As newly empowered computer users sought to share work, new communications infrastructures emerged. Local area networks (LANs) allowed business users to share spreadsheets, word processing, and other documents and to use common printers to obtain hard copies of their work. PCs and LANs became more sophisticated as users' computing needs evolved and as underlying technologies that were fundamentally different from earlier mainframe technologies advanced. The client-server movement was the culmination of this model: higher-powered but still distributed computers (servers) combined with more elaborate networks and desktop PCs (clients) to provide IT services (i.e., payroll, order management, sales support, and beyond) formerly delivered by mainframe.

In the early 1990s, the rise to prominence of the commercial Internet, the Web, and underlying protocols (rules for how data would be moved across networks) led to new stages of evolution.[5] Transmission Control Protocol and Internet Protocol, together known as TCP/IP, provided a robust standard for routing messages between LANs and created the potential to connect all computers on an ever-larger wide area network (WAN). These Internetworking technologies were the legacy of U.S. Department of Defense (DOD) research conducted in the 1960s against the backdrop

---

[4]Paul Frieberger and Michael Swaine, *Fire in the Valley: The Making of the Personal Computer* (New York: McGraw-Hill, 2000), p. 20.
[5]The Internet was not new in the 1990s. It had been in use by the military and by researchers since the 1960s. But commercial uses of these technologies accelerated dramatically in the 1990s.

FIGURE 5.3
A Graphical
Illustration of
Metcalfe's Law

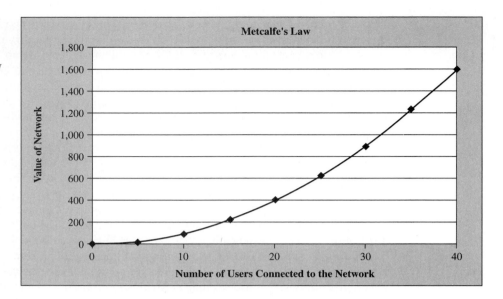

of the Cold War with the Soviet Union that sought to develop communication networks without critical communication lines or nodes that could be targeted by an enemy. Because of their publicly funded origins, TCP/IP and other Internet protocols and technologies were open standards, not owned by any person or company. Computers, therefore, could be connected at low cost and with minimal central orchestration. Self-service hookup facilitated rapid growth in the worldwide Internet.

At first, the Internet was useful primarily for exchanging e-mail and large data files, but the Web, with its graphical user interfaces, made Internet communication very valuable to those who were not computer specialists. Just as PCs had made computing accessible to a wide variety of nontechnical users, the Web made network resources (such as distant databases) and capabilities (such as over-the-Net collaboration) accessible. The number of connected computers shot upward, and the value of the network increased according to Metcalfe's law: "The usefulness of a network increases with the square of the number of users connected to the network" (see Figure 5.3).[6] As the number of users grew, commercial potential mounted and network capacity expanded. Network capacity followed a curve steeper than the one that applied to chips (see Figure 5.4). The combination of powerful chips and large communication "pipes," both at low cost, fueled a process that would lead to qualitatively different computing infrastructures.

These related exponential trends—reduction in the cost of computing power and reduction in the cost of exchanging information between computers—have been fundamental drivers of changes in the business landscape that we continue to experience and try to understand. Because changes have been rapid, many business en-

[6]Metcalfe's law is commonly attributed to Robert Metcalfe, one of the inventors of the Ethernet standard and the founder of 3Com Corporation.

FIGURE 5.4
The Bandwidth Explosion

Source: Adapted from
http://www.stanford.
edu/~yzarolia/
Challenges.htm.

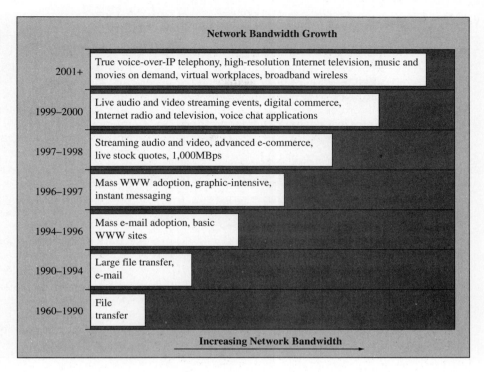

vironments contain a mix of technologies from various computing eras. Some companies still rely heavily on mainframes; as recently as 1997, for example, Ford Motor Company had over 300 million lines of COBOL software running vital company functions on mainframe computers, and it is likely that much of that code remains in use today.[7] At the same time, companies have moved boldly to seize the benefits of newer technologies. Mainframes have been redefined and reborn as enterprise servers. The constant intermingling of old and new technologies adds to the complexity of infrastructure management problems. Understanding how shifting technology might combine with "legacy" systems to result in changes in business capabilities, the choices facing businesses, and the structures of industries is a prerequisite for understanding how to manage IT infrastructures.

The Basic Components of Internetworking Infrastructures

For our purposes, Internetworking infrastructures can be conceptually divided into three categories: network, processing systems, and facilities. *Network* refers to the medium and supporting technologies (hardware and software) that permit

[7]For more details on this, see Robert D. Austin and Mark Cotteleer, "Ford Motor Company: Maximizing the Business Value of Web Technologies," Harvard Business School Case No. 198-006.

TABLE 5.1   **Fundamental Components of Internetworking Infrastructure**

	Core Technologies	Key Management Issues
Network	Fiber optics, cable systems, DSL, satellite, wireless, Internetworking hardware (routers, switches, firewalls), content delivery software, identity and policy management, net monitoring	• How to select technologies and standards • How to select partners • How to manage partner relationships • How to assure reliability • How to maintain security
Processing systems	Transaction software (enterprise systems offered by companies such as SAP and Oracle or more targeted solutions offered by companies such as Trilogy and i2), servers, server appliances, client devices (PCs, handhelds)	• What to keep internal and what to outsource • How to deploy, grow, and modify • Enterprise system or best-of-breed hybrid? • Relationships with legacies • How to manage incidents • How to recover after a "disaster"
Facilities	Corporate data centers, collocation data centers, managed services data centers, data closets	• Internal or external management? • Choosing a facilities model suited to one's company • How to assure reliability • How to maintain security

exchange of information between processing units and organizations. As network capacity increases, the network takes on greater importance as a component of IT infrastructure. *Processing systems* encompass the hardware and software that together provide an organization's ability to handle business transactions. They are newly interesting in the age of Internetworking because they are being redesigned to better capitalize on the advantages offered by Internetworking technologies. *Facilities,* the physical systems that house and protect computing and network devices, are perhaps the least glamorous infrastructure components. But they too are growing in importance as demand increases for high levels of availability, reliability, and security and as greater network capacity makes new facilities models possible.

Each of these infrastructure components generates opportunities and issues managers must understand and be able to address effectively. Table 5.1 lists some of the supporting core technologies and identifies some of the key management issues that arise for each component. A major theme underlying the evolution of these components is that *Internetworking creates many more degrees of freedom in how components can be arranged and managed.* Having more degrees of freedom creates possibilities for cost reduction, new capabilities, and new business models but also poses challenges in understanding the implications of possible infrastructure designs and management actions.

FIGURE 5.5
A Simple LAN

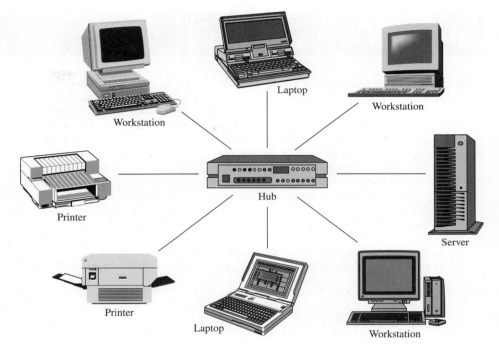

The Technological Elements of Networks

The network component of IT infrastructure can be decomposed into several technological elements; these are the key components that managers must understand, arrange, and maintain. Although the underlying technologies that constitute these elements vary, anyone involved in managing networks will need to make decisions about the design, management, and improvement of the following.

Local Area Networks

Local area networks (LANs), as the name implies, provide a way for computers that are physically close together to communicate (see Figure 5.5). LAN technologies define the physical features of technological solutions to local communication problems and needs (e.g., should we use coaxial or unshielded twisted pair cabling? should we go wireless?) and also the protocols—the rules—for "conversations" between computers (e.g., should we use Ethernet or Token Ring standards?). Choices between different technologies and standards involve trade-offs, often in terms of cost versus capabilities but sometimes also, as in the case of wireless technologies, in terms of convenience versus data capacity or even information security.

Hubs, Switches, and Network Adapters

Hubs, switches, and network adapters allow computers to be connected in LANs. Hubs and switches serve as central junctions into which cables from the computers

How LAN Protocols Work

The problem of computers "conversing" on a LAN is much like the problem of students conversing in a classroom. In a classroom, the air in the room (the "ether") readily supports students in speaking to each other. But if two people speak at the same time, they cannot be sure of communication. To avoid such problems in the classroom we employ protocols—rules—that govern our interactions. One possible set of rules might require that students speak in turn. To keep track of whose turn it is, we might pass a small object (a "token") in a pattern (maybe a "ring") around the room. Whoever has the token at the moment has speaking rights; everyone else must listen.

These rules are very much like those used by computers as they speak onto the captive ether of LAN network cables by using the Token Ring protocol. The popular Ethernet protocol is a little different. With Ethernet, computers speak out whenever they (1) have something to say and (2) hear silence on the network for a moment. If two or more computers speak at the same time, the computers notice this—they detect the "collision"—and stop talking. Each waits a random amount of time and tries again. The Ethernet protocol works well as long as the amount of time it takes a computer to say something is small relative to the time available.

on a LAN are connected. Hubs are simple connection devices, but switches vary in complexity and capability from very simple to very large and sophisticated. Sophisticated switches connect LANs and larger networks to each other. Network adapters that are physically fitted into the computers on a LAN translate the computer's communications into a language that can be broadcast over the LAN and understood by listening computers. Network adapters also listen for communications from other computers and translate them into terms that can be understood by the connected computers (see the accompanying feature).

Wide Area Networks

Wide area networks (WANs), as the name implies, provide a way for computers physically distant from each other to communicate (see Figure 5.6). WANs are networks of networks, which enable multiple LANs and smaller WANs to connect and communicate. WAN technologies define the physical features of technological solutions and the standards for conducting conversations between computers and communication devices over long distances (e.g., should we use gigabit Ethernet or Asynchronous Transfer Mode to transmit large volumes of data over long distances?). A WAN inside the boundaries of a company's physical premises is sometimes called an Intranet. A WAN that extends outward from a company's physical premises to business partners is sometimes called an Extranet. Choices between different technologies and standards in building Internetworks, whether they are Intranets or Extranets, involve trade-offs of cost versus data capacity, reliability, and security.

FIGURE 5.6
An Example of a WAN

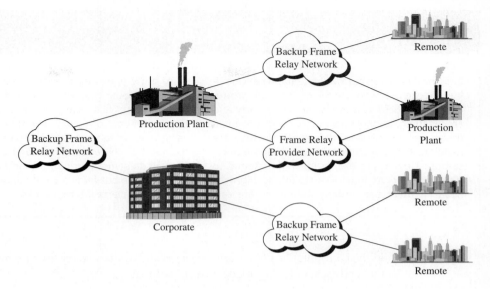

Routers

Routers are the devices that enable Internetworking, the means by which messages are relayed across large distances. A router listens in on LAN conversations and recognizes messages intended for computers that are not on that LAN. The listening router relays those messages to other routers. Each router has some notion of the approximate direction of the message's destination across the larger network. As a message makes its way through a series of between-router "hops," it gradually arrives at routers that know more details about the location of the destination computer. Eventually a message finds a router that knows the destination machine's LAN and can complete the delivery of a message. Like switches, routers come in simple and sophisticated varieties. They are the glue with which networks are connected to each other and provide many degrees of freedom in network design (see the accompanying feature).

Firewalls and Other Security Systems and Devices

As we discuss in more detail in the next chapter, managers of computing infrastructure have reason to worry about the security and confidentiality of the information that traverses networks. A variety of network systems and devices addresses these worries. Firewalls act as security sentries at the boundaries of an organization's internal network to protect it from intrusion from the outside. Because firewalls are imperfect, network managers employ intrusion detection systems (IDSs) composed of a variety of software tools such as network monitoring software and hardware devices such as sensors and probes. Other network security devices help users open secure virtual "tunnels" across public and private networks to create virtual private networks (VPNs). The complexity

An Internetworking Analogy

Imagine a complex highway system on which millions of cars are always moving. There are groups of cars that belong to the same travel party and are heading to the same place. But individual drivers know only the address where they are heading. They have no maps and no sense of direction. Members of groups make no attempt to stay together. At junctures along the highway network there are routing stations where cars stop, show their destination addresses, and are told, "Try going that way." A single routing station may send cars heading for the same destination in different directions. Eventually, though, a car arrives at its destination. It waits for other members of the travel party to arrive, and then they all do something useful together. This is an overly simple but fairly accurate analogy for how messages traverse Internetworks.

of the configurations of security systems and devices increases with the changing nature and escalating magnitude of security threats.

Caching, Content Acceleration, and Other Specialized Network Devices

As the commercial uses of Internetworks proliferate, so do devices aimed at accomplishing specialized network functions. Some devices help accelerate the delivery of information across the network, sometimes by "caching" (e.g. storing) information in a location close to the destination machine. This approach is used for information that does not change often. Other specialized devices help assure the efficient transmission of time-dependent information such as the sound and image data that accompany Internetwork-based video delivery or video teleconferencing. As infrastructure evolves, there will be continuing growth in specialized network systems and devices for metering and management of messages and transactions to assure timely and error-free quality of services (QoS), facilitate information-based transactions, and accomplish a variety of other functions.

The Technological Elements of Processing Systems

The processing systems component of IT infrastructure can be decomposed into technological elements managers must understand, arrange, and maintain. Although there is tremendous variety in the underlying hardware and software that constitute these elements, anyone involved in managing a company's processing systems will need to make decisions about the design, management, and improvement of the following.

Client Devices and Systems

Until quite recently it was safe to think of client devices as PCs; in the last few years, however, variety in client devices has exploded to include handheld devices, cell phones, and even automotive components. Client systems are the software that runs on these devices to perform business functions, manage interactions with other computers, and handle certain low-level client machine operations (such as storing saved information). As the name implies, clients are often on the receiving end of IT services delivered from elsewhere in the network. Business users experience Internetworking infrastructure primarily through client devices and systems. Unlike the terminals of the mainframe era, modern clients are not dumb; often they are capable of performing significant business functions even when separated from a network. Mobile users often use clients in both network-connected and unconnected modes; client software must manage intermittently connected devices and systems in a way that provides business advantage to users.

Server Devices and Systems

Servers occupy a role in Internetworking infrastructure roughly equivalent to that of mainframe computers in an earlier era. Although based on microcomputer technology, servers handle the heavy processing required for high-volume business transactions and permit sharing of information across a large number of computer users. Servers are the source of many of the IT services that clients receive from across the network. Server systems consist of software to carry out mainline business functions (such as order or inventory management), manage transactions from other computers (such as those that update inventory information), and handle low-level machine operations (such as storing saved information). In essence, clients perform front-end processing (interaction with users) while servers perform back-end processing (heavy computation or interaction with other back-end computers). Servers are often physically located in data centers and managed by central staffs, as their mainframe ancestors were. Servers and their systems are increasingly designed as specialized appliances targeted at specific functions: database servers, Web servers, and application servers, for example (see Figure 5.7). Software systems that run on distributed, specialized architectures must be designed very differently from those of mainframe systems in which all processing happens on the same machine.

Mainframe Devices and Systems

Mainframe computers remain very much a part of modern Internetworking infrastructure. In many companies, mainframes still do the vast majority of business-critical transaction processing. Some of these mainframes are modern, high-performance machines, the equivalent of very powerful servers that interoperate well with Internetworks. Others are relics of an earlier era that are still performing vital business functions. As computing infrastructures become more interconnected, legacy mainframe systems pose complications. The open protocols of the Internetworking world are not the native language of older mainframe computers. Mainframe manufacturers have developed systems that enable interaction between legacy mainframes and Internetworks. These advanced systems allow users to access information on mainframes via new technologies, such as Web browsers. But interfaces between legacy mainframes and Internetworks sometimes cannot overcome the problems associated with the interaction of such different technologies. For example, some mainframe systems still process jobs in batches. Native Internetworking systems and more modern mainframe systems, in contrast, usually are designed to operate in real time, to process new orders at the time they occur. Overcoming fundamental operational

FIGURE 5.7
Servers in a Typical E-Commerce Configuration

Source: Robert D. Austin, Larry Leibrock, and Alan Murray, "The iPremier Company: Denial of Service Attack (A)," Harvard Business School Case No. 9-601-114.

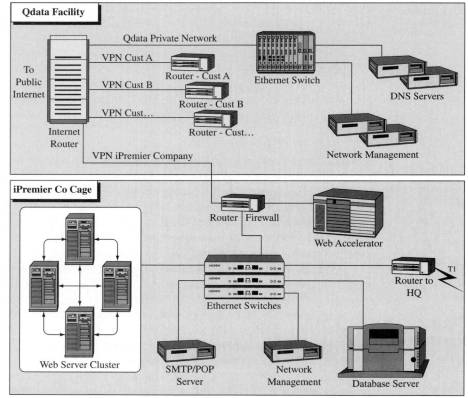

Diagram simplified for illustration purpose

incompatibilities often eventually necessitates the replacement of a legacy system. This takes time and money, though, and cannot be accomplished overnight. Where mainframes remain in more modern renditions, their mission has changed so that they function effectively as real-time transaction processors.

Middleware

Middleware is the hodgepodge of enabling utilities, message handling and queuing systems, protocols, standards, software tool kits, and other systems that help clients, servers, mainframes, and their systems coordinate activities in time and across networks. Middleware, which often runs on servers, could be considered a category of server system, but it is important enough in orchestrating the activities of Internetworking infrastructure to deserve its own category. Many managers know little and understand less about middleware; it is a classic example of difficult-to-manage infrastructure. Few people know enough about both the technology and the business needs to make intelligent decisions in this area.

Infrastructure Management Systems

A company must have systems for managing its computing infrastructure. These systems monitor the performance of systems, devices, and networks. They include systems that support the help desks when users are having trouble with computers or networks and the systems that deliver new software to computers throughout an organization. The quality of infrastructure management systems influences how efficiently a company obtains value from its computing assets. Without strong systems management, expensive Internetworks may become tied in knots; for example, too many transactions may flow to one computer while another is underused.

Business Applications

Computer users interact with the business applications layer of infrastructure constantly and directly. Most companies house an immense variety of installed business applications. Many applications are custom built by the IT staffs in the companies that use them. Others are off-the-shelf packages ranging from small client applications, such as a spreadsheet program, up to huge packages that cost tens of millions of dollars and take years to install, such as enterprise resource planning (ERP) systems. As the name suggests, business applications deliver actual business functionality. In a real sense, it is the job of the rest of an Internetworking infrastructure to make possible the delivery of business functionality by this top layer.

The Technological Elements of Facilities

The facilities component of IT infrastructure also can be decomposed into technological elements. Once a backwater left to real estate managers, facilities management has become an important aspect of infrastructure management, primarily due to the demands for always on, 24-hour, 7-days-a-week (24 × 7) operations. Consequently, anyone involved in managing a company's processing systems eventually will face decisions about the design, management, and improvement of the following.

Buildings and Physical Spaces

The physical characteristics of the buildings and rooms that house computing infrastructure strongly influence how well devices and systems function and how efficiently and effectively they can be managed (see Figure 5.8). The size of a facility, its physical features, how readily it lends itself to reconfiguration, and how well it protects its contents from external disruptions are important factors to consider in managing physical structures.

Network Conduits and Connections

The way in which systems within a facility are connected to wider networks also influences IT infrastructure performance. Among the factors managers must consider are the amount of redundancy in physical network connections, the number and selection of partners who will provide "backbone" connectivity to external networks, and the capacity of the data lines leased from service providers. All these

FIGURE 5.8
A Modern Data Center

Source: Allegiance Telecom.

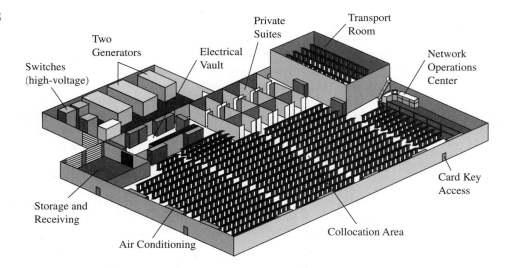

factors involve trade-offs in terms of cost, performance, availability, and security. At stake in trade-off decisions are nothing less than relationships with customers, suppliers, and other business partners.

Power

Computers do not run without power, and many businesses do not run without computers. Assuring that firms will have power when they need it is, then, a major concern for infrastructure managers. Decisions in this area involve trade-offs between cost and redundancy. Systems can obtain power from multiple power grids and utilities, uninterruptible power supplies (UPSs), backup generators, and even privately owned power plants. Determining which measures are worth their cost is a management decision.

Environmental Controls

Computers are delicate devices (although less so than in the past). They do not tolerate wide variations in temperature or combine well with moisture. Shielding computers from environmental hazards is another effort that can be pursued more or less thoroughly and at varying cost. As with power, how much should be paid for additional degrees of protection is a management decision.

Security

Computer devices and systems also must be protected from malicious attacks, both physical and network-based. Physical security requires facilities and methods that control access to machines, such as security guards, cages, and locks. Network security—a field of growing complexity—has numerous facilities implications. The threat from hacker attacks and intrusions is a growing problem. As with other facilities elements, security involves trade-offs, in this case between cost and level of protection.

How Information Is Transmitted through an Internetwork

First the information is divided into packets. A "header" is then attached to each packet; the header contains a "sequence number" and the packet's origin and destination "IP addresses." IP addresses are composed of four numbers, 0 to 255, separated by decimal points (19.67.89.134, for example). Packets are then transmitted via a router—a specialized computer that keeps track of addresses—across an available communication line to other computers in the rough direction of the destination address. The process is repeated until a packet finds its way to its destination. A packet waits at its destination for the arrival of the other information packets sent with it. When all the packets in a group arrive, the sent information is reconstructed by using the sequence numbers in packet headers. If a packet has not arrived after a certain period of time, the receiving machine transmits a resend request to the origin address found in the headers of other packets in the group.

Operational Characteristics of Internetworks[8]

Taken together, Internetworking technologies have operational characteristics that distinguish them from other information technologies. In many ways, these characteristics determine the challenges of managing infrastructures based on Internetworking technologies. Important operational characteristics of Internetworking technologies that make them different from the technologies of previous eras in terms of how they perform and should be managed include the following (see the accompanying feature).

Internetworking Technologies Are Based on Open Standards

We have already mentioned this, but it bears repeating because of its importance. TCP/IP is the primary common language of Internetworking technologies. TCP/IP standards define how computers send and receive data packets. Because the standards were developed using public funds, they are public, not owned by anyone; they are open, not proprietary. The fact that TCP/IP can be freely used by anyone makes Internetworks less dependent on solutions developed and marketed by private companies. Decreased reliance on proprietary technologies has generated huge economic benefits for purchasers of new technology by making systems from different vendors more interoperable and thus increasing competition. Prices are lower and performance better than they might have been if these technologies had remained proprietary. Insistence on open standards and solutions has become part of the ethos of the Internetworking community of administrators and developers. This ethos has

[8]This section is based in part on Thomas Rodd and Robert D. Austin, "The Worldwide Web and Internet Technology: Technical Note," Harvard Business School Case No. 198-020.

TABLE 5.2 Measuring Network Bandwidth

Term	Definition
Bandwidth	Maximum rate at which information can be transmitted along a communication link
Bit	Smallest unit of information handled by computers
Bits per second (bps)	Bandwidth measurement unit

Information Measure	Bit Equivalent	Information Transfer Speed
1 kilobit (Kb)	1 thousand bits	1,000 bits/second
1 megabit (Mb)	1 million bits	1,000,000/second
1 gigabit (Gb)	1 billion bits	1,000,000,000/second

led to development of other important open standards, such as Hypertext Transport Protocol (HTTP), used to deliver Web content.

Internetworking Technologies Operate Asynchronously

Information sent over an Internetwork does not employ dedicated, bidirectional connections between sender and receiver, as for example, a telephone call. Instead, packets of information with accompanying address information are sent toward a destination, sometimes without any prior coordination between the sender and the receiver. Network services that exchange information quickly, such as the Web, require the sender and the receiver to be connected to the Internetwork at the same time. But such communication is still asynchronous in that no dedicated link is established. For other services, such as e-mail, the receiver's computer need not even be switched on at the time the message is sent. As with postal mail, an e-mail recipient has a mailbox where mail can accumulate until it is accessed. Unlike regular mail though, e-mail messages can be sent around the globe almost instantaneously.

Internetwork Communications Have Inherent Latency

The computers that make up Internetworks are connected by links of varying capacity (see Table 5.2). As packets carry information along different paths toward a common destination, some packets flow quickly through wide links while others move more slowly through narrow links. Packets that together constitute a single message do not arrive at the destination in the same moment. Thus, there is variable wait time between the sending of a message and the arrival at the destination of the last packet in a message. Because traffic volume is somewhat unpredictable, wait time—often called *latency*—can be difficult to predict. Managers can take actions to make it likely that latency will be within certain tolerances. At the very least, they can assure that network capacity between two points is great enough to avoid unacceptable wait times. New routing technologies provide more options; some make it possible to move high-priority packets to the top of the queues that form at narrow network links. But some degree of latency, and hence unpredictability, is inherent in

Internetworking technologies and must be taken into account in the design and management of Internetworking systems.

Internetworking Technologies Are Naturally Decentralized

Largely due to their Defense Department heritage, which dictated that computer networks contain no single points of failure, Internetworks have no central traffic control point. Computers connected to the network do not need to be defined to a central control authority, as is the case with some networking technologies. There is, in fact, no central authority that oversees or governs the development or administration of the public Internet except the one that assigns TCP/IP addresses. As a result, individuals and organizations are responsible for managing and maintaining their own facilities in a way that does not hinder the operation of the network as a whole.

Internetworking Technologies Are Scalable

Because communication is intelligently routed along multiple paths, adding to an Internetwork is as simple as connecting to another machine. An Internetwork as a whole is not affected significantly when a path is removed (packets simply get routed a different way). Additional paths can be added in parallel with overworked paths. Furthermore, Internetworking technologies allow relatively easy reorganization of subnetworks; if a network segment has become overloaded, the network can be split up into more manageable subnetworks. In general, these new technologies allow more flexible expansion than do most other network technologies.

The Rise of Internetworking: Business Implications

Dr. Eric Schmidt, Google chief executive officer (CEO), former Novell CEO, and former Sun Microsystems chief technology officer (CTO), has observed that high-capacity networks enable a computer to interact just as well with another physically distant computer as with one that is only inches away. Thus, given excess bandwidth, the physical location of computers ceases to matter much. Operationally, the communication pathways inside a computer become indistinguishable from the pathways that connect computers. The network itself becomes part of a larger processor composed of the network and all of its connected computers. To paraphrase a Sun Microsystems slogan: The network *becomes* a computer.

For business computer users who do not have access to this level of network bandwidth, Schmidt's observation remains largely theoretical (see Table 5.3). Nevertheless, the idea of an increasingly connected network, both inside and beyond the boundaries of organizations, in which the physical location of processors matters less and less is of great practical importance. Improved connections between machines, departments, companies, and customers mean *quicker realization of economic value* when parties interact; Internetworking infrastructure is the means by which value is created and captured in real time. Transactions are initiated and consummated quickly. Activities that once were sequential occur simultaneously. Because the physical location of processing is less important, new

TABLE 5.3 **Communication Technology, Bandwidths, and User Groups**

Communication Technology	Bandwidth*	User Groups
Telephone modem	33.6–56 kbps	Individuals and small businesses
Integrated Services Digital Network (ISDN)	128 kbps	Individuals and small businesses
Cable modem	128–512 kbps	Individuals and small businesses
Digital subscriber line (DSL)	128 kps–1.5 mbps	Individuals and small businesses
Ethernet LAN	10–100 mbps	Most businesses and organizations
Leased Lines (T1, T3)	1.544–45 mbps	Government, universities, medium-size and large businesses
Asynchronous Transfer Mode (ATM)/ Gigabit Ethernet	155 mbps–25.6 gbps	Government, universities, and large corporations

*We have listed the typical bandwidth performance. Some of the technologies are theoretically capable of higher bandwidths. Additionally, some technologies perform at different speeds upstream and downstream.

possibilities for outsourcing, partnerships, and industry restructuring emerge. Along with these beneficial outcomes come drawbacks: rising complexity, unpredictable interactions, and new types of threats to businesses and consumers. As a result, executives must understand the business implications of these powerful and pervasive networks.

The Emergence of Real-Time Infrastructures

In the mainframe era, scarcity of processing capacity required business transactions to be accumulated and processed in batches. A telephone calling card account might, for example, be updated by a batch run once each day. A stranded traveler who needed to reactivate a mistakenly deactivated card might have to wait for the once-a-day batch run for the card to be reactivated. As processing and communication capacity became more abundant, however, batch processing became less necessary. Delays between initiating a transaction and completing its processing have been greatly reduced. With real-time Internetworking infrastructures, customers are serviced and economic value is realized immediately rather than over hours, days, or weeks. The potential benefits of real-time infrastructures are discussed below.

Better Data, Better Decisions

In most large organizations, people in different locations need access to the same data. Until recently, organizations had to keep copies of the same data in many places. But keeping the data synchronized was difficult and frequently did not happen. Discrepancies between copies of data led to errors, inefficiencies, and poor decision making. Abundant communication capacity has not completely eliminated the need for multiple copies, but it has reduced it. In addition, it has made it much easier to keep copies synchronized. For the first time it is becoming possible to run a large business based on a set of financial and operational numbers that are consistent throughout an enterprise.

Improved Process Visibility

Older IT systems based on proprietary technologies often communicated poorly with each other. Consequently, viewing the progress of orders or other transactions across system boundaries was difficult. People in a company's sales organization could not access data in manufacturing, for example, to obtain information about the status of an order. New technologies based on open standards and compatible back-office transaction systems let users instantaneously view transactions with each step in procurement and fulfillment processes, beyond specific system boundaries, and even beyond the boundaries of a company into partners' systems.

Improved Process Efficiency

Many efficiency improvements result directly from enhanced process visibility. In manufacturing, workers who can see what supplies and orders are coming their way tend to hold less buffer stock ("just-in-case" inventory) to guard against uncertainty. Holding less buffer stock reduces working capital, shortens cycle times, and improves return on investment (ROI). A manager in charge of supplying plastic cases for portable radios, for example, can notice that orange radios are not selling well and quickly reduce orange in the color mix.

From Make-and-Sell to Sense-and-Respond[9]

Real-time infrastructures are a prerequisite for achieving highly responsive operations, those based on "sense-and-respond" principles rather than make-to-sell principles. The fundamental insight here is that if operating infrastructures can come close enough to real time, value-adding activities can be performed in response to *actual* customer demand rather than *forecasted* customer demand. Sense-and-respond organizations avoid losses caused by demand-forecasting errors. The most celebrated example is Dell Computer Corporation's make-to-order manufacturing process, which makes computers only in response to actual customer orders. But many other companies in both manufacturing and service industries are seeking ways to move to sense-and-respond models, including some with very complex products, such as automobiles.

In many companies, especially older ones, moving to real-time systems involves reengineering transaction systems to take advantage of greater processing and network capacities. Some companies have renewed transaction infrastructures by implementing large enterprise systems made, for example, by SAP, Oracle, and

[9]See Richard L. Nolan and Steven P. Bradley, *Sense and Respond: Capturing Value in the Network Era* (Boston: Harvard Business School Press, 1998).

Peoplesoft. Others have designed best-of-breed transaction infrastructures by connecting what they consider the best products from a variety of niche vendors. Whichever approach a company takes, the objective is to remove elements from the transaction infrastructure that do not operate in real time, thereby realizing almost immediate economic value from transactions.

A company that succeeds in reengineering transaction and communication systems to operate more or less in real time has ascended to a new and important stage of evolution. When a company achieves real-time IT operations, it not only creates value more quickly, it also creates options for fully leveraging a shared public infrastructure, the Internet, for that company's private gain. But there are drawbacks in how real-time infrastructures operate. The same characteristics that allow immediate value creation also allow crisis acceleration. The connections to public networks that create leverage also increase exposure to external threats. While the drawbacks do not outweigh the benefits, they must be understood and managed.

Broader Exposure to Operational Threats

On October 19, 1987, the Dow Jones Industrial Average plummeted more than 500 points in the 20th century's single largest percentage decrease. The 22.6 percent plunge was almost double the 12.9 percent drop in 1929 that foreshadowed the Great Depression. Unlike 1929, the market in 1987 quickly recovered, posting major gains in the two days after the crash and regaining its precrash level by September 1989. Nevertheless, the suddenness of these events prompted a search for explanations.

Many singled out the role of computerized program trading by large institutional investors as a primary cause of the 1987 crash. In program trading, computers initiate transactions automatically, without human intervention, when certain triggering conditions appear in the markets. What no one anticipated was that automatic trades could lead to a chain reaction of more automatic trades. Automatic trades themselves created market conditions that set off more automatic trades, which created conditions that set off more automatic trades, and so on, in a rapid-fire progression that was both unexpected and difficult to understand while it was in progress.

This example reveals a dark side of real-time computing that extends to Internet-working infrastructures. As batch-processing delays are eliminated and more transactions move from initiation to completion without intervention by human operators, the potential grows for computerized chain reactions that produce unanticipated effects. Favorable effects such as value creation happen more immediately, but so do ill effects. Malfunctions and errors propagate faster and have potentially broader impacts. Diagnosis and remediation of problems that result from fast-moving, complex interactions present major challenges to organizational and, indeed, human cognitive capabilities. Just figuring out what is going on during or in the immediate aftermath of an incident is often difficult.

IT infrastructures of the 21st century therefore must be less prone to malfunctions and errors that might trigger a chain reaction and more tolerant of them when they occur. Real-time operations demand 24 × 7 availability. Because some unintended effects will occur despite the best intentions and plans, responsible managers need to think in advance and in detail about how they will respond to incidents. Effective "disaster recovery" requires anticipating that incidents will occur despite the fact that one cannot anticipate their exact nature and practicing organizational responses. The range of incidents that require detailed response plans also includes those of a more sinister sort: malicious attacks. Infrastructure managers must anticipate and protect systems from the many exploits creative individuals—hackers—use.

Technologies of the past were designed to deny access to systems unless someone intervened specifically to authorize access. Internetworking systems are different. Because they evolved in an arena not oriented toward commerce but intended to support communities of researchers, Internetworking technologies allow access unless someone intervenes to disallow it. Security measures to support commercial relationships, therefore, must be retrofitted onto the base technologies. Moreover, the universality of Internet connections—the fact that every computer is connected to every other computer—makes every computer a potential attack target and a potential base from which to launch attacks.

The average computer is connected to the Internet for only a few minutes before it is "port scanned," or probed for vulnerability to intrusion or attack. Many attempted incursions are the electronic equivalent of school kids playing a prank. But recent evidence shows that more serious criminals have begun to explore the possibilities presented by the Internet. The threat is real, even from pranksters. Damaging attacks are alarmingly simple to initiate.

In February 2000, the business community received a wake-up call concerning its vulnerability to electronic attack (see Table 5.4). Total damages from a series of high-profile, centrally orchestrated "denial of service" attacks were estimated to be in excess of $100 million; the estimated costs incurred in more recent attacks reached into the billions of dollars. As the Internet and the Web have risen to commercial prominence, computer security problems have progressed from being tactical nuisances that could be left to technicians into strategic infrastructure problems that require the involvement of business executives at the highest levels.

New Models of Service Delivery

In the early days of electric power generation, companies owned and managed their own power plants. Later, as standardization and technological advances made it possible to deliver power reliably via a more centralized model, companies began to purchase electric power from external providers. A similar shift is under way in the IT industry.

In today's companies, as increasingly reliable networks make the physical location of computers less important, services traditionally provided by internal IT departments can be acquired externally, across Internetworks, from service providers. Fundamental economic forces such as the scarcity of IT specialists and the desire to reduce costs are driving this shift. The shift, which parallels the maturation of other industries, reveals a common pattern: Standardization and technology advances permit specialization by individual firms in value chains, resulting in economies of scale and higher service levels.

The transition under way is analogous to the move from telephone answering machines to voice mail. Telephone answering machines were purchased by companies and attached to individual telephones. When they broke, it was the company's job to

TABLE 5.4   **Wake-Up Call: Denial of Service Attacks in February 2000***

Date	Target Company	Results of Attack
February 7	Yahoo!	• Overwhelming spike in traffic that lasted 3 hours. • Network availability dropped from 98% to 0%. • Attack originated from 50 different locations and was timed to occur during middle of business day. • Stock was down 3.2% for a week in which Nasdaq rose almost 3%.
February 8	Buy.com	• Attack occurred within an hour of the company's initial public offering (IPO). • Stock was down at week's end more than 20% from IPO price.
	eBay	• Stock was down 7.3% for a week in which Nasdaq rose almost 3%.
	CNN.com	• Service disrupted.
February 9	E*Trade	• Attacked during peak trading hours. • Stock was down 7.6% for a week in which Nasdaq rose almost 3%.
	ZDNet	• Service disrupted.
February 18	Federal Bureau of Investigation (FBI)	• Service disrupted.
February 24	National Discount Brokers Group (NDB)	• Attacked during peak trading hours. • Operators accidentally crashed site as they attempted to defend against the attack.

*Overall performance of the Internet degraded by as much as 25% during the peak of the attacks as computers resent messages repeatedly and automatically, trying to recover interrupted transactions.
Source: Adapted from NetworkWorldFusion, www.nfusion.com, compiled by LeGrand Elebash.

fix or replace the machines. Messages were stored on magnetic tape inside the machine. In contrast, companies acquire voice mail from service providers for a monthly fee. The hardware that supports the service is owned by the provider and physically resides in a central location unknown to most voice mail users. When voice mail breaks, the service provider is responsible for fixing it. Fixing it is easier and less expensive because the infrastructure that delivers the service is centralized and easily accessible. The potentially sensitive contents of voice mail messages no longer reside on the end user's desk; instead, the service provider is entrusted with their care and security.

The move to over-the-Net service delivery has been gradual. As supporting infrastructure matures, however, the economic advantages become more compelling. Even if actual software functionality is not acquired externally, external infrastructure management may still make sense. For example, a company may rent space in a vendor-owned IT hosting facility rather than incur the capital expenses required to build a data center even as it retains internal management of the software.

As IT service models proliferate, service delivery depends on a growing number of service providers and other partners. One implication is that the reliability of vital services is only as good as the weakest link in the service provider chain. Selecting strong partners and managing relationships are vital to reliable service delivery.

New service models that offer new capabilities and cost reduction cannot realize their full potential without being integrated into the rest of a company's IT infrastructure. Ideally, over-the-Net services would exchange data seamlessly, in real time, with a company's installed base of systems. Unfortunately, this is not easily accomplished. The questions involved in deciding how new services should interact with existing IT and organizational systems leads to the subject of managing legacies.

Managing Legacies

Few companies are so new that they have no artifacts left over from earlier eras that must be managed even as the companies move forward with new technologies. Legacy systems present one set of challenges. They are often based on outdated, obsolete, and proprietary technologies. Yet they are vital to the business as it operates from day to day. Fitting new infrastructure into complex legacy infrastructure, or vice versa, presents formidable challenges and uncertain outcomes.

But systems are not the only legacies companies must manage. Even more significant are legacy processes, organizations, and cultures. Changing the IT infrastructure has unavoidable effects on nontechnical elements of a company's operations. New technologies change how people work and interact. Managers must decide how much they want the company's culture to drive the design of its infrastructure or vice versa. In some companies, managers go to great lengths to make sure the IT infrastructure does not constrain culture or process. In others, managers use IT systems as "sledgehammers" to bring about organizational change. Both approaches can work, but the issues and decisions involved are complex.

The Future of Internetworking Infrastructure

The basic technology that supports moving data packets around an Internetwork has existed in something like its present form since the late 1960s. The technologies we use to access Internetworks—PCs, e-mail packages, and Web browsers, for example—have been appearing and maturing over the last 20 or so years. Although Internetworking infrastructure continues to evolve significantly in both of these areas, there is a third area in which Internetworking technologies are evolving even more rapidly.

The smooth functioning of markets and other kinds of business interactions presumes prerequisites that Internetworking infrastructure still does not perfectly fulfill. We have mentioned some of these already. Markets do not tolerate the uncertainties of unreliable or unavailable infrastructure. Customers of a financial services firm, for example, will not abide loss of access to stock market trading. Similarly, business transactions cannot flourish when infrastructure is not highly secure. As we have seen, Internetworks already are reasonably good at reliability, availability, and security, and they are getting better. But there are other, more subtle aspects of business support for which these technologies are not yet mature.

Ultimately, Internetworking technologies must support all or nearly all the elements of business transactions that can occur in face-to-face transactions. If you are videoconferencing, for example, you need to be able to purchase guaranteed network bandwidth sufficient to make the conference approximate a productive face-to-face work experience; this is not yet possible everywhere. Consider another example: In business, you need to be sure the party you are interacting with is who he says he is so he cannot later say, "That was not me you contracted with." This "non-repudiation" requirement still presents difficulties between some Internetworks. In general, the elements of infrastructure that support financial transactions are works in process; they constitute the above-mentioned third area in which infrastructure is evolving most rapidly. How we transport information within Internetworks and how we access network resources are well defined, if continually changing, at this point in history. How companies will in the long run engage each other in real-time transactions, negotiate the terms of transactions, establish business linkages, and settle accounts depends on standards and technologies not yet fully developed.

Summary

Internetworking infrastructures include the totality of existing client-server systems, new externally provided services, and older legacy systems. They interact with living organizations and have distinctive characteristics that are coming into clear view in the 21st century. They offer many more degrees of freedom in designing organizations and contain larger numbers of smaller components that interact in complex ways. Some of the components exist outside a firm's boundaries and thus are not fully under the control of internal executives. The overall effect on a company's business is that there is *more inherent uncertainty in the operational environment*. This is at least partially offset by *more incremental options for managing that uncertainty*. Our ability to predict how a planned system will perform is limited, but options for experimenting to improve our understanding of emerging infrastructures are becoming more numerous and less expensive. Not surprisingly, our management frameworks are evolving in a way that reflects the uncertain and incremental nature of emerging infrastructure.

In this chapter we have described the technologies, functions, and components of Internetworking infrastructure and how they are changing. We have explained how the changes at work generate new benefits, challenges, and threats. Approximately 75 percent of most companies' IT dollars go to infrastructure investments. If you are like many companies, that 75 percent approaches half of all your capital expenditures. Executives can use the following questions to assess the implications of the emergence of new technologies and infrastructures for their companies' operational capabilities:

1. What does the public infrastructure of the Internet mean to our business operations? Are we leveraging this infrastructure to maximum advantage? How dependent are we still on proprietary technologies?

2. How close do our company operations come to running in real time? What value creation opportunities can still be obtained by moving more in the direction of real-time value capture?

3. Has our company taken appropriate advantage of the many degrees of architectural and operational freedom offered by Internetworking technologies? Have we thought through the inherent complexities and risks in those additional degrees of freedom?

4. Are we exploring new service delivery models aggressively enough?

5. Have we reexamined our management frameworks in light of the new and more adaptive capabilities that Internetworking technologies offer? Most important, do senior business managers play an active and informed role in infrastructure design and planning decisions?

Chapter 6

Assuring Reliable and Secure IT Services[1]

The emergence of Web-based commerce has accelerated the expansion of a worldwide network capable of transmitting information reliably and securely across vast distances. The inherent reliability of modern Internetworks is a legacy of U.S. Department of Defense research in the 1960s that led to technologies robust enough to withstand a military attack. The key to this inherent reliability is *redundancy:* the exceptionally large number of potential paths a message can take between any two points in a network. Because Internetworking technologies automatically route messages around network problems, transmissions are highly likely to be successful.

Unfortunately, some components of a firm's infrastructure are not inherently reliable. The reliability of processing systems, for example, is a function of how they are designed and managed. As with Internetworks, the key to reliable systems is redundancy; however, reliability through redundancy comes at a price. It means buying extra equipment (computers, switches, software, electric generators, etc.) to guard against failures. Every increment of additional redundancy makes outages less likely, but every increment increases expenses as well.

How much reliability to buy is a management decision highly contingent on numerous, mostly business, factors. How costly is a 15-minute failure of the order management system? How costly is a 3-hour failure or a 12-hour failure? How likely are these failures? How about the e-mail system and the human resources system? Answers to these questions differ across businesses. Some costs of failures are intangible and hard to quantify. It may be possible to estimate, for example, the direct revenues your company will lose if your Web-based retail site goes down for two hours in the middle of the day, but it is much harder to gauge how many customers

[1]This chapter is adapted from materials in Professor Robert D. Austin's *Managing Information Technology Infrastructure* course module, Harvard Business School Publishing No. 601-181.

frustrated by the outage will never return. In addition, it is difficult to estimate the probabilities of such events.

Redundant systems are more complex than nonredundant systems, and this complexity must be managed. Businesses need policies that determine how to integrate redundant elements into a company's overall infrastructure: how backup systems and equipment will be brought online, how problems will be diagnosed and triaged, and who will be responsible for responding to incidents. Since the efficacy and efficiency of incident response improve with practice, the frequency and structure of rehearsals are also management decisions. Charles Perrow suggests in *Normal Accidents: Living with High Risk Technologies* that failures are inevitable in "tightly coupled" complex systems (as real-time infrastructures are by definition). Typical precautions, Perrow writes, such as adding redundancy, help create new categories of accidents by adding complexity.[2] Thus, our efforts to make infrastructure designs more robust also make operational management more difficult.

Managers also must guard against malicious threats to computing infrastructure. Malicious threats, which are similar to accidental failures in their potential cost and unintended ripple effect, are designed specifically to damage a company's business. Attacks, intrusions, viruses, and worms have no legitimate uses when perpetrated against others' systems. Their designers, who are often extremely creative, are motivated by a desire to cause mayhem.

Instigators of malicious threats, who often are called *hackers,*[3] range from pranksters to organized criminals and even international terrorists. Securing systems against malicious threats is an arms race, a high-stakes contest requiring constantly improving defenses against increasingly sophisticated weaponry. Some businesses have particular reason to fear being targeted. But even the most unobtrusive firms cannot count on low profiles (security through obscurity) as a defense. Increasingly, attacks are automated and systematic, carried out by wrecking routines turned loose on the Internet to probe for vulnerabilities and inflict damage wherever they find them.

In an age of real-time systems, global operations, and customers who expect always-on performance, reliability and security have taken on new importance. Technologies to assure 24×7 operations[4] get better all the time, but every increment of capability comes with additional infrastructure complexity and additional management challenges. Add new malicious threats to the mix and we see that 21st century infrastructure managers indeed have their hands full. Making the wrong decision in designing or maintaining infrastructure or in responding to incidents can severely harm a business.

---

[2] Charles Perrow, *Normal Accidents: Living with High Risk Technologies* (Princeton, NJ: Princeton University Press, 1999).

[3] The term *hacker* is controversial. Although the word is now used to describe a computer expert with malicious intent, it originally had no negative connotations. UNIX programming enthusiasts, beginning in the 1960s, called particularly excellent programmers hackers. Some have tried to preserve the positive interpretation by proposing the word *cracker* to describe malicious hackers. In the popular perception, however, this battle seems largely lost; to most people, *hacker* implies malicious intent, so that is how we use it in this book. We extend our apologies to purists on this point.

[4] That is, operations that run 24 hours per day, 7 days per week.

Availability Math

The reliability of computing infrastructure is often discussed in terms of the *availability* of a specific information technology (IT) service or system. A system that is 98 percent available is on average up and ready to be used 98 percent of the time. It is down, or not available for use, 2 percent of the time. In a day, 98 percent availability translates into just under one-half hour of downtime, which might be fine for some systems and businesses.

A business's tolerance for outages varies by system and situation. Downtime that occurs in large chunks, say, a two-hour outage every four days, might be more of a problem than the same total amount of downtime occurring in increments that never exceed three minutes in a single outage. Whether outages occur at predictable times matters too. A half-hour outage that always happens at 3:00 A.M. may not be a problem. Some systems require planned outages; for example, a system might need to be shut down each night to have all its data files copied to a backup tape. But planned outages are increasingly rare in the world of real-time infrastructures, and unplanned outages are not usually well behaved.

In modern contexts, a 98 percent availability rating for a system usually means that its probability of being up and running at any given time is 98 percent—period. A strong underlying presumption is that planned outages will be minimized, if not eliminated. Moreover, for real-time infrastructure 98 percent is not nearly good enough. In fact, the availability of today's IT infrastructure is often expressed in terms of a number of "nines." "Five nines" means 99.999 percent availability, which equates to less than a second of downtime in a 24-hour day, or no more than a minute in three months, on average. Not surprisingly, keeping systems available at such a high level requires much redundancy and highly sophisticated operations management.

We can better appreciate how difficult it is to achieve very high levels of reliability if we consider how rates of availability for components combine into overall system or service availability. Most IT services are not delivered by a single component but by a number of components working together. For example, a service that sends transactions from one server to another via a corporate Internetwork might require two or more routers, one or more switches, and both servers—all up and running at the same time. Each of these devices has its own individual availability. Thus, overall *service* availability is generally lower than the availability of individual components. Many managers do not appreciate how rapidly service availability decreases as components are added in series. Let's consider how this works.

The Availability of Components in Series

Suppose you have five components connected in *series* that together deliver an IT service (see Figure 6.1). Assume that each component has an availability of 98 percent, which means, as we have noted, a half hour per day of downtime for each component on average. Computation of service availability is straightforward.

For the service to be up and running, all five components must be up and running. At any given time the probability that a component is up and running is .98 (that's what 98 percent availability means), and so the probability that Component 1 *and*

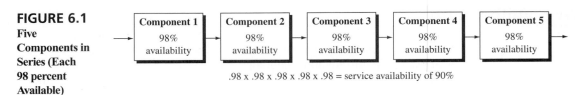

FIGURE 6.1

Five Components in Series (Each 98 percent Available)

.98 x .98 x .98 x .98 x .98 = service availability of 90%

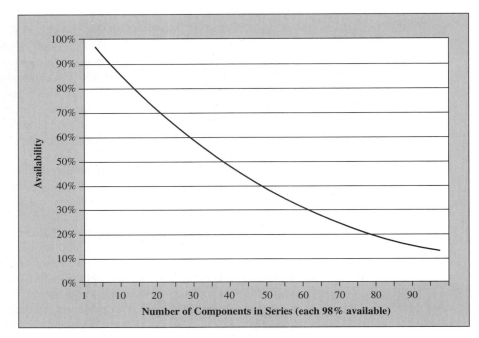

FIGURE 6.2

Combining Components in Series Decreases Overall Availability

Component 2 *and* Component 3 *and* Component 4 *and* Component 5 are all up and running is .98 × .98 × .98 × .98 × .98 = .9.

The overall service availability is 90 percent, which means the service is unavailable 10 percent of the time, or almost two and a half hours a day. If we take into account the fact that most services rely on many more than five devices operating in series, we can see that service availability degrades quite severely as we add components in a chain.

Figure 6.2 shows how service availability falls as we add components, assuming that individual components are 98 percent available. Notice that by the time we get to 15 devices in series—which is not hard to imagine in a modern IT infrastructure—downtime exceeds 25 percent. Reversing this logic leads to an important conclusion: If we need overall service availability of 99.999 percent (five nines) and service provision relies on 10 components, the availability of the individual components must average 99.9999 percent. For each of the 10 individual components, that equates to about 30 seconds of downtime per year. Thirty seconds is not enough time

FIGURE 6.3
Five
Components in
Parallel (Each
98 percent
Available)

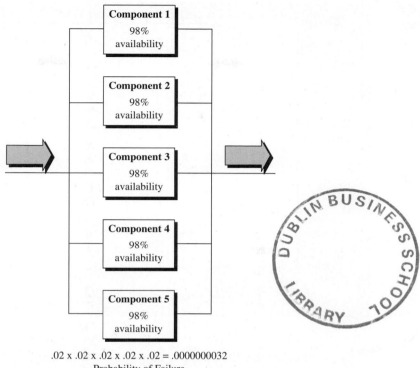

.02 x .02 x .02 x .02 x .02 = .0000000032
Probability of Failure

to restart most servers. If only one server needs rebooting in a year, that blows a five nines availability rating. Unfortunately, many popular server operating systems need to be rebooted much more often than once a year. How, then, can we achieve five nines of availability? The answer to this question is redundancy.

The Effect of Redundancy on Availability

Suppose you have five components connected in *parallel* involved in the provision of an IT service (see Figure 6.3). The components are identical, and any one of them can perform the functions needed to support the service. As in the earlier example, each individual component has an availability of 98 percent and each component experiences outages randomly. The computation for the overall availability of these parallel components is also straightforward.

Because any of the individual components can support the service, all five must fail at the same time to render this combination of components a failure. At any given time, the probability that a component is down is .02 (98 percent availability means 2 percent downtime), and so the probability that Component 1 *and* Component 2 *and* Component 3 *and* Component 4 *and* Component 5 will all fail at the same time is .02 × .02 × .02 × .02 × .02 = .0000000032.

FIGURE 6.4
Redundancy Increases Overall Availability

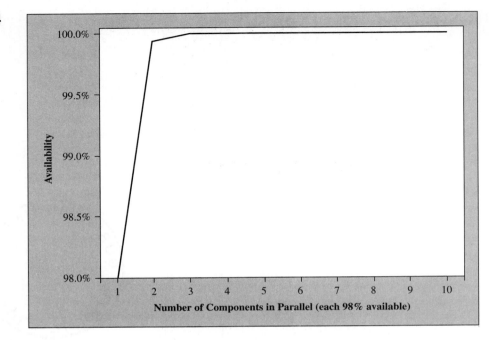

The overall availability of these components combined in parallel therefore is 99.99999968, which is eight nines of availability. Figure 6.4 shows how availability increases when components that are 98 percent available are combined in parallel. Of course, these components in parallel cannot deliver a service by themselves. To deliver a service, we must place the parallel combination in series with other components. From this example and the previous one, however, we can see that even if a component does not satisfy our five nines availability requirement, several connected in parallel may.

High-Availability Facilities

A close look at modern data centers provides a concrete sense of the availability decisions faced by infrastructure managers. Data centers physically house Web, application, database, and other servers; storage devices; mainframes; and networking equipment in a robust environment that enables them to function reliably. They supply space, power, and Internet connectivity as well as a range of supporting services. Although there is considerable variation in designs, today's state-of-the-art facilities tend to offer the following features.

Uninterruptible Electric Power Delivery

High-availability facilities provide redundant power to each piece of computing equipment housed in them, literally two power cables for each computer (high-availability computing equipment accepts two power inputs). Power distribution inside the facility is fully redundant and includes uninterruptible power supplies (UPSs) to maintain power even if power delivery to the facility is interrupted. Connections to outside sources of power are also redundant; usually facilities access two utility power grids. Diesel generators stand by for backup power generation; on-site fuel tanks contain fuel for a day or more of operation. Facilities managers have a plan for high-priority access to additional fuel in case of a long-lasting primary power outage (e.g., delivery by helicopter). High-end data centers may obtain primary power from on-site power plants, with first-level backup from local utility power grids and second-level backup from diesel generators; UPSs may employ batteryless, flywheel-based technologies.

Physical Security

Security guards posted in bulletproof enclaves protect points of entry and patrol the facility regularly. Closed-circuit television monitors critical infrastructure and provides immediate visibility into any area of the facility from a constantly attended security desk. Access to internal areas requires photo ID and presence on a prearranged list. Entry is through a buffer zone that can be locked down. Guards open and inspect the items (e.g., boxes, equipment) people bring into the facility. The building that houses the data center is dedicated to that use, not shared with other businesses. In some high-end facilities, the building is "hardened" against external explosions, earthquakes, and other disasters. Advanced entry systems force everyone through multiple, single-person (hostageproof) buffers with integrated metal and explosive detection. Biometric scanning technologies such as retinal scanners, palm readers, and voice recognition systems control access to zones within data centers. Motion sensors supplement video monitoring, and perimeter fencing surrounds the facility.

Climate Control and Fire Suppression

Facilities contain redundant heating, ventilating, and air-conditioning (HVAC) equipment capable of maintaining temperatures in ranges suitable for computing and network equipment. Mobile cooling units alleviate hot spots. Integrated fire suppression systems include smoke detection, alarming, and gas-based (i.e., no equipment-damaging water) fire suppression.

Network Connectivity

External connections to Internet backbone providers[5] are redundant, involve at least two backbone providers, and enter the building through separate points. The company that owns the data center has agreements with backbone providers that permit significant percentages, say, 50 percent, of network traffic to travel from origin to destination across the backbone company's private network, avoiding often-congested public Internet junctions. A 24 × 7 network operations center (NOC) is staffed with network engineers who monitor the connectivity infrastructure of the facility; a redundant NOC on another site is capable of delivering the same services

---

[5]Backbone providers own the very large data transmission lines through which large quantities of data are moved long distances.

of equal quality as those provided by the primary NOC. High-end facilities have agreements with three or more backbone providers that allow even more traffic, up to 90 percent, to stay on private networks.

Help Desk and Incident Response Procedures

Customers can contact facility staff for assistance at any time during the day or night. The facility has procedures for responding to unplanned incidents. Automated problem-tracking systems are integrated with similar systems at service delivery partner sites, and so complex problems involving interactions between services can be tracked down and quickly solved.

N + 1 and N + N Redundancy

Most modern data centers try to maintain an "N + 1" level of redundancy of mission-critical components. N + 1 means that for each type of critical component there should be at least one unit standing by. For example, if a facility needs four diesel generators to meet power demands in a primary power outage, N + 1 redundancy requires five such generators, four to operate and one to stand by. N + 1 redundancy provides a higher level of availability if the underlying number of components, the N in the N + 1, is small (you can verify this for yourself by using probability calculations such as those that we demonstrated earlier).

Some companies aspire to higher levels of infrastructure redundancy. "N + N" redundancy requires twice as many mission-critical components as are necessary to run a facility at any one time. For example, a facility that needs four diesel generators to meet its power demands needs eight generators to achieve N + N redundancy. Where N + 1 facilities are able to commit to service levels in the 99.9 percent availability range, N + N facilities can ensure availability levels at the 99.999 percent (five nines) level. Facilities are sometimes categorized according to the level of uptime they support. Level 1 data centers, which employ N + 1 redundancy, are available 99 to 99.9 percent of the time. Level 2 and level 3 centers feature more redundancy. They guarantee availability at 99.9 to 99.99 percent and 99.99 to 99.999 percent levels, respectively. Level 4 data centers, the highest level of availability in current common usage, have N + N or better redundancy and achieve uptime in the range of 99.999 to 99.9999 percent. Downtime at a level 4 facility, literally seconds per year, is unnoticeable by most users.

Not surprisingly, high levels of availability are costly. Forrester Research estimates that increasing the availability of *a single website* from 99 percent to 99.999 percent would require additional initial spending of $3.7 million and additional annual fees of $1.8 million.[6] According to Morgan Stanley Dean Witter, the cost of building a 99.999 percent availability data center in 2000 was $400 to $550 per square foot; a data center capable of 99 to 99.9 percent uptime costs about $150 per square foot to build.[7]

[6]Randy K. Souza with Harley Manning, Hollie Goldman, and Joyce Tong, "The Best of Retail Site Design," Forrester Research white paper, October 2000.
[7]Jeff Camp, April Henry, Jamie Gomez Surado, and Kristen Olsavsky, Morgan Stanley Dean Witter, November 2000.

FIGURE 6.5

A Representative E-Commerce Infrastructure

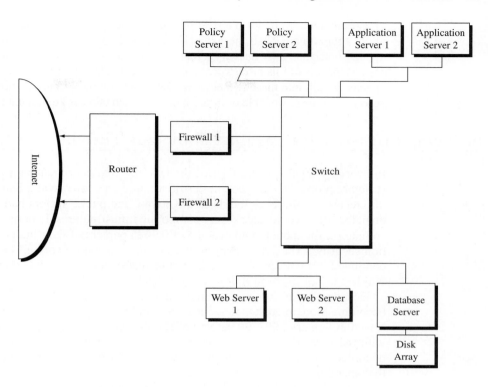

Indeed, management decisions about the design of IT infrastructures always involve trade-offs between availability and the expense of additional components. Figure 6.5 depicts an e-commerce infrastructure used by a real company for delivering a basic Web-based IT service. Notice that many infrastructure elements are redundant: the firewall devices, the Web servers, the application servers, and the policy servers. Notice, though, that the switch and the database server are not redundant. Why?

Although you cannot tell from the diagram, both the switch and the database servers have built-in redundancy. Both have redundant power supplies. In addition, the switch has redundant modules. The database server is shown connected to an array of disks that is set up in a 'RAID' (redundant array of inexpensive disks) configuration to write data to at least two separate disks at the same time.[8] Nevertheless, there are single points of failure in these two components. Thus, the question remains: Why would managers leave these two obviously central components without redundancy when they have made all the other components redundant?

[8]Notice that there are usually many options for adding redundancy, some more expensive than others. For most high-availability equipment, redundancy is a matter of degree and can be purchased incrementally. Note also that redundancy does not necessarily mean purchasing another instance of exactly the same technology platform; cheaper platforms are sometimes used as temporary backups for expensive system components.

The answer boils down to one word: money. The two nonredundant components represent approximately half the cost of this several hundred thousand dollar setup. Making the switch and database server redundant would add about 50 percent to the overall cost. Managers of this infrastructure have made a deliberate decision to rely on the redundancy built into these two devices. Depending on the company's business, this decision might be reasonable or it might not be. Such choices are not unusual, however.

Securing Infrastructure against Malicious Threats

In February 2002 Richard Clarke, the U.S. national coordinator for security, infrastructure protection, and counterterrorism, told an audience at a San Jose, California, security conference that both the private and public sectors had much work to do before they would have secure computing infrastructures. In particular, he chided companies for spending an average of 0.0025 percent of their budgets on information security. "That's less than most companies spend on coffee," he observed. He continued: "If you spend as much on information security as you do on coffee, you will be hacked, and you'll deserve to be hacked."[9]

Despite Clarke's ominous words, there *are* indications that business leaders are becoming more interested in security. According to a Booz Allen Hamilton study released in January 2002, 90 percent of chief executive officers (CEOs) at companies with yearly revenues of $1 billion or more had personally reviewed disaster-planning documents in the last three months. Two-thirds of the 72 CEOs surveyed suggested that spending on security would increase in 2002.[10] The September 11, 2001, terrorist attacks against the United States seem to have prompted much of the new visibility for information security, but even before that a series of high-profile attacks, viruses, and worms had been drawing attention to security concerns.

The threat is growing. Ninety-one percent of companies and government agencies that responded to a 2001 survey conducted by the Computer Security Institute (CSI) and the U.S. Federal Bureau of Investigation (FBI) said they had detected security breaches in the last 12 months. Sixty-four percent acknowledged security-related financial losses. Only 35 percent, or 186 respondents, were willing to quantify their losses, but those alone totaled about $378 million; in 2000, by comparison, 249 respondents reported losses of about $266 million. Thirty-six percent of 2001 respondents said they had been targets of attacks intended to take down computing infrastructure components during the year.[11]

Who are the attackers? Some are thrill seekers with too much time on their hands, people who like the challenge of defeating defenses or getting in where they are not supposed to be. Even if they intend no damage, they are unknown elements inter-

[9]*InformationWeek Daily,* February 20, 2002, http://update.informationweek.com.
[10]*InformationWeek Daily,* January 24, 2002, http://update.informationweek.com.
[11]"2001 CSI/FBI Crime and Security Survey," *Computer Security Issues & Trends,* VII, no. 1, Spring 2001. Note that these estimates probably underrepresent the problem to a large degree. There are many reasons why firms fail to disclose or underreport losses from security incidents.

acting with the complexity of IT infrastructure in unpredictable ways, which can precipitate accidents. Other attackers have taken a specific dislike to a company and intend to do it harm. Attackers of this kind are a significant problem because every defense has cracks and persistent attackers eventually will find one. Another sinister type of attacker attempts to steal a company's proprietary data, such as information a company is storing in confidence for others (e.g., credit card numbers). Industrial espionage and terrorism are a concern, especially for high-profile corporations.

All attackers represent serious threats. Even a thrill seeker who gains access but does no damage can harm a company's reputation if word of the breach gets out. And even apparently harmless breaches must be investigated to determine that nothing more serious has occurred. Many hackers who penetrate a company's defenses set up routes through which they can return, opening doors that they hope company managers will not notice. Many also share information with each other about how to break in to certain companies or open doors they left behind after their own break-ins. A thrill seeker who intends no real harm may pass information to people with more malevolent aims.

Responsible managers must build defenses to secure a company's information-related assets—its data, infrastructure components, and reputation—against this escalating threat. When it comes to securing IT infrastructure, one size does not fit all, and so defenses must be customized to a company's situation, business, infrastructure technologies, and objectives. Sound approaches to securing IT infrastructure begin with a detailed understanding of the threats.

Classification of Threats

Hackers are always inventing new ways to make mayhem. There are many kinds of attacks, and there are subtle variations on each kind. Some threats are common, only too real in actual experience, while others are hypothetical, theoretically possible but never yet observed. Despite the variety, threats can be divided (very roughly) into categories: external attacks, intrusions, and viruses and worms.

External Attacks

External attacks are actions against computing infrastructure that harm it or degrade its services without actually gaining access to it. The most common external attacks are "denial of service" (DoS) attacks, which disable infrastructure devices (usually Web servers) by flooding them with an overwhelming number of messages. Attackers send data packets far more rapidly than the target machine can handle them. Each packet begins what appears to be an authentic "conversation" with the victim computer. The victim responds as it usually does to the beginning of a conversation, but the attacker abruptly terminates the conversation. The resources of the website are consumed by beginning a very large number of bogus conversations. Figure 6.6 compares how a normal and DoS conversation proceed between network-connected computers (also see the accompanying feature).

If attacks always came from a single location on the Internet, defeating them would be easy. Network monitoring software can automatically read the origin IP address from incoming packets, recognize that the flood is coming from a single address, and

FIGURE 6.6
Normal and DoS Handshakes

Source: Robert D. Austin, "The iPremier Company, (A), (B), and (C): Denial of Service Attack," Harvard Business School Teaching Note 602-033.

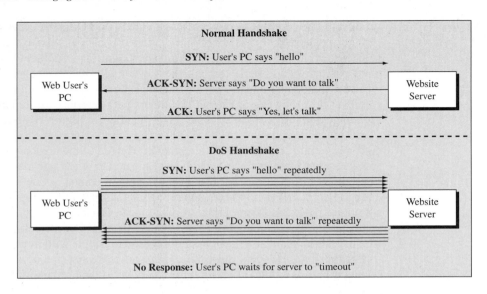

Normal Handshake

SYN: User's PC says "hello"

ACK-SYN: Server says "Do you want to talk"

ACK: User's PC says "Yes, let's talk"

Web User's PC   Website Server

DoS Handshake

SYN: User's PC says "hello" repeatedly

ACK-SYN: Server says "Do you want to talk" repeatedly

Web User's PC   Website Server

No Response: User's PC waits for server to "timeout"

FIGURE 6.7
A Distributed Denial of Service Attack

Source: Robert D. Austin, "The iPremier Company, (A), (B), and (C): Denial of Service Attack." Harvard Business School Teaching Note 602-033.

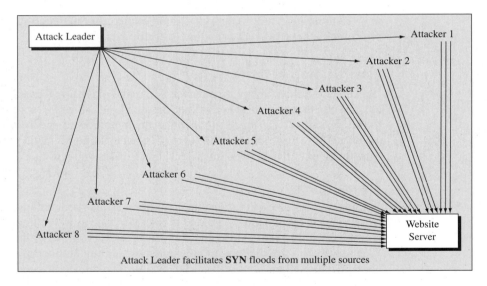

Attack Leader

Attacker 1
Attacker 2
Attacker 3
Attacker 4
Attacker 5
Attacker 6
Attacker 7
Attacker 8

Website Server

Attack Leader facilitates **SYN** floods from multiple sources

filter out flood traffic before it reaches its target. Attackers counter this defense, however, by sending packets that originate from multiple locations on the Internet or appear to originate from multiple locations (see Figure 6.7). *Distributed* denial of service (DDoS) attacks are carried out by automated routines secretly deposited on Internet-connected computers whose owners have not secured them against intrusion (a large percentage of DSL and cable modem–connected PCs fall into this unsecured category). Once implanted on the computers of unsuspecting users, these routines

How Computers Start Conversations . . . with a Handshake

A normal "conversation" between a Web user's computer and a website begins with a three-part exchange of greetings commonly referred to as a "three-way handshake." The Web user's computer says "Hello" (actually "Synchronize" or "SYN") to the website. The website replies, "Do you want to start talking?" ("Synchronize Acknowledged" or "SYN-ACK") back to the Web user's machine. Finally, the Web user's computer responds, "Yes, let's start talking" ("Acknowledged" or "ACK"). At this point, the two ordinarily consider communications to be established and move to the next step of interaction, which is usually more content-based (for

example, sending a page image to the Web user's computer from the website).

In a common form of DoS attack called a SYN flood, the attacker sends swarms of SYN packets (that say, in effect, "Hello" to the website). The website responds with SYN-ACKs ("Do you want to start talking?"), but the attacker never completes the handshake by sending the final ACK. The contacted site will devote a certain amount of its resources to waiting for the final ACK before giving up on it. This use of resources, multiplied thousands of times in a few seconds, is what the attacker is counting on to paralyze the website.

FIGURE 6.8
"Spoofing"

Source: Robert D. Austin, "The iPremier Company, (A), (B), and (C): Denial of Service Attack." Harvard Business School Teaching Note 602-033.

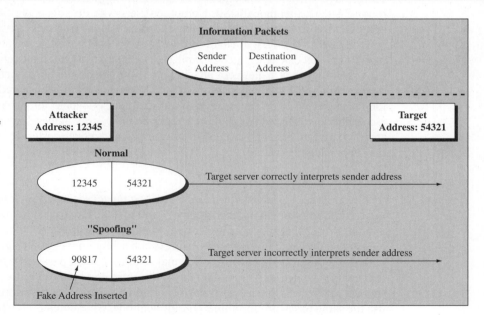

launch packets at targeted websites for a predefined duration or during a predetermined interval. Because the flood comes from many different addresses, network-monitoring software cannot easily recognize the flood as an attack. Clever attackers can simulate a distributed attack by inserting false origin information into packets to mislead filtering software at a target site (providing packets with false origin addresses is called "spoofing;" see Figure 6.8).

Like a Tour Bus at a Fast Food Restaurant: A DoS Attack Analogy

Have you ever stopped for fast food while driving on a major highway only to discover that a full tour bus has just unloaded its passengers at the restaurant? The restaurant is overwhelmed by the sudden burst of business. A DoS attack is like this, only worse. In a DoS attack, it is as if tour bus customers were standing in line, interacting with the cashier at the front of the line, and then deciding not to buy anything. Customers who really intend to buy food are stuck at the back of the line. The restaurant wastes resources on fake customers who are indistinguishable from real customers.[12]

Unfortunately, DoS attacks are extremely easy to execute. Attack routines are available for downloading from sources on the Internet. Using the routines is almost as easy as sending e-mail. Attackers need not be programming experts; many, in fact, are "script kiddies," relatively unsophisticated computer users who run routines that others have written. Although DDoS and spoofing attacks are more difficult, they require no great technical skill. Computer users who do not secure their computers against mischievous use provide unintended assistance to attackers.

DoS attacks are very difficult to defend against. Most defensive methods rely on monitoring that can detect recognizable attack patterns, but it is relatively simple for attackers to vary their patterns of attack. Patterns of attack can be very similar to legitimate e-commerce traffic. A slow-motion DoS attack—recently observed attacks of this kind have been called "degradation of service" attacks—looks almost exactly like real e-commerce traffic. Although these attacks do not cause outages, they do affect infrastructure performance, waste company resources, and reduce customer satisfaction (see the accompanying feature).

Intrusion

Unlike external attackers, intruders actually gain access to a company's internal IT infrastructure by a variety of methods. Some methods involve obtaining user names and passwords. Most people's user names and passwords are not hard to guess; user names usually are constructed by using a consistent convention (e.g., John Smith's user name might be jsmith). An informal scan of student passwords at a major U.S. university revealed that more than half had something to do with sex, drugs, or rock 'n' roll.[13] Many people use birthdays or children's names for passwords; many more use the same password for numerous applications, which means an intruder can gain access to many systems with the same password. Few people change passwords frequently, and it is not uncommon to find passwords taped to computer monitors or sent out in the trash to dumpsters behind high-tech buildings. The term *social engi-*

[12]We first heard this analogy from Dr. Larry Liebrock of the University of Texas at Austin.
[13]Dr. Larry Leibrock is the source of this amusing fact.

neering describes low-tech but highly effective hacker techniques for getting people to freely divulge privileged information. Many people will reveal a password to an official-sounding telephone caller who pretends to be a company network engineer.

There are also high-tech ways to get inside a company's defenses. Hackers who gain physical access to a network can acquire passwords by eavesdropping on network conversations by using "sniffer" software; because network traffic often traverses many local area networks (LANs), a sniffer need not be attached to the LAN where traffic originates to get a password. Or intruders can exploit vulnerabilities left in software when it was developed to gain access to systems *without* first obtaining passwords. In some cases, software development mistakes allow hackers to trick a company's computer into executing their own code or to cause a failure that leaves them in control of the computer. Such vulnerabilities in software are common. New vulnerabilities in widely deployed software systems are discovered daily, sometimes by good guys, who notify vendors so that they can fix the problem, and sometimes by bad guys, who take advantage of the opening. Computers are "port scanned"—probed for vulnerability to intrusion—within a few minutes of connecting to the Internet. Hackers use automated routines that systematically scan IP addresses and then report back to their masters which addresses contain exploitable vulnerabilities.

Once inside, intruders have the same rights of access and control over systems and resources as legitimate users. Thus empowered, they can steal information, erase or alter data, or deface websites (internal and external). Or they can use a location inside a company to pose as a representative of the company. Such an imposter could, for example, send a message canceling an important meeting or send scandalous information (e.g., racist or pornographic) that appeared to originate from official sources inside the company. Intruders also can leave behind routines that use the company's computers as a base for attacks against other companies. Or they can deposit time bombs, seemingly innocuous bits of code scheduled to explode unexpectedly into catastrophic action at a future date.

One of the most difficult problems arising from intrusion is figuring out what exactly intruders might have done while they were inside company defenses. It can take companies a long time to discover trespassing on their systems or networks. Hackers generally try to cover their tracks. They may make subtle changes in a system, opening obscure doors, adding a small file to a disk drive, or slightly altering some data. Finding out what intruders have done, or whether they have done anything, can be very costly for victim companies, yet it must be done. A company that does not know exactly how its systems have been compromised may have difficulty deciding what to tell customers, business partners, and others about the security of data entrusted to the company. There is a very high public relations penalty for not knowing something consequential about your infrastructure that you should have known or, perhaps worse, for issuing assurances about the security of your systems that turn out to be spectacularly inaccurate.

Viruses and Worms

Viruses and worms are malicious software programs that replicate, spreading themselves to other computers. The damage they do may be minor, such as defacing a website, or severe, such as erasing the contents of a computer's disk drive. Although

The Code Red Worm

On Friday the 13th in July 2001, computer system administrators around the world began to notice that their websites had been defaced with a message: "Welcome to http://www.worm.com! Hacked by Chinese!" Subsequent investigation revealed that this message was the work of a worm named Code Red. It was not immediately obvious what other damage the worm might do.

Over the next several days investigators learned that the worm infected only Microsoft's popular Internet Information Server (IIS) through a point of weakness accidentally left in the software. The worm spread by selecting 100 random IP addresses, scanning the computers associated with them for vulnerability, and then migrating to vulnerable machines. In this way, it spread to 15,000 computers by July 18 and an estimated 350,000 by July 31. Ironically, systems were vulnerable only if their administrators had failed to administer a "patch" that Microsoft had made available on June 18.

Close study of Code Red revealed that it was programmed to launch a DoS attack on July 20 from every machine it had infected against the U.S. White House website. The White House changed its IP address in time to dodge the attack. The worm became dormant again on the 28th. A second version of the worm, Code Red II, appeared in August but lacked the DoS attack feature. Instead, it installed "back doors" in systems it infected—openings that intruders could return to later.

people disagree about the exact definitions of viruses and worms, they often are distinguished by their degree of automation and ability to replicate across networks. Simply put, viruses require assistance (often inadvertent) from users to replicate and propagate (e.g., opening a file attached to an e-mail message or even opening a Web page), whereas worms replicate and move across networks automatically.

What is perhaps most alarming about viruses and worms is that they increasingly incorporate and automate other kinds of attacks. The Code Red Worm, for example, which caused widespread consternation in July 2001 (see the accompanying feature), moved across networks, automatically invaded systems with certain vulnerabilities, deposited a program to launch a DoS attack against another computer, and replicated itself across the Internet at an exponential rate. Although Code Red did little damage to infected systems (it defaced their websites), it is significant for the possibilities it suggests. Human hackers can attack companies at human speeds only, but self-propagating, automated attackers can potentially wreak havoc much faster and against arbitrary targets.

Defensive Measures

Defense against hackers is difficult. The threats are varied, sophisticated, and ever-evolving, and security is a matter of degree rather than absolutes. There is no master list against which a company can compare its defenses and, after checking off everything, declare its infrastructure secure. There are defensive measures that are effective in combination, elements of fortification that companies can erect around vital networks, computers, and systems. Like the fortifications of ancient castles, they must be able to repel hostile forces while admitting friendly parties. Elements of information security often marshaled for this task include security policies, firewalls, authentication, encryption, patching and change management, and intrusion detection and network monitoring.

Security Policies

To defend computing resources against inappropriate use, a company must first specify what is meant by "inappropriate." Good security policies specify not only what people should avoid doing because it is dangerous but also what people should do to be safe. A good policy also explains company decisions not to offer certain services or features because the security risks more than outweigh the benefits.

Security policies address questions such as the following:

- What kinds of passwords are users allowed to create for use on company systems, and how often should they change passwords?

- Who is allowed to have accounts on company systems?

- What security features must be activated on a computer before it can connect to a company network?

- What services are allowed to operate inside a company's network?

- What are users allowed to download?

- How is the security policy enforced?

Because a security policy cannot anticipate everything users might want or all situations that might arise, it is a living document. It must be accessible to the people who are expected to comply with it and not be written in overly technical language. And it must be reasonable from the standpoint of a user; a policy people perceive as unreasonable usually is ignored or subverted.

Firewalls

A firewall is a collection of hardware and software designed to prevent unauthorized access to a company's internal computer resources. Computer users outside a company's physical premises often have a legitimate need to access the company's computers. An employee who is traveling, for example, may need to access a system he or she often uses at work. A primary function of a firewall, then, is to facilitate legitimate interactions between computers inside and outside the company while preventing illegitimate interactions.

Firewalls usually are located at points of maximum leverage within a network, typically at the point of connection between a company's internal network and the external public network. Some work by filtering packets coming from outside the company before passing them along to computers inside the company's production facilities. They discard packets that do not comply with security policies, exhibit attack patterns, or appear harmful for other reasons. Others use a sentry computer that relays information between internal and external computers without allowing external packets direct entry.

Firewalls are also useful in other ways. They enforce aspects of a security policy by not allowing certain kinds of communication to traverse the internal network. They have a limited ability to filter out viruses as they enter company networks. Because they are located at the boundary of company systems, firewalls are excellent points at which to collect data about the traffic moving between inside and outside networks. They sometimes are used between segments of an internal network to divide it into regions so that an intruder who penetrates one part will not be able to access the rest. Firewalls also conceal internal network configurations from external prying and thus serve as a sort of electronic camouflage that makes breaking in harder.

Firewalls do not provide perfect protection. Every design has weaknesses, some of which are not known at any point in time. They provide no defense against malicious insiders or against activity that does not traverse the firewall (such as traffic that enters a network via an unauthorized dial-up modem behind the firewall). It is best to think of a firewall as part of an overall strategy of defense. Although it reduces risks, it does not eliminate them.[14]

Authentication

Authentication describes the variety of techniques and software used to control who accesses elements of computing infrastructure. Authentication can occur at many points. *Host* authentication controls access to specific computers (hosts); *network* authentication controls access to regions of a network. Host authentication and network authentication almost always are used in combination. When used with sophisticated and well-managed directory technologies, which keep track of user identities and access rights, access control can be very granular, allowing many layers of access control throughout the infrastructure.

Strong authentication takes as given that passwords expire regularly and that forms of passwords are restricted to make them harder to guess. For example, a company might require that passwords be changed weekly and be composed of a combination of at least eight alphanumeric characters. What minimally constitutes strong authentication is a matter of debate, but simple user name and password authentication does not meet the test for many security experts. A common definition holds that strong authentication requires user name/password authentication plus one other factor, such as certificate authentication (see the accompanying feature) or biometric verification of identity (e.g., iris scanning).

Encryption

Encryption renders the contents of electronic transmissions unreadable by anyone who might intercept them. Modern encryption technologies are very good and provide a high degree of protection against the vast majority of potential attackers. Legitimate

---

[14]Elizabeth D. Zwicky, Simon Cooper, and D. Brent Chapman, *Building Internet Firewalls,* 2nd ed. (Sebastapol, CA: O'Reilly, 2000), is an excellent reference on firewalls and their capabilities.

Digital Certificates

Digital certificates are analogous to the official physical documents people use to establish their identity in face-to-face business interactions. When someone writes a check at a retail store, the store may ask for proof of identity. To provide proof, people often offer a driver's license. Businesses trust a driver's license because they trust the issuing authority (the state agency that regulates motor vehicle use) to verify identity by using a rigorous procedure and because driver's licenses are difficult to forge. A digital certificate is much like the driver's license, a signed document that a trusted third-party organization stands behind that provides evidence of identity. Digital certificates are in fact much harder to forge than physical documents, although it is possible to trick people into issuing real certificates in error. Also, digital certificates are "bearer instruments," rather like driver's licenses with no photo on them; it is possible that the person presenting a certificate is not the person the certificate represents her or him to be.

recipients can decrypt transmission contents by using a piece of data called a "key" (see the accompanying feature). The recipient typically possesses the key for decryption as a result of a previous interaction. Like passwords, keys must be kept secret and protected from social engineering, physical theft, insecure transmission, and a variety of other techniques hostile forces use to obtain them. Encryption does little good if the key that decrypts is available to attackers. Nevertheless, modern encryption techniques provide excellent concealment of the contents of messages if the key is secret regardless of what else hackers might know about the encryption algorithm itself. By setting up encryption at both ends of a connection across public networks, a company can in effect extend its secure private network (such network extensions are called virtual private networks; see the accompanying feature).

Encryption does not conceal everything about a network transmission. Hackers still can gain useful information from the pattern of transmission, the lengths of messages, or their origin or destination addresses. Encryption does not prevent attackers from intercepting and changing the data in a transmission. The attackers may not know what they are changing, but subtle changes can still wreak havoc, especially if the intended recipient is a computer that expects data to arrive in a particular format.[15]

Patching and Change Management

A surprising number of attacks exploit weaknesses in systems for which "patches" already exist at the time of the attack. Successful attacks of this kind sometimes represent administrative failures, but there are also a large number of contributing factors, such as shortage of IT staff to apply fixes to existing systems, or legitimate concerns about the unintended negative consequences of a system patch.

[15]Jalal Feghi, Jalil Feghi, and Peter Williams, *Digital Certificates: Applied Internet Security,* (Reading, MA: Addison-Wesley, 1999), is an excellent reference on the subject of encryption and digital certificates.

Public-Private Key Encryption and Digital Signatures

Public-private key encryption uses a mathematical algorithm with an interesting characteristic: If one unique key is used to transform a plain text message into encrypted form, a different unique key must be used to decrypt the message back into plain text at its destination. Typically, one key is made public and the other is kept private. A message can be sent confidentially if it is encrypted using the public key; then only a person possessing the private key can decrypt the message. A message can be "signed" by using the same process in reverse; if the public key can successfully decrypt the message, only the person in possession of the private key could have encrypted it; hence, it must have come from the person known to possess the private key.

Keeping track of the variety of systems in a company's infrastructure, their security weaknesses, the available patches, and whether patches have been applied is nontrivial. Consequently, attacks against known and presumably patched weaknesses often are successful.

Knowing exactly what software is running and whether it is patched is important for another reason: After an attack this knowledge is essential to discerning whether attackers have changed anything within a company's infrastructure. Detecting a change in a file size or finding a file that "should not be there" would be an obvious sign of intruder activity. Best practice calls for keeping detailed records of all files that are *supposed* to be on production computers, including file sizes or even file "fingerprints."[16] Sadly, many companies fall short of this practice, sometimes for what seem to managers like good business reasons. For example, managers hurrying to fix a customer-impacting problem may be tempted to shortcut formal change management procedures. The result is a gap in formal knowledge about what files and programs ought to be present on company systems.

Intrusion Detection and Network Monitoring

Intrusion detection and network monitoring work together to help network administrators recognize when their infrastructure is or has been under attack. Network monitoring automatically filters out external attack traffic at the boundary of company networks. Sophisticated intrusion detection systems include combinations of hardware probes and software diagnostic systems. They log activity throughout company networks and highlight patterns of suspicious activity for further investigation. Along with formal change management, which provides a baseline description of company system configurations, the information logged by intrusion detection systems can help companies reconstruct exactly what an intruder did as quickly as possible.

---

[16]There are technologies available to capture images of disk drives that act as a sort of fingerprinting.

Virtual Private Networks

Virtual private networks (VPNs) use encryption to create a connection across public networks that extend a company's private network. Traffic between two points—for example, a remote user and a computer inside a company's network—is encrypted at one end of the transmission, encapsulated inside new packets, and sent on to a destination where the packets are unencapsulated and decrypted. VPNs allow a secure private network to be extended securely across a public network to arbitrary points. There is a dark side to this, however. If an attacker can gain access to a remote VPN node, a company's network can be attacked as if from the inside. Thus, although VPNs extend security usefully, they also add to the complexity of the security management task.

A Security Management Framework

Securing a company's infrastructure involves design decisions, operating policy and procedure development, and steely execution. Information security is an evolving field with an evolving state of the art. Nevertheless, the following principles of security management remain relevant.

Make Deliberate Security Decisions

This may seem obvious, but too many companies rely on a combination of blissful ignorance and security through obscurity. These are not reasonable approaches for companies seeking to connect to and leverage the public Internet. Ignorance is neither a strategy nor an excuse. General managers must educate themselves on security-related subjects and take responsibility for decisions in this area.

Consider Security a Moving Target

The forces of digital darkness are constantly searching for new ways to attack. Companies must maintain a solid defense, attack their own systems (do a safety check), and hire outside firms to audit their defenses for vulnerability to new threats on a regular basis. Indeed, companies must stay plugged in to sources of information about threats, such as the Computer Emergency Response Team (CERT) (www.cert.org). Information security is not something a company can do once and then forget about.

Practice Disciplined Change Management

The fix that needs to be rushed into production may be important, but if shortcutting formal procedures makes reconstructing the facts of a subsequent attack impossible, the costs of informality ultimately may be far greater. Companies need to know what they have running at all times and need a disciplined process for migrating infrastructure changes through testing and into production use. Not following such procedures represents reckless behavior for which general managers are ultimately responsible.

Conversely, failure to promptly install available patches to counter known threats also risks unnecessary incidents. Best practice requires the prompt installation of patches while remaining within change management procedures.

Educate Users

Make sure users understand the dangers inherent in certain activities, such as sharing passwords and connecting behind-the-firewall dial-up modems to their desktop computers. Help them understand the reasons for security measures that may inconvenience them in some situations. Enlist them as allies in maintaining security.

Deploy Multilevel Technical Measures, as Many as You Can Afford

Use security at the host and network levels. Acquire defensive technologies as they develop. No company can afford an infinite amount of security, but managers need to be sure they have thought through the consequences of a breach of security. Managers must prioritize security measures appropriately.

Risk Management of Availability and Security

Companies cannot afford to address every threat to the availability and security of IT infrastructure with equal aggressiveness. Even if they could, doing so would not make business sense. Instead, risks must be characterized and addressed in proportion to their likelihood and potential consequences. Management actions to mitigate risks must be prioritized with an eye to their costs and potential benefits. The promise of new capabilities adds another wrinkle to availability and security management challenges. New capabilities usually entail new risks, and so decisions about what capabilities should be supported and when they should be introduced are also matters of risk management.

Figure 6.9 suggests a way of thinking about potential failures in terms of their probabilities and consequences. Incidents in the upper right corner are both likely and costly; mitigating these risks is obviously important. Risks in the other quadrants must be prioritized. One method of prioritizing involves computing the *expected loss* associated with incidents in these quadrants by multiplying the probability of an incident and its cost if it occurs. Incidents with higher expected losses get higher priorities. Needless to say, incidents in the upper left and lower right quadrants receive higher priorities than do the low-probability, low-cost incidents in the lower left quadrant.

For most companies, however, the logic of risk management is more complicated. Managers' attitudes toward risk may be too complex to be summarized by simple probabilities and costs. For example, managers may dread high-cost incidents so much that they prefer to address high-cost incidents first even if those incidents are very unlikely to occur and their associated expected loss (probability × cost) is small. Or managers may fear specific events for reasons that go beyond cost. A further complication arises from the difficulty of estimating costs and probabilities in some situations. As we have suggested, the intangible costs of some incidents are exceedingly difficult to predict, and estimating probabilities often is no easier.

FIGURE 6.9
**Managing
Infrastructure
Risks:
Consequences
and
Probabilities**

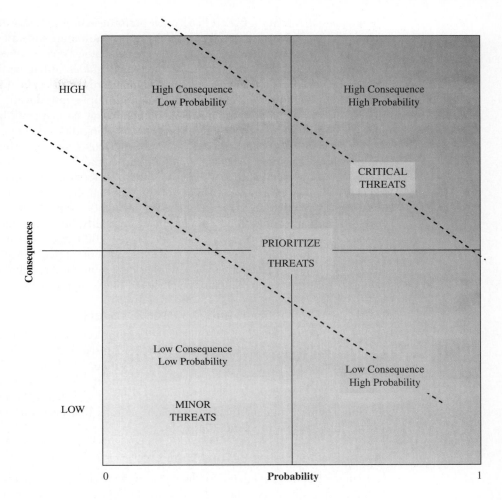

In addition, not all risks can be countered with well-defined management actions. Most companies choose between courses of action that vary in cost and address risks to varying degrees. Sometimes none of the possible actions address some serious risks. Sometimes addressing a serious risk is prohibitively expensive. Thus, after assigning priorities to risks, most companies perform an additional assessment step to decide which actions to take. This step takes into account not only the expected losses from incidents but also the costs of actions to reduce or eliminate risks.

New capabilities that come with new technologies generate another wrinkle in risk management thinking. Although new capabilities provide benefits, they often require taking on new risks to availability or security. Thus, managers also engage in risk management as they decide which new services to offer. A new service to support the business—for example, a collaborative videoconferencing technology—increases the complexity of infrastructure, which generates challenges for both availability and security.

There is almost always a trade-off between performance or richness of features of a technology and infrastructure robustness. For example, running software with high levels of "logging" so that the details of activity are meticulously recorded will help a company detect intrusions more quickly. But logging degrades system performance, perhaps to a point where users complain or additional hardware must be purchased.

Consider the infrastructure configuration example introduced earlier: an e-commerce company that purchased some redundant components but left single points of failure in its infrastructure (Figure 6.5). Should this company buy another $65,000 switch? We could estimate the relevant costs and probabilities, and we could compute the expected loss from the failure of the current single switch. A second switch dramatically reduces the probability of a loss of switching, which in turn reduces the expected cost due to a loss of switching. If the improvement in expected loss from buying the second switch exceeds the $65,000 that the extra switch would cost, the company ought to buy it—in theory. In reality, however, other factors may intervene. The company may not have an extra $65,000, managers may not believe the cost and probability estimates, or there may be more urgent places to spend that $65,000. Whatever managers decide, deliberately thinking through the logic of risk management improves a company's chances of realizing business objectives.

Incident Management and Disaster Recovery

No matter how available and secure they make a company's infrastructure, managers can expect incidents. Infrastructure incidents present a rare business challenge: a need to solve problems under the pressure of a ticking clock. Though they are rare, the stakes are often high when real-time incidents occur. Managers' actions in a crisis can make a huge difference to the well-being of a company. We consider incident management in terms of actions that need to be taken before, during, and after an incident.

Managing Incidents before They Occur

The range of options available to managers in the middle of a crisis is largely determined by decisions made before the crisis. Precrisis practices that make incidents more manageable include the following:

Sound infrastructure design. If infrastructure has been designed with an eye to recoverability and tolerance for failures, the losses associated with an incident are more likely to be contained.

Disciplined execution of operating procedures. Change management procedures make the diagnosis of problems more effective by maintaining a baseline of knowledge about infrastructure configurations. Data backup procedures preserve data in case the data are lost. Scheduled infrastructure health audits uncover lurking problems or vulnerabilities.

Careful documentation. If procedures and configurations are carefully documented, crisis managers need not guess about crucial details. Reliable documentation saves time and increases certainty in dealing with a crisis.

Established crisis management procedures. Procedures for managing incidents guide the diagnosis of problems, help managers avoid decision-making traps, and specify who should be involved in problem-solving activities. Managing in a crisis is difficult enough without having to make up every response as you go. Crisis management always involves creativity, but familiar and useful procedures serve as bases from which managers can innovate under fire effectively.

Rehearsing incident response. Rehearsing responses to incidents makes decision makers more confident and effective during real crises. Even if the way an incident unfolds is different from the way it was practiced, practice makes the situation more familiar and better prepares managers to improvise solutions.

These preparations may seem basic, but a large number of companies do not make them. There is a tendency for other urgent business concerns, such as growing revenues, profits, product functionality, and the customer base, to take priority over hypothetical problems nobody wants to think about. In most companies, staff members who execute responses to incidents have no training in that area and are not necessarily trained in the nature of threats. Nevertheless, managers clearly bear responsibility when they do not foresee exposure to availability and security incidents. Good infrastructure managers find the time to plan for high-cost events.

Managing during an Incident

When faced with a real-time crisis, human decision makers have numerous psychological obstacles to surmount in addition to the usually very serious technical difficulties inherent in the crisis. These obstacles include the following:

- Emotional responses, including confusion, denial, fear, and panic

- Wishful thinking and groupthink

- Political maneuvering, diving for cover, and ducking responsibility

- Leaping to conclusions and blindness to evidence that contradicts current beliefs

Awareness of psychological traps helps decision makers avoid them when situations turn dire.

Another difficulty managers face in crises is "public relations inhibition." Sometimes managers are reluctant to admit the seriousness of a problem because they do not want to take actions that communicate to others (customers, the public) that a serious incident has occurred. For example, the managers of an e-commerce company might not want to shut down their online retail site to confound a hacker until they have definitive proof of an intrusion. A shutdown would have to be explained to the press and might alarm customers. Obviously, the stakes of such a decision are very high.

Managing after an Incident

After an incident, infrastructure managers often need to rebuild parts of the infrastructure. Sometimes erasing and rebuilding everything from scratch is the only way to be sure the infrastructure is restored to its preincident state. If configurations and procedures have been carefully documented in advance, recovery can happen swiftly. But if records of how systems should be put together are not exact, rebuilding can run into hiccups: problems that must be solved under the time pressure of getting the business back online. Rebuilding processes may have to be reinvented "on the fly." Furthermore, if there have been change management lapses—for example, if changes made to systems have not been documented—a rebuild can result in lost functionality (a problem solved earlier by an informal change in production may reappear).

To avoid future incidents of the same type, managers need to understand what happened. Figuring out exactly what caused an incident is sometimes difficult, but it must be done regardless of the cost. Typically, a company owes business partners information about the nature of a failure so that those partners can determine the consequences that might flow to them as a result. There is no one best way to explain or disclose an incident to partners, customers, or the press and public. In formulating actions after an incident, however, it is essential to communicate the seriousness with which a company protects the information entrusted to it. A possible intrusion need not be a public relations disaster if subsequent steps to secure infrastructure are framed as "taking no chances."

Summary

The rate of adoption of Internetworking technologies has outrun efforts to establish effective frameworks and policies for managing them. In no area is this truer than availability and security. The challenges of keeping real-time infrastructures always operational are formidable and evolving. Nevertheless, in this chapter we have outlined management actions and frameworks that will, if applied with discipline and effort, improve the chances of success. The economic consequences of ignoring or failing to take effective action in these areas may be dire indeed (see the accompanying feature).

We have demonstrated how the arithmetic of availability calls for increasing sophistication in infrastructure design and how redundancy, the primary means of increasing robustness, also adds operational complexity and management challenges. We have outlined a series of new and serious malicious threats to IT infrastructure and proposed frameworks for reducing the threats and for managing incidents when they occur. Executives can use the following questions to access their own preparedness for these 21st-century challenges:

1. How available do the systems in our application portfolio need to be? Are our infrastructure investments in availability aligned with requirements?

2. Are we taking security threats seriously enough? How secure is our current infrastructure? How do we assess information security on an ongoing basis? Have IT staff members received adequate training? How do we compare with information security best-in-class organizations?

3. Do we have a solid security policy in place? Were business managers as well as IT managers involved in creating it? Do users know about it and understand it? Do they accept it? How is the policy enforced?

A Dark Scenario for 2009

There are over two billion Internet enabled devices in the United States now in 2009, each with its own Internet protocol, or IP, address. Worldwide the number of devices is six billion. . . . Elevators, appliances, cars, trucks, manufacturing machinery, photocopiers and traffic lights all have IP addresses. All are connected in some way to the single global network of networks loosely known as the Internet. . . .

In the private sector, IT security and reliability spending accounts for almost one in every three dollars spent on information systems. Despite that expenditure, there are chronic security problems and system outages.

The routing tables for the six billion IP addresses are immense and unmanageable. Packets of messages routinely are lost in transmission, especially messages sent to large numbers of addressees. The result is that messages are frequently retransmitted, slowing already overburdened routers.

In addition to slowdowns and failures caused by the size of the system, malicious activity frequently confuses or corrupts the servers and routers that maintain IP addresses and pathway information, resulting in parts of the Internet (and on seven occasions by 2009, all of it) not working for days. During those "Down Days," clean copies of the address tables were distributed around the country on special military flights that were allowed to fly using visual flight rules (since the new air traffic system shuts down when the Internet does). . . .

Most of the attention to malicious activity in 2009 is . . . focused on Affinity Worms . . . [which enter] an Internet enabled device using a vulnerability in an operating system and then branch out in a "chain letter" fashion. . . . A major brokerage house was attacked in 2004 by an Affinity Worm that entered the wireless connection of the CEO's home security alarm system (from a laptop in a car two blocks away) and then wormed its way to the CEO's home PC and then through the Virtual Private Network to the brokerage house's trading records, which it hopelessly scrambled. The Market closed for three days that time . . . the power grid collapses of 2005 were the result of an Affinity Worm that infected devices throughout the power grid (probably through wireless connections) and then had the devices simultaneously launch message traffic every second to flood the key routers supporting the grid. This technique was originally called a Distributed Denial of Service attack when it first surfaced in February, 2000. In the 2005 attack, the network operators had a choice of blocking traffic from their own devices (thereby collapsing the grid) or letting the flood of messages, or tsunami as it is now known, crash the routers. They chose the latter, which collapsed the grid.

After the success of that attack, a similar technique collapsed the key routers in the Tier 1 backbone providers in 2006 during the international crisis. No one could ever prove the attack was connected to the crisis because the IP addresses of the attackers were spoofed and anonymous accounts were used. Whoever did the attack, it did halt the rail and air traffic systems, causing the US military buildup to slow. A diplomatic solution was quickly found, although not one favorable to US interests.

How much had all of this cost the US? The Federal Reserve Bank published an econometric analysis toward the end of 2009 that attempted to estimate the effects on GDP growth over the last seven years caused by the cyber attacks on the markets, the power grids, and the telecommunications systems. The report concluded that in the absence of those attacks and their cascading effects on the economy, growth could have averaged between 2.1% and 2.8%, instead of the seven-year average of 0.3%. Two days later the Fedwire was hit with a Data Base Scrambler attack that corrupted data on the Fed's main transaction data base and its two geographically separated backups. The resulting Bank Holiday caused the seven-year average to be readjusted to 0.28% growth in GDP.[17]

[17]Excerpt from Richard Clarke's "Straight Line Scenario: 2009." Presented by Howard A. Schmidt, vice chair, President's Critical Infrastructure Protection Board at the 2002 Internet2 Conference on May 8, 2002, in Arlington, VA. Reprinted by permission.

4. Do we have plans for responding to infrastructure incidents? Do we practice them on a regular basis? Are staff members trained in incident response? What are our plans and policies for communicating information about incidents to external parties such as customers, partners, the press, and the public?

5. Do we practice risk management in availability and security decisions? Is our approach to dealing with hypothetical problems deliberate, structured, and well reasoned? Have the company's general managers embraced responsibility for availability and security?

Managing Diverse IT Infrastructures[1]

Before the emergence of the commercial Internet in the 1990s,[2] companies accomplished much that they now achieve through public Internetworks entirely on their own by using proprietary technologies installed and managed inside each firm. For several reasons, this approach was expensive and unsatisfactory:

- To reach business partners and customers, every company had to develop its own communication infrastructure, a process that led to massive duplication in infrastructure investment. Often the multiplicity of technologies confused and confounded the partners and customers businesses wanted to reach.

- The technologies did not interoperate well. Many companies maintained complex software programs that had no purpose except to serve as a bridge between otherwise incompatible systems.

- Reliance on proprietary technologies meant that companies were locked in to specific vendor technologies. Once locked in, firms had little bargaining power and were at the mercy of the margin-maximizing inclinations of their technology providers.

Companies that installed hardware and software from many vendors suffered performance and reliability difficulties. IT managers, seemingly trapped in a losing game, were perennially blamed by business managers for delivering expensive systems that performed poorly or, worse, never worked at all.

---

[1]This chapter is adapted from materials in Professor Robert D. Austin's *Managing Information Technology Infrastructure* course module, Harvard Business School Publishing No. 601-181.
[2]The Internet itself arose much earlier, of course, but the *commercial* Internet really took off only with the introduction of Web browsers in the early 1990s. Some companies were using the Internet productively in the 1980s, but not very many.

The emergence of an accessible public Internet based on open standards has changed the way companies build IT capabilities. Corporate systems now gain leverage from their connections to public infrastructure. The new approaches compare favorably with and in many cases enhance previous approaches in numerous ways. Today, for example,

- Companies can share a communication infrastructure common to all business partners and customers. Customers and business partners can interact via common interfaces (usually Web browsers). This seamless interaction dramatically reduces complexity and confusion.

- Because of the open Transmission Control Protocol/Internet Protocol (TCP/IP) standard, communication technologies interoperate very well. Software that bridges systems is simple, standardized, and inexpensive. In some cases it can be acquired for free.

- Companies are much less locked in to specific vendor technologies, a fact that creates more competition among vendors. More competition leads to lower prices and better-performing technology.

At last, companies can combine technologies from numerous vendors and expect them to interconnect seamlessly. Although the job of the information technology (IT) manager remains formidable, it is not the losing game it once was.

As we have seen, reliable and secure connections to public networks provide new options for delivering IT services. Services historically provided by IT departments now can be acquired in real time from service providers. This is outsourcing, but of a kind different from large-scale outsourcing programs (those still very important programs are discussed in Chapter 9). As communication technologies improve and become more compatible and modular, firms can obtain smaller and smaller increments of service from outside vendors, with shorter lead times and contract durations. Futuristic "Web services" visions take incremental service ideas to a logical extreme, depicting a world in which functions as narrow as, say, currency conversion will routinely be obtained externally for prices and from sources automatically negotiated in real time whenever a currency conversion is needed.

Although the standards and infrastructure necessary to bring this vision to reality are not yet available, major IT vendors such as IBM and Microsoft profess a commitment to it. In any case, the underlying trend toward external acquisition of increasingly incremental services is irresistible. Infrastructure that lends itself to incremental improvement enjoys favorable management attributes; for example, investment management and implementation risks are easier when improvements involve a series of many small steps rather than a few large "all-or-nothing" steps. Incremental improvement also facilitates experimentation and learning.[3]

---

[3]David Upton has written extensively on the benefits of incremental improvement strategies, especially the need to design operational infrastructures so that they can be incrementally improved. See, for example, *Designing, Managing, and Improving Operations* (Upper Saddle River, NJ: Prentice-Hall, 1998).

Incremental service delivery also makes new business models possible, and those models act as catalysts for restructuring in service delivery industries. In general, the trend is toward providers that specialize in particular aspects of IT service delivery and collaborate with other providers to deliver services. More and more, IT services are delivered by chains of service partners, each of which must perform well to deliver the service reliably and securely. Having many service providers means that IT managers must be especially careful in selecting and managing relationships with these business partners. Managing service provider relationships means sharing information—"virtually integrating," if you will—which requires surmounting technical communication challenges as well as challenges of incentive design. Service-level contracts provide a vital foundation for aligning incentives between parties collaborating in service delivery, but successful relationship management, as we will see, goes beyond mere contract administration.

When evolving service models connect to corporate systems, diverse IT infrastructure is the result. In many companies, legacy systems still perform vital functions and must be supported. In most companies, there is an accelerating trend toward heterogeneity in supported client devices. Increasingly, cell phones and personal digital assistants (PDAs), not personal computers (PCs), are the tools people use to interact with IT systems to conduct business. The variety of service delivery models and technologies creates complexity, which, as we have seen, generates management challenges. Not surprisingly, new ways of thinking are needed to manage diverse, distributed, and complex information and technology assets.

New Service Models

Since the emergence of PC and client-server computing, end-user software has been designed to execute on PCs or on servers that are housed locally. Saved work—documents and other forms of data—usually remains on a PC's hard drive or on storage devices connected to a nearby server or mainframe. In this scenario, when the software malfunctions, the user contacts his or her IT department, which owns and operates most, if not all, of the IT infrastructure.

With the advent of reliable, high-capacity networks, however, local software execution no longer is the only alternative, nor is it necessarily the best alternative. Increasingly, software is designed to operate in geographically distant facilities that belong to specialized service providers, each of which deliver software services across the Internet to many different customers. In this scenario, data are stored in a distant location, and the end user's company owns little of the infrastructure involved in service delivery. The end user's company pays a monthly fee for a service bundle, which usually includes technical support services as well.

Even if actual software applications are not acquired externally, other increments of outsourcing may make sense. A company, for example, can rent space in a vendor-owned hosting facility rather than incur the capital expenses required to build a data center even when it retains internal management of the software that delivers services to users. The benefits of incremental outsourcing include the following:

Managing the shortage of skilled IT workers. According to the U.S. government, there may be as many as 4 million unfilled IT jobs in the United States by 2003. Incremental outsourcing helps individual firms overcome the shortage of skills by reducing the need for internal staff a firm must hire. This benefit is especially important to small and medium-size businesses that have difficulty attracting and retaining IT talent.

Reduced time to market. With the rise of the Web, companies can use IT to enhance revenues by rapidly creating new business models, products, and services. New revenue opportunities sometimes offer early mover advantages. Seizing these advantages depends on rapid deployment. Network-based service delivery models help companies develop new capabilities quickly. For example, existing companies can use externally hosted retailing packages to sell over the Web without the delays involved in having to purchase equipment or develop software.

The shift to 24 × 7 operations. As we discussed in Chapter 6, consumers expect company websites and supporting systems to be always available. Real-time operations require that computers always be on. But in many enterprises, facilities and equipment are not designed for such high levels of availability. High availability requires large capital investments in a highly redundant infrastructure. Because specialized vendors are able to spread capital investments across many customers, they can achieve economies of scale that justify large investments. In fact, specialized vendors often can invest in levels of availability and security that individual firms cannot afford. In addition, by acquiring services externally, companies can skip painful start-up difficulties. The reliability of the core services vendors offer usually is already proven; service delivery kinks have been worked out on other customers.[4]

Favorable cash flow profiles. Traditionally, IT investments required large up-front cash outlays that only yielded deferred and often uncertain (because of high IT project failure rates) benefits. Subscription-based IT services have a different cash flow profile. Firms pay a monthly fee to acquire services equivalent to those provided by internal systems in the past. With limited up-front purchases, payback flows in more quickly. This benefit is particularly important to small and medium-size companies that cannot afford the large up-front investments associated with some IT services. Figure 7.1 compares the cash flow profile of a traditional IT investment with that of a subscription-based service delivered through a prebuilt external infrastructure.

---

[4]A corollary observation here is that if you are the first customer or even an early customer of a service provider, you have some chance of being the company that experiences the start-up pain on behalf of other companies. Clearly, this is a factor that should be taken into account in deciding whether to acquire a service externally or from a certain vendor.

FIGURE 7.1
Purchase
versus
Subscribe Cash
Flows

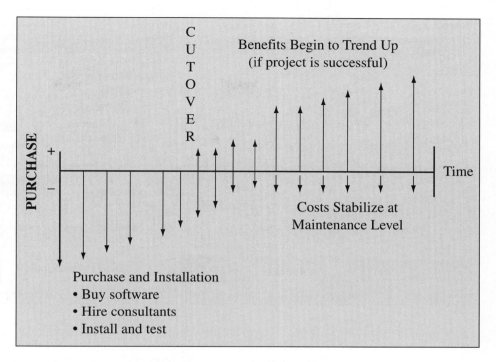

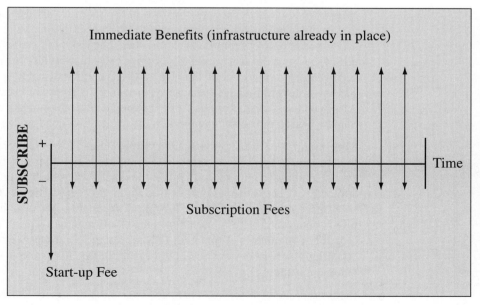

FIGURE 7.2 An IT Service Chain

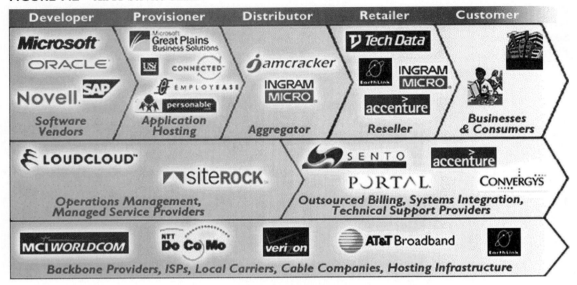

Cost reduction in IT service chains. Centralized service delivery can reduce support costs in many ways. With business functionality delivered from centralized servers, upgrades to new versions of the software are done centrally, eliminating the need for support personnel to upgrade individual client computers. This service delivery approach also reduces the risk (and costs) of software piracy, because the software is never physically distributed. In addition, there is no inventory of physical media (e.g., CD-ROMs) for distributors and systems administrators to manage because services are distributed in real time to users. Also, vendors realize savings from economies of scale in using staff, which may be passed along to customers in the form of reduced prices.

Making applications globally accessible. When IT services are delivered over the Net, the geographic location of a computer is unimportant. Services are available at any computer with a Web browser for any user who has the authority to access the service. Traveling employees can access the same virtual workspace regardless of where they are in the world. Because the IT infrastructure is geography-neutral, much of the cost of moving a worker from one location to another is eliminated. This advantage combines with the continuing evolution in client devices (cell phones and PDAs, for example) to create new value opportunities.

Figure 7.2 shows a service chain for over-the-Net service delivery. Independent software vendors (ISVs) develop software that operates across networks. This software operates in vendor-owned, secure 24 × 7 availability facilities. Aggregators (distributors) collect the offerings of ISVs and hosters into coherent packages, which they sell

Web Services: An Example

Suppose a software program needs to convert euros into U.S. dollars. The software program is not designed to perform this conversion internally and therefore must request conversion functionality from an external source. In a Web services model, the process might go something like this:

1. The software program sends out a request for the service over the Internet to a known "registry" that lists service providers. The registry sends back information about currency conversion routines that vendors have listed with the registry. Information about each routine includes details of its functionality, the price charged by the vendor for use of the routine, and the quality of service experienced by others that have used it.
2. The software program automatically evaluates the criteria provided by the registry and chooses a routine to use.
3. The software program contacts the provider of the chosen routine across the Internet and

contracts with the provider for one-time use of the routine.
4. The provider sends a description across the Internet telling the software program how to interact with the routine: the format in which the program should send its amount in euros and the format in which the program will receive the U.S. dollar amount back.
5. The software sends the request for conversion and the conversion data to the provider; the provider's routine responds.
6. The provider and the user of the conversion service exchange the information necessary to assure payment reconciliation.

All this happens automatically as the program runs, and all interactions are across the Internet. The next time this program needs currency conversion, it might choose a different provider for any of a number of reasons. The price of the service might have changed, or there might be updated information in the registry about the quality of service of the routine.

through resellers (retailers) that offer additional value-added services (such as tech support and consulting). In addition, supporting players include network providers and outsourcing partners that specialize in back-office businesses such as billing or help desk services, and of course communication carrier providers, such as backbone providers, telephone companies, DSL services, and wireless providers.

Figure 7.2 shows one possible version of an IT services chain. An interesting variation is the Web services model that, unlike the previously described service chain, allows for highly dynamic provision and aggregation of services. Rather than establishing long-term relationships with retailers and aggregators, customer firms using Web services negotiate and acquire services in real time from a dynamic and fluid market for those services. For example, a user in need of currency conversion might obtain it from one vendor at 11:00 A.M. and from a different vendor at 11:15 A.M., perhaps because the 11:15 A.M. vendor has lowered its price for the service. All the negotiating and contracting would be automatic and behind the scenes, seamless to the user, who would never know the two conversions had been done by different vendors. Reliability and quality of service are automatically factored in to protect companies from services that do not work well (see the accompanying feature).

The advantage in a service chain of specialized players is that each player focuses on what he or she does well, thereby realizing economies of scale and scope. Resellers focus on managing relationships with end customers. Aggregators focus on combining the offerings of different software vendors so that they interoperate. Hosters focus on the reliable and secure operation of a type of system (e.g., e-mail). ISVs focus on developing software.

This is not a hypothetical model; players already conduct business in this way. For example, Microsoft (an ISV) has cooperated with Personable (a hoster) to develop an over-the-Net version of Microsoft's Office productivity suite. In the spring of 2002, Personable offered this version of Office to customers for $19.95 per month. Microsoft Great Plains Business Solutions (a hoster) provides IT services for financial and service management to small and medium-size businesses also via a subscription model. Jamcracker (an aggregator) combines the offerings of hosters such as Employease (which offers IT services for human resources management) and Connected (which offers automated PC backup services) into coherent packages. Accenture resells Jamcracker's packages and technology.

Managing Risk through Incremental Outsourcing

As IT service chains proliferate and mature, companies often face the question of which services to outsource. Figure 7.3 outlines the steps many companies consider in making this decision. IT services that are unique to a company and provide it with significant advantages over competitors tend not to be outsourced, at least not to vendors that are trying to sell similar services to all of their customers. Such services are so core to a company's business that an internal capability to manage and extend them must be maintained. The exception to this rule arises when companies find themselves unable to develop a vital capability internally and must therefore rely on outsourcing to acquire the capability.

Many IT services do not provide competitive advantage. These services are essential in running a modern business, but there may be no reason one company's service must be different from that of its competitors. A company probably needs, for example, e-mail and word processing software, but the success or failure of a company usually has little to do with the features of these products. For these commodity-like services, the priorities are reliability and low cost (or a more favorable cash flow profile).

The logic of incremental outsourcing decisions parallels the logic of outsourcing large segments of the IT function, which we discuss fully in Chapter 9. But there are also differences. With incremental outsourcing, the economic stakes are not as high and the potential consequences of mismanagement are not as far-reaching. When a firm outsources only its travel expense reporting, for example, as opposed to its entire IT organization, risk is contained. Mistakes are more reversible and less painful. Also, because mistakes cost less, more experimentation is feasible. Trying something does not mean managers must suffer its effects for the duration of a long-term contract.

FIGURE 7.3
Internal versus
External
Service
Delivery

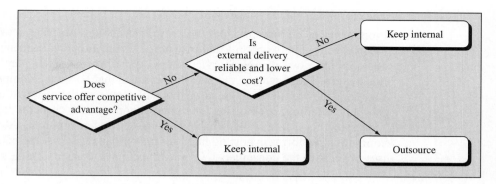

However, incremental outsourcing decisions cannot be taken lightly. A decision to outsource hosting or network management can have serious across-the-company implications if there are service problems. Furthermore, many individually correct incremental decisions can add up to a significant negative overall impact. Incremental decisions made in isolation must not add up to an incoherent or inconsistent business strategy.

Incremental outsourcing, however, offers new and attractive choices to managers seeking to improve IT infrastructure. In the past, managers often felt they faced two equally unpleasant choices: (1) do nothing and risk slipping behind competitors or (2) wholesale replacement of major components of computing infrastructure, which risks huge cost overruns and potential business disruptions as consequences of an implementation failure. Decisions to replace wholesale legacy networks with TCP/IP-based networks have run this second risk, as have decisions about whether to implement enterprise systems. With the TCP/IP networks installed today, however, managers have intermediate options that lie between all-or-nothing choices. The importance of these options cannot be overemphasized. For perhaps the first time in the history of IT, it is possible to imagine incremental improvement paths, ways of getting from A to B and then to C and capturing significant economic benefits without putting the entire future of the firm at stake each time.

An Incremental Outsourcing Example: Hosting

Outsource hosting of a company's systems involves deciding where they should be located physically. Although on the surface this may seem like an all-or-nothing choice, a company can in fact precisely determine which management functions it turns over to a vendor when moving computers to a vendor's site. Some basic support functions, such as electrical power, are necessarily ceded, but beyond those, managers can choose the size of the increment of outsourcing. By doing so, managers exercise control over the risks that executing the outsourcing initiative entails. In this chapter, we consider hosting as an illustration of the incremental nature of modern service delivery options even in cases when at first glance outsourcing seems to present all-or-nothing options.

The Hosting Service Provider Industry

Proponents of service provider–based infrastructures describe a world in which companies routinely obtain a majority of the IT functionality needed for day-to-day business from over-the-Net service chains. Hosting companies play a vital role in this picture. They own and manage the facilities that house the computers that provide over-the-Net services. In some industry segments the vision already is reality. In online retailing, back-office functions (shopping cart, checkout, and credit card processing, for example) that enable Web-based consumer purchases often reside on computing platforms in hosting facilities rather than on the selling company's premises or local to the consumer. J. Crew, for example, hosts its online retailing infrastructure with Digex.

The benefits of outsourcing hosting are many. An International Data Corporation (IDC) study in 2000, for example, found that companies reduce downtime by an average of 87 percent when they move Web servers into vendor-owned hosting facilities. IDC also calculated that the return on investment (ROI) from outsourcing hosting can reach 300 percent, with a payback time on the investment of only 120 days.[5] Morgan Stanley Dean Witter estimates that outsourcing hosting and data center management can reduce costs by as much as 80 to 90 percent.[6]

Although the hosting industry (and in fact the entire telecommunications sector of the world economy) recently has been beset by a downturn, including spectacular bankruptcies, the fundamental economic advantages of hosting remain. The successes of hosting providers such as Digex in attracting enterprise customers suggest that large companies eventually will provide the most significant customer base for the industry.[7]

Incremental Service Levels in Hosting[8]

Table 7.1 shows the layers of services a hosting provider can offer. The base service level—real estate services—is similar to the business of leasing office space. Although this level of outsourcing provides robust facilities, it leaves the management and ownership of networks, computers, and software applications to the customer. All that has changed is the physical location of the computers delivering IT services. The same development and maintenance staff members care for the computers, and the customer continues to own all application computing equipment.

In addition to space and utilities, most hosting providers can manage networks, physical computing equipment, application performance, and even applications. As

---

[5]Melanie Posey, Beryl Muscarella, and Randy Perry, "Achieving Rapid Return on Investment in Outsourced Web Hosting," IDC white paper, 2000.

[6]Jeff Camp, April Henry, Jaime Gomezjurado, and Kristen Olsavsky, "The Internet Hosting Report," Morgan Stanley Dean Witter, November 2000.

[7]Much of the economic malaise experienced by so-called new economy hosting companies such as Exodus can be traced to the high density in their client base of dot-coms.

[8]Some of the material in this section is adapted from Robert D. Austin, "Web and IT Hosting Facilities: Technology Note," Harvard Business School Publishing Note No. 601-134.

TABLE 7.1   Levels of Service from Hosting Providers

Level of Service	Description of Service
Business operating services	Administering and operating an application
Application support services	Support for software above the operating system level; application support; application performance monitoring and tuning; design of applications for scalability, reliability, security
Platform services	Support for hardware, operating system; reboot services; data backup and disaster recovery services; URL monitoring
Network services	Connectivity within the facility and externally to the public Internet and to private peering networks; monitoring of network traffic at the transport layer; service-level assurances at the packet loss and network availability layers; network security
Real estate services (lowest level)	Suitable floor space and physical facilities; maintenance of the space and facilities

we move up the levels of service in Table 7.1, the outsourcing increment—the dollars the customer spends and the percentage of effort outsourced—grows larger.

Hosting industry models align with customer requirements for different service levels. Some providers specialize in particular models. For example, some focus on lower real estate and network management service levels only. But the trend is toward supporting higher levels of service as well. Hosting models can be roughly categorized along service level lines, as follows:

Colocation hosting. Colocation hosting companies provide no-frills access to a facility and its infrastructure. Customers rent floor space, connectivity, and power. Everything beyond these basics is provided à la carte and not necessarily by the hosting provider. Customer space is usually enclosed inside floor-to-ceiling cages, and the customer owns and retains responsibility for all the servers and equipment inside the cages. Often the hosting company knows little about the equipment or business operations inside customers' cages. This model requires customers to have (or acquire from a third party) the expertise to design, maintain, and operate the equipment inside the cages. This model, which supports a wide range of architectural possibilities, generally offers high availability.

Shared hosting. In shared hosting, servers are owned and operated by the hosting provider and customers purchase space on servers. Multiple customers share a single physical server. Some providers use sophisticated clustering technologies to achieve highly secure and reliable performance. This model, however, is considered best suited to non-mission-critical hosting for small companies or individuals when low cost is an important requirement. Some customers are wary of the degree of sharing implicit in this model because of its perceived negative implications for security and reliability.

Dedicated hosting. Just as with shared hosting, in dedicated hosting, servers are owned and operated by the hosting provider. Unlike a shared model, however, customers do not share servers; the servers are "dedicated" to individual customers. Other infrastructure components that provide network, storage, and some other services are shared across customers. Usually, dedicated hosting providers offer a complete managed services package that includes everything needed to run the customer's systems at the required level of security and availability. Dedicated servers, in fact, support high levels of security and availability.

IDC separates the dedicated hosting category into three subcategories, in which service offerings are divided into even smaller increments:[9]

- **Simple dedicated hosting.** This option relies on server "appliances" (i.e., simplified Web servers) to deliver a narrow menu of highly standardized functions such as basic Web hosting. Server appliances, which do not require complex configurations, are simple and inexpensive to operate. In this dedicated hosting model, server appliances are typically allocated one per customer. Although it is inexpensive, dedicated hosting supports a limited range of functions only.

- **Complex dedicated hosting.** This option uses two or more servers with different functions (e.g., Web, application, database servers) to meet a single customer's business needs. It supports a wider range of functions than does simple dedicated hosting, but standardized hardware and software configurations are still emphasized. The hosting company partners with the manufacturers and developers of the components that constitute the hoster's standard offerings, and the hosting provider's staff becomes vendor-certified to support those components. By focusing on more complex standard configurations than those in simple dedicated hosting, this model facilitates reliable and economical operation of larger computer systems whose functions are still somewhat limited.

- **Custom dedicated hosting.** As the name suggests, hosting offerings in this category are designed specifically to support custom functionality. Custom configured architectures involve multiple servers beyond the hosting company's established standards. To reliably design, build, and operate custom architectures, hosting providers often have to team with systems integrators and other service providers, who work and bill on a one-time, project basis, to design and deploy the custom infrastructure. This hosting model provides, in essence, a completely customized service offering composed of exactly the service level increments a customer wants to purchase.

It should be apparent from this variety of hosting model alternatives that outsourcing data center infrastructure management is not an all-or-nothing choice. Connectivity service providers—to take another example—offer increasingly incremental service levels with much more attractive risk and expense management pro-

---

[9]Melanie A. Posey and Courtney Munroe, "Web Hosting Service: US Web Hosting Market Forecast, 1999–2004," IDC Research Report, December 2000.

files for customers. Do you want 1 megabit per second (mps) of connectivity to the Internet backbone? Ten mps? How about 1 mps "burstable"[10] to 10 mps? Gigabit Ethernet? The options in service provision are multiplying, and infrastructure managers now often can purchase exactly the service increments they want.

Managing Relationships with Service Providers

When they acquire IT services externally, companies inevitably find themselves engaged in relationships with a growing number of service providers. As the operations of service providers and their customers become intertwined, the customer firm comes to rely on the provider's capabilities as a basis for its own capabilities. Consequently, as with all outsourcing of important business functions, whether supplying just-in-time parts to a manufacturing assembly line or managing computing platforms, healthy relationships with vendors are critical to how well a company performs its primary business mission. Mistakes by vendors can be costly. Services are only as good as the weakest link in the service provider chain. Choosing reliable service providers and managing strong vendor relationships therefore are critical skills for an IT manager.

Selecting Service Provider Partners

The most critical step in assembling an IT service chain is the selection of providers. Providers differ greatly in the service increments they offer, how they charge for services, the guarantees they *can* make, and the guarantees they are *willing* to make. No expertise in relationship management can overcome choosing an unreliable service provider. Infrastructure managers therefore must take tremendous care in selecting business partners that perform vital service chain functions.

The most common process for selecting service providers involves writing a "request for proposal" (RFP) and submitting it to a set of apparently qualified vendors. An RFP asks prospective providers for information relevant to their service capabilities across a spectrum that includes financial, technical, and operational information. Responses become a primary basis for deciding between vendors. Companies, however, rarely rely entirely on RFP responses but instead gather additional information from industry analysts, from other companies that have used providers' services, and from visits to service provider sites. Many companies employ elaborate scoring mechanisms for combining information gathered from all sources into comparable bases. But selection always comes down to the judgment of management.

There is no single format for RFPs, nor are there universally agreed on categories of information or sources that should be consulted in selecting providers. RFPs, however, typically request information in the following categories:

Descriptive information. How it describes its business reveals much about a service provider's priorities and likely future direction. Descriptive information

---

[10]Burstable bandwidth options allow customers to use extra bandwidth if they need it for short periods in return for a higher per megabit price.

is equally relevant in evaluating the prospective provider's capacity to provide services (e.g., is it big enough to meet your demands?).

Financial information. A service provider's financial strength is a critical factor in evaluating the continuity of service and service quality a vendor is likely to provide. Providers that struggle financially may have trouble maintaining service quality or may require financial assistance that reduces or eliminates the economic benefits of acquiring a service externally. Worse, they may fail and shut down, leaving the customer firm to navigate the provider's bankruptcy.

Proposed plan for meeting service requirements. How the provider offers to meet the requirements laid out in the RFP indicates whether it truly understands the requirements. The plan for meeting the requirements can be evaluated on its merits and compared with proposed plans from other vendors. Partner firms that will be involved in the vendor's plan should be identified so that the customer firm can be assured of the qualifications of all the parties involved in service provision.

Mitigation of critical risks. A good RFP asks specific questions about potential service risks. Availability and security are two areas where it pays for customers to be sure they understand a service provider's approach.

Service guarantees. A service provider's guarantees (the levels of performance it is willing to back with penalty clauses in a contract) are important signals of the real level of confidence vendor managers have in their services. Often there is a substantial gap between what the performance service providers claim is their norm and what they are willing to guarantee. If the gap is too wide, often the services will not be as robust as advertised. Service guarantees are essential to aligning incentives between service providers so that overall, the service chain performs well.

Pricing. Pricing usually includes one-time and variable components and may be structured in other ways as well. Although pricing is important for most companies, it usually is not the most important factor in deciding between vendors.

Table 7.2 shows a summary of information about three hosting providers that might be gathered from an RFP and other sources.[11] A close look at the information demonstrates that often choices between vendors are nontrivial. Providers that are strong in one area may be weak in another, and often no clear choice emerges.

For example, in Table 7.2 the fact that Provider 1 seems unwilling to supply financial information is probably a red flag that signals further investigation. Even if Provider 1's funding sources are gold-plated, customers need specific assurance that a service provider has a viable business model and will be a strong partner well into the future. Similarly, infrastructure managers might reasonably be worried about

[11]This example is taken from Robert D. Austin, "Selecting a Hosting Provider," Harvard Business School Exercise No. 601-171.

TABLE 7.2 Summary Grid for Comparing Hosting Providers

Comparison Dimension	Provider 1	Provider 2	Provider 3
Company description	Regional hosting and broadband (backbone, DSL) service provider	National hosting services provider	Regional telco, backbone and broadband service provider
Employees	1,600	3,300	28,000
Financial profile	Declined to provide (private company)	After-tax loss $180 million on sales of $600 million; strong cash position; new facilities building offered as explanation for lack of profitability	After-tax profit of $1.1 billion on sales of $13 billion (most not from hosting business)
Number of data centers managed/ total square feet	3 data centers/ 160,000 sq. ft.	28 data centers/1.6 million sq. ft.	5 (2 operational)/ 220,000 sq. ft. (45,000 operational)
Space offered (RFP specified space for six racks of equipment)	3 8′×8′ cages (192 sq. ft.), partitions removed to provide contiguous space	3 8′×7′ cages (168 sq. ft.), partitions removed to provide contiguous space	280 sq. ft. enclosed room
Physical security	Fully meets requirement	Fully meets requirement	Some concerns (see notes from site visit)
Power	Fully meets requirement	Fully meets requirement	Connected to only one power grid; two promised within 6 weeks
Connectivity	Fully meets requirement	Fully meets requirement	Not redundant to backbone; promised redundancy in 6 weeks
Service-level guarantees	Fully meets requirement	Fully meets requirement	Partially meets requirement
One-time setup cost, space	$6,500	$7,800	$10,800
Monthly space rental	3 × $6,500	3 × $6,800	$9,800
One-time setup cost, connectivity	$1,200	$1,500	$1,600
Variable connectivity cost	$1,200 per month plus $525 per month for each mbps above 10	$1,500 per month plus $589 per month for each mbps above 10	$900 per month plus $412 per month for each mbps above 10

Source: Adapted from Robert D. Austin, "Selecting a Hosting Provider," Harvard Business School Exercise No. 601-171. Although based on real cases, these data are fictitious and do not pertain to any real hosting provider.

Provider 2's lack of profitability. Provider 2 relates the losses to its expansion plans, but prospective customers might wonder if the company can transition as easily to profit-making as its managers suggest. In this scenario, Provider 3 looks like the solid choice because it is large and profitable and its fees are lower.

Unfortunately, there are reasons to worry about Provider 3. Most of the company's revenues come from business other than hosting services. This situation may translate into a lack of focus on the hosting business. Furthermore, Provider 3 seems to have some serious operational problems. Table 7.3 shows a discouraging report from a team that visited Provider 3's data center. In light of the report, one wonders whether Provider 3's lower prices are a miscalculation and perhaps evidence of the company's inexperience in hosting services. If so, the low prices eventually may become a problem for Provider 3's customers as well, especially if low profitability in the hosting business causes that provider's managers to further reduce their attention to hosting. Worse yet, if Provider 3 discovers it is losing money on hosting, it may seek to reduce costs in ways that affect service levels or even discontinue its hosting business.

We have stumbled here onto a general truth of outsourcing that we will return to in Chapter 9: *An outsourcing deal that is too one-sided, too favorable to one party at the expense of the other, usually ends up as a bad deal for both sides.* As they realize the deal is a loser, the managers of a disadvantaged vendor almost always divert resources away from the relationship. This realization brings us to the next subject: managing relationships with providers once they are in place.

Relationship Management

Relationships with service provider partners require ongoing attention. Processes must be in place so that partners can share information and problems in the service chain can be solved quickly even when they result from complex interactions of infrastructure components owned by different players. Problem-tracking and customer relationship systems, for example, must be able to exchange problem-tracking information as well as, sometimes, customer account information. Procedures and technical interfaces between partner systems must be properly designed and maintained.

More significant than problems with information-sharing systems, though, are the many incentive problems that attend collaborative service chain relationships. The most formidable obstacles are sometimes not technical but "political." When avoiding responsibility for a problem intrudes into the process of solving it, the service collaboration becomes less effective. A key to effective relationships is aligned incentives among partners.

A service-level agreement (SLA) is the prevalent contractual tool used to align incentives in relationships with service providers. SLAs describe the specific conditions by which the service provider is held liable for a service interruption and the penalties that the service provider will incur as a result. Table 7.4 illustrates the kinds of contractual terms one finds in an SLA. In keeping with our earlier examples, this SLA is for a hosting provider. Notice that failure is specifically defined, penalties apply only when the service provider is responsible for the service interruption, and

TABLE 7.3   Sample Facility Visit Report for Hosting Provider 3

Initial walk around exterior: Renovated warehouse building (conventional brick, not hardened) shared with a delivery service. Urban setting amid a complex of warehouses. City workers doing roadwork near the facility, with heavy-duty digging (potentially fiber cable slicing) equipment. Data center on third floor. First floor and basement include a garage used by the delivery service. Panel trucks come and go on the lower levels on the north side. Second floor includes offices and appears to be empty. Never spoke to anyone who could tell us definitively how the second floor would be built out or if even that was the plan.

CCTV cameras visible around the perimeter of the facility. Diesel generators enclosed in 12-foot-high chain link, HVAC on roof. West side of building composed of a series of loading doors. On day of visit, three loading doors were open. We succeeded in climbing up onto the loading dock and walking right into a power infrastructure room where many UPSs were housed. Waited there, expecting CCTV or alarm to summon security; no one ever showed up. (Staff later explained this lapse by saying that the door was open to facilitate construction and renovation and that the guard who was posted there had been reprimanded.)

Entering facility: First-level security is building security. Guard appeared not to realize that there was a data center in the building. Ushered us up to the third floor, where we encountered an unoccupied security desk behind a sliding glass partition. One CCTV console visible at desk. It would have been easy to climb through the opening to the security desk and let ourselves into the facility. Biometric palm reader visible but dust-covered at door. Security guard who had walked us up called someone on radio, and someone came to let us in. Person who let us in came from somewhere outside the data facility, then let us in by leaning through the opening and hitting the buzzer, which was in reach. We stood inside the door while he made out visitor badges for us. He did ask to see picture IDs, but security was kind of a farce by this point and everyone was a little embarrassed (including us for them). The room we were standing in while he prepared badges approximated a man trap in that there was another door about 20 feet away that opened into the data center proper. Unfortunately, that door was propped open.

Cages: No cages. Everyone gets an enclosed room with keypad access. No raised floor; power comes in from above, as do comms. Bolt-in racks and shelves provided. Walls of rooms do not extend to roof, so possible to climb over walls or to toss something into enclosed room.

Verification of redundancy, security, etc.: Redundant power and connectivity not yet in place, although promised within six weeks. Network hardware for facility was exposed in an open area anyone walking to his or her own enclosed space would need to pass. No on-site NOC, although they expressed willingness to provide specific network monitoring on site on a contract basis; noted too that network operations were monitored from a regional NOC. Guy giving tour kept apologizing for the construction.

Concerns: This facility is not fully built yet, although some customers are operational. Provider promises to have it in shape in time consistent with our project, but fact is that we cannot compare this facility on an equal basis with the others. Facility being under construction did not explain all the lapses we saw.

Overall assessment: These guys don't appear to have the hosting business figured out yet. Maybe it's just that they are in a construction phase. But there was little that we saw that offered warm feelings during our tour.

Source: Robert D. Austin, "Selecting a Hosting Provider," Harvard Business School Exercise No. 601-171. Information in this report is fictitious and not intended to pertain to real hosting provider.

TABLE 7.4 An SLA Offered by a Hosting Provider

- Downtime—defined as sustained packet loss in excess of 50% for 15 consecutive minutes due to the failure of the hosting provider to provide services for that period (does not include scheduled maintenance time).
- Excess latency—defined as transmission latency in excess of 120 milliseconds round-trip time between any two points within the hosting provider's U.S. network.
- Excess packet loss—defined as packet loss in excess of 1% between any two points in the hosting provider's network.
- Each downtime period entitles customer to receive a credit equal to one day's recurring connectivity charge.
- Hosting provider guarantees two-hour response time in diagnosing problems within hosting provider and customer network.
- If problem is not within hosting provider and customer network, hosting provider will determine source within an additional two hours.
- Customer will be advised of reason for problem within one hour of hosting provider's discovery of the reason for the problem.
- If problem is within control of hosting provider, remedy for problem is guaranteed in two hours from diagnosis of the problem.
- Inability to deliver diagnosis or remedies within the times stated above entitles customer to an additional service credit for each two-hour period of delay.
- Customer can collect credits for no more than seven days' charges in a calendar month.
- Customer must request credits in writing within seven days of the event for which credits are compensation.
- Credits are granted at the sole discretion of the hosting provider.

penalties are prespecified and limited. Why a service provider insists on careful definitions is clear: to limit its liability for problems not under its control. But the specific nature of the agreement complicates service quality assurance. What matters to the client company is any failure regardless of which service provider causes it.

Managers of customer firms must therefore manage a *web* of SLAs with many service providers. SLAs in the web must interlock so that penalty payments flow through the service chain in a way that provides appropriate incentives. Suppose, for example, a company offering over-the-Net software functionality agrees to an SLA with a customer firm that requires the software company to pay a penalty if the system is not available for a period longer than 10 minutes. Suppose also that the actual cause of a failure is a different vendor, say, an Internet service provider (ISP). In that case an SLA in place between the software company and an ISP should specify that the ISP will reimburse the software company for the penalty it owes to the client company. Although the SLA arrangement between the software company and the ISP might seem a matter best left to those two entities, it is to the customer company's advantage to ensure that incentives are aligned. Disputes between partners in a service chain can have dire implications for the user of the service.

The conventional wisdom in defining SLAs calls for designing them with "teeth," that is, so that service providers feel pain when failures occur. In practice, however, it is difficult to determine appropriate penalty levels. SLAs provide service providers with both incentives and a way to credibly express their intention to deliver reliable service, and so it is important that they be in place. But setting penalties too low has little impact. Setting them too high is detrimental to a provider's willingness (and, if penalties are high enough, ability) to be a strong partner. Thus, whereas SLAs are important, it is a mistake to consider them the only means by which partners are managed. The most successful relationships emphasize shared objectives and helping all the partners earn a reasonable return.

Since many outsourced services involve entrusting data to service providers, contractual relationships need to contain provisions about a customer firm's rights to control its own data. The concern here is not that a vendor might try to claim ownership of customer data but that the vendor might try to lock the customer into a relationship by making it inconvenient to switch vendors. A company needs to retain its right to move data to another vendor. In its contract, the service provider must guarantee the customer's right to transfer data back to the company or to another vendor. Such a contractual provision addresses a common case, but the point is more general: The interests of service providers and their customers are poorly aligned when it comes to the degree of entanglement in their relationship. Regardless of the type of service, managers who use IT service providers must work to preserve service delivery options. Managers who take insufficient care in avoiding unnecessary entanglements will find themselves at the mercy of service providers, forfeiting a principal benefit of incremental outsourcing: the ability to alter and improve IT infrastructure in small steps in an ongoing manner.

Managing Legacies

Not too long ago, tax accountants at a major U.S. company discovered they were not taking full advantage of a benefit they could claim under the U.S. tax code. The tax law details of this story are unimportant, but the benefit was worth a substantial amount of money to the company if the accountants could claim it. But to claim the tax benefit, the company needed to process receivables in a very specific way. The tax accounting managers therefore convened a large meeting of all the people in the company who might have something to say about a change in how receivables were processed.

The meeting was nearly two-thirds finished when a relatively young, relatively junior employee seated near the back of the room interrupted the smooth flow of the meeting to the mild irritation of the senior manager from tax accounting.

"Excuse me," the young man said. Everyone knew he was from the IT department. "Can you help me . . . do I understand . . . ?" the young man stuttered as the glare of the room's attention turned entirely to him. "What you are proposing? Is it . . . ?" He then summarized his understanding of the proposal.

"Yes," the senior tax accounting manager answered. "That is the proposal, although we are working it through in detail with everyone here to make sure no one sees any issues with the change."

The young man smiled. "I've got news for you," he said. All those in the room braced themselves, expecting an explanation in incomprehensible IT terms of why the change could never be made within the company's IT infrastructure, at least not at a reasonable cost. What he said surprised everyone:

"We've been processing our receivables that way for the last 20 years. That's the way the system does it. That's how the program logic works."

The meeting was quickly adjourned as the tax accountants returned to their offices to see if they could figure out a way to apply for the benefit retroactively.

This story illustrates two very serious points. First and most obvious, company operations often are constrained by the way legacy systems process information. Old computer code often disturbingly manifests what have been called "core rigidities," the ossified remains of what were once capabilities.[12] Second, business managers often do not even know how their company performs certain vital business functions because the details are buried in how legacy systems operate. In this story, the managers' discovery about their company's operations was a happy one; more often, though, such discoveries are less welcome.

The difficulties that arise from legacy systems can be roughly categorized as follows:

Technology problems. Sometimes the constraints embedded in legacy systems result from inherent incompatibilities in older technologies. As we have seen, proprietary technologies that predate the Internetworking era were not designed to converse easily with technologies from other vendors. This kind of problem must be worked around in modern Internetworking infrastructures.

Residual process complexity. Some difficulties with legacy systems arise because the systems address problems that no longer exist. One example is the substantial amount of batch processing some companies still perform. Legacy systems were designed to operate in batch mode because processing power needed to be rationed and because the bandwidth available at that time did not allow computers to operate in real time. Now computing power and bandwidth are relatively abundant, but many batch systems have not been redesigned or replaced because of other priorities.

Local adaptation. Many legacy systems were developed for very focused business purposes within functional hierarchies. When such systems were designed, their architects had little inkling of the enterprise systems and real-time architectures of the then-distant future. Instead, systems were intended to solve a particularly narrow business problem. Not surprisingly, a system

---

[12]For a deeper discussion of core rigidities, see Dorothy A. Leonard, *Wellsprings of Knowledge: Building and Sustaining the Sources of Innovation* (Boston: Harvard Business School Press, 1998, paperback edition).

TABLE 7.5 Key Questions in Managing Legacies

Legacy systems	• How will new infrastructure exchange data with legacy systems? • Will new infrastructure obtain needed real-time interaction with legacy systems? • What work-arounds are necessary? Are they sustainable? • What is long-term strategy for renewing legacy systems?
Legacy organizations and cultures	• How will new infrastructure affect ways of working and communicating? Are anticipated changes acceptable? • Should technology drive organizational and cultural change? • Should organization and culture be protected from technology effects? • What are organizational expectations about common processes in different parts of the organization? • What are criteria for deciding whether systems or process will change when the two are not compatible?

designed for order processing of replacement parts for the aftermarket in the 1970s, for example, does not facilitate global uniform parts management in 2002, although it still may do its narrowly defined job very well.

Nonstandard data definitions. Throughout most companies, business units and divisions have used different conventions for important data elements. For example, the parts division might use a 15-character part number whereas the product development organization uses a 13-character part number. This may seem like a small difference (only two characters), but the legacy system implications are far-reaching. Differences in fundamental data definitions are built into a company's IT infrastructure in many specific places. They are difficult to change not only because they touch so many elements of the IT infrastructure but because making definitions common requires an expensive and difficult to achieve companywide consensus.

Because of the tremendous variety in legacy systems across companies, it is not possible to develop a prescriptive approach to dealing with legacy issues. Tactics for solving legacy problems must fit individual companies and their specific situations. However, there are questions managers should think through carefully before they contemplate growing infrastructure by adding new systems or services on top of existing systems.

Table 7.5 lists questions managers might ask about legacy systems that will have to interact with a new system or service. The first issue is whether legacy systems can, in any modified or enhanced form, perform consistently with real-time infrastructure objectives. If the answer is no, replacement may be the only option. Often, though, the answer is not definitively negative. Questions then focus on "work-arounds," contrivances needed to facilitate interaction between new and old infrastructure elements: whether they are sustainable and whether they represent reasonable cost/functionality trade-offs.

Many businesses have succeeded in adding interfaces to legacy systems that enable them to interact with Internetworking systems. This interfacing approach sometimes is called enterprise application integration (EAI). EAI practitioners recommend "noninvasive" interfaces that minimize changes to the internal operations of legacy systems. Even EAI enthusiasts, however, acknowledge limits to how well legacy systems can perform as components of real-time infrastructure. Sooner or later the problems of getting work-arounds to operate satisfactorily become more difficult and more expensive to solve than just replacing the old systems. Infrastructure managers always must ask whether the complexity of work-arounds is unreasonable.

When installing new infrastructure or acquiring new services, infrastructure managers also run up against organizational rather than technical legacies. Changing IT infrastructure unavoidably affects nontechnical elements of a company's operations, especially how people work and interact. A complex interrelationship exists between core rigidities that manifest themselves in ossified legacy systems and a firm's social systems and processes. Sometimes the rigidity of workers' attachment to how a system works (the process it follows) is as much or more of an obstacle to change as any technology factor. Moreover, changes in how systems work almost always force changes in how people work to a greater or lesser degree. The degree to which systems force cultural and process changes is a key management decision. The second half of Table 7.5 suggests questions that managers should ask as they confront organizational legacies that interact with system legacies.

Managing IT Infrastructure Assets

In the mainframe era, keeping track of the assets that made up a company's IT infrastructure was relatively easy. The majority consisted of a small number of large mainframe machines in the corporate data center. A company's investment in IT had a tangible presence. Senior business managers could point to it, even rap their knuckles against it if they wished. Because a company's infrastructure was centralized and because services were deployed from mainframe assets, companies found it relatively easy to track how systems were being used and estimate how much value they were providing.

After the emergence of PCs, clients and servers, the Web, portable devices, and distributed network infrastructure, a company's investments in IT became much more diffuse. Computing assets were scattered in a large number of small machines located in different buildings. Some (i.e., laptops) moved around with their users and left the company's premises on a regular basis. As we look forward, some new service delivery models could cause assets (e.g., servers) to migrate back to the corporate data center, which might seem to herald a return to centralized management models. Other model variations, such as outsourced hosting, make it clear, though, that complexity of infrastructure and distribution of IT assets are here to stay. As service delivery models proliferate and improve, the variety of IT asset configurations will increase.

The variety of asset configurations in modern IT infrastructures makes certain business questions hard to answer: How are IT investments deployed across business lines or units? How are IT assets being used? Are they being used efficiently? Are they deployed to maximum business advantage? How can we adjust their deployment to create more value? Although never easy to answer, these questions were at least reasonable when assets were centralized. Some of the thinking about IT management frameworks over the past decade or so has focused on reclaiming management control over IT assets.

One approach to this problem has been called total cost of ownership (TCO) analysis. IT services are analyzed in terms of the costs and benefits associated with service delivery to each client device. For example, the total cost of delivering office productivity services to a PC desktop within an enterprise might be expressed as "$250 per client per month." Arriving at this number requires a detailed study to determine the total monthly costs associated with the delivery of each service available on that client, including costs shared with other clients and costs not necessarily accounted for as line items in budgets or accounting systems. Once monthly costs are computed, they must be allocated on a per client basis. Totaling costs without missing any that are material is difficult, as is allocating costs to clients in a way that preserves the management usefulness of the information.

Completing the analysis on the benefit side of the equation is also difficult but essential if IT assets are to be used efficiently. Many who attempt TCO analyses settle for usage information—what services are used and with what frequency—on the benefit side of the equation rather than attempting to estimate the actual benefits to each user. Usage information on a per client, per month basis can be helpful compared with cost of service delivery on a per client, per month basis. Usage information also may be useful when computed on the basis of other platform types. For example, usage information on a per server basis might be useful in server-to-server comparisons, in planning for growth in server capacity, or in discovering opportunities for consolidating underused servers into a smaller number nearer their capacities.

Cost and benefit analysis for IT assets and platforms provides a basis for evaluating a company's current IT services against new service alternatives. Outsourcing vendors often are asked to bid on a per platform basis. These prices can be compared to study results to evaluate a company's options and identify incremental opportunities for service delivery improvement. Where a firm's costs of delivering an IT service are out of line with the price at which it can be acquired externally, outsourcing becomes comparatively appealing.

Summary   This chapter has explored the increasingly diverse nature of the infrastructure used to deliver IT services in 21st-century companies. We have described how more available and secure network connections are creating more service delivery options and how new options have led to the creation and restructuring of the service provider industry. Today companies acquire services externally from chains of service providers and integrate those external services into their internal legacy infrastructures. The shift toward incremental outsourcing and multiple, collaborating service delivery partners dictates a shift in management emphasis. The following questions should help a company assess the opportunities and the risks:

1. What services within our IT infrastructure are candidates for incremental outsourcing? Where are there opportunities to convert large up-front IT investments into spread-over-time subscription services?

2. Are our service delivery partners technically and financially capable enough to support our evolving IT service needs? Do we have well-defined processes for partner selection to ensure that we will continue to have highly capable partners?

3. Do we have detailed service-level agreements in place with our service providers? Have we made sure that the SLAs in our service delivery chains interlock and that incentives are aligned up and down the chain? Do we have systems in place for virtually integrating with service delivery partners? Have we specified contract terms with service providers that preserve our options for incrementally improving our infrastructure?

4. What are our short-term and long-term strategies for dealing with legacy system issues? What systems should we replace, and when should we replace them?

Managing and Leading a Networked IT Organization

by F. Warren McFarlan

Module

4

Although much has changed as information technology (IT) organizations have become networked, some core management issues have persisted. How should IT staff be organized to support business activities? Which IT functions should be performed inside the firm and which should be performed outside? How should we manage IT projects, especially megaprojects that have increased in size beyond anything in our past experience? We have inherited these questions from the past, but they have changed somewhat in this new era. Some of the answers are also changing.

The chapters in this module provide a basis for discussing these questions in their 21st-century form. We adopt a contingency approach intended to identify the factors that differ between organizations, business situations, and projects and to make recommendations appropriate to specific markets, firms, and projects. The overall result of our analysis is a portfolio framework that allows questions and recommendations to be formulated into policies consistent with a company's overall strategic direction.

8

Organizing and Leading the IT Function

The management structures needed to introduce new technologies into a company are quite different from those needed to maintain older, established technologies. A guiding principle is to encourage the information technology (IT) staff and business users to innovate with newer technologies while simultaneously focusing on control and efficiency of the existing systems. In the early 21st century, as we shift into the world of Internetworking, technology innovation is probably the more important of these concerns. In this chapter we discuss the range of alternatives in assigning responsibility and roles to business users, the IT staff, IT suppliers, and general managers in conducting IT activities and formulating IT policy.

Organizational Issues in the Control of IT Activities

Two sets of tensions guide policies for developing, deploying, and managing IT systems. The first set is between innovation and control. The emphasis a firm should place on aggressive innovation depends on a broad assessment of the potential strategic impact of IT on a firm and on management's willingness to take risks. If IT can greatly help a firm achieve its strategic objectives and managers are not too risk-averse, a significantly greater investment in innovation is called for than is the case if IT is considered merely helpful or if managers want to avoid all unnecessary risks. In today's IT environment the benefits promised by real-time Internetworking systems have shifted the emphasis toward more innovation.

As a company selects priorities and enlists resources to pursue its objectives, a second set of tensions may develop between the IT staff and business users. Users often are inclined to focus on short-term need fulfillment, solving today's problems right now, frequently at the expense of long-term IT architectural concerns, maintenance needs, or orderly deployment. The IT department, in contrast, tends to be preoccupied with standardization of solutions, mastery of technology, maintenance difficulties, and orderly deployment at the cost of a slow response, or no response, to legitimate business needs. Balancing the tension between the two groups is difficult and must take into account many factors, including corporate culture, IT's potential strategic impacts, and the urgency of short-term problems.

Table 8.1 illustrates the consequences when either the IT staff or business users inappropriately dominate IT resource allocation and project priorities. Very different application portfolios and operating problems emerge in the two circumstances. Because it is difficult to anticipate the implications of the introduction of new technology, neither the IT perspective nor the user perspective is more correct. Decisions about the proper balance between innovation and stability and the degree of IT or user control of priorities and resources are highly contingent on the business situation. In particular, when rapid innovation is required, managers must be sure that rigid policies do not interfere with experimentation and learning. As the following four examples demonstrate, there is no perfect prescription for successful IT innovation.

1. From Centralized, IT-Driven Innovation to Decentralized, User-Driven Innovation

Over a four-year period in the early 1990s a major textile company invested heavily in new systems for electronic commerce and order management. By executing a few very large, centrally managed projects, the company's IT department assured adherence to companywide standards for software, computing platforms, and communications. The new systems were considered a success by all involved. In 1998, however, management moved systems development activity from the central IT department to the divisions, a change that involved some 80 people. The goal was to align the development of new applications more quickly and effectively with the needs of senior divisional management. With IT standardization problems largely solved, the company was able to install a new organizational structure that enabled the divisions to innovate more rapidly around individual agendas. The results since the reorganization suggest that it has been extremely effective. In addition, IT standards have not yet been eroded.

2. User-Driven Innovation over IT Department Protests

The number one priority in a large machine-tool manufacturer's engineering department was implementing computer-aided design (CAD). Early success led the company to expand the CAD system scope significantly: Engineers modified the digital output from the system so that department personnel could feed it directly to computer-driven machine tools. To maximize the speed of deployment, engineers deliberately kept the project separate from concurrent work by the IT department on a related bill of material system. Although the CAD project was a major success, integration into the bill of material system remained an outstanding requirement.

TABLE 8.1   Possible Implications of Excessive IT and User Dominance

IT Dominance	User Dominance
Too much emphasis on database and system maintenance	Too much emphasis on problem focus
All new systems must fit data structure of existing system	IT feels out of control
	Explosive growth in number of new systems and supporting staff
All requests for service require system study with benefit identification	Multiple suppliers deliver services; frequent change in supplier of specific service
Standardization dominates with few exceptions	Lack of standardization and control over data and systems
IT designs/constructs everything	Hard evidence of benefits nonexistent
Benefits of user control over development are discussed but never implemented	Soft evidence of benefits not organized
Study always shows construction costs less than outside purchase	Few measurements/objectives for new system
Headcount of distributed minis and development staff growing surreptitiously	Technical advice of IT not sought; if received, considered irrelevant
IT specializing in technical frontiers, not user-oriented markets	User buying design, construction, maintenance, and operations services from outside
IT spending 80% on maintenance and 20% on development	User building networks to own unique needs, not to corporate need
IT thinks it is in control of everything	Some users growing rapidly in experience and use, while others feel nothing is relevant because they do not understand
Users express unhappiness	No coordinated effort between users for technology transfer or learning from experience
Portfolio of development opportunities firmly under IT control	Growth in duplication of technical staffs
No strong user group exists	Dramatically rising communications costs because of redundancy
General management is not involved but concerned	Duplication of effort and input everywhere because different data, hardware, and communications will not allow seamless movement

Because it was short-staffed, the IT department delayed the integration with the bill of material system. Emboldened by their success with the CAD system, the engineers proceeded with the integration on their own over the objections of IT management. IT managers feared that the engineers would not adhere to standards and, consequently, major operational problems would result. Nevertheless, because of the project's potential to immediately affect the company's product development life cycle, the engineering department received full support from senior management.

The enthusiastic engineers made the project work: The project slashed new product development time by half. The IT department remained decidedly unenthusiastic throughout the project. Although some integration issues remained after completion, the project was judged a great success.

3. From Decentralized, User-Driven Innovation to Centralized IT Management

A division of a large consumer products company made a substantial investment in desktop services with modest up-front cost justification. Even though it had only cursory direction and training, the IT department encouraged managers and administrative support personnel to "use" desktop systems. In the first year a number of uncoordinated projects emerged within the user community, including several sales force support applications and a number of spreadsheet applications. Users gained confidence and pursued new programs with enthusiasm.

Six months later the IT department was asked to develop a program to support these "experienced" users and bring some commonality and order to their disparate activities. By then business user applications were so fragmented that an IT manager estimated that it would take roughly two years to deploy an effective support program. Two years seemed like a long time to company managers. They asked themselves whether they should have developed the support program in advance and deployed desktop services with more centralized IT control in place.

The consensus answer to that question was no. Both IT and business management felt that an IT-driven desktop services project would have been viewed as an IT initiative and therefore would not have been embraced enthusiastically by business users. The two years it would take to gain management control of distributed user initiatives was a price the company was willing to pay for the zeal with which users had embraced the new technology. This decentralized approach stood in marked contrast with the company's traditionally centralized approach to managing its mature data processing technologies.

4. From Decentralized, User-Driven Innovation to Unexpected Centralized Innovation

A large South African retail chain installed a point-of-sale (POS) inventory tracking system in each of its 50-plus stores. The company's retail division initially funded the project for a narrow business purpose: to assist store managers in controlling inventory. POS information was to be used inside individual stores exclusively in order to accumulate daily sales totals and trigger reorders. The project was successful, and stores quickly achieved significant inventory savings.

Later, senior business managers asked the IT department to link store POS systems with central systems at corporate headquarters. The proposed links would feed data to new corporate software designed to measure product performance across stores and help manage warehouse stock levels throughout the retail chain. Because the communication protocols used by POS systems were incompatible with the protocols in use by IT at headquarters, implementing the project was expensive. Managers asked themselves whether the expensive incompatibility between POS system and corporate systems was evidence of a deficiency in their planning process.

The consensus answer to that question was no. A planning process that explored all possible future uses of POS data would have taken too long and delayed inventory savings in individual stores. Furthermore, planning stage estimates of the benefits of linking POS and corporate systems would have been highly speculative (if they could have been identified at all). The excess time necessary to link corporate systems might have weakened the cost/benefit case to the point where the project might have been canceled. The success of the first system set a baseline for future systems. The firm has since used the POS-to-corporate network to implement a customer loyalty card and gain a detailed understanding of the individual buying habits of its key customers.

Implications and Conclusions

These examples powerfully illustrate the impossibility of foreseeing the full impact of new technology and the consequent difficulty of specifying a single best way to allocate control over priorities and resource allocation in systems development and deployment. Too much focus on prescriptive policies, centralized control, or rapid proof of favorable results in the early stages of the adoption of new technology can prevent important learning that may lead to even more useful applications. Neither IT professionals nor business users have outstanding records in anticipating how new technologies will affect organizations. A general manager's role therefore is to facilitate the assimilation of new technology by continuously monitoring tensions and shifting emphases as appropriate between centralized and decentralized IT and user control-driven innovation.

In the balance of this chapter we discuss three aspects of the organizational issues in more detail. First, we address the key drivers in business users' desire to gain control over IT development, deployment, and management activities. Second, we analyze the need for centralized coordination of systems deployment and the pitfalls of uncontrolled proliferation of user-developed systems. Third, we identify and discuss core policies that IT management, user management, and general management must implement to balance tensions and produce favorable results. As we shall see, the general manager's role is particularly critical in creating an environment that facilitates technological change and organizational adaptation to that change.

Drivers toward User Dominance

A number of critical drivers encourage users to exercise control over internal systems development resources and sometimes to engage external IT resources (consultants or systems integrators) to address business needs. These drivers can be grouped into the following five categories.

Pent-Up User Demand

IT departments and suppliers often do not have the staff and budget needed to handle the volume of IT activities and projects. There are a number of causes for this disparity. Existing systems, for example, require sustained maintenance to accommodate changing regulatory and business requirements. As the number of automated systems in a firm increases and as systems age, the total volume of change requests increases. Ongoing customization of existing systems increases system complexity and makes enhancements more difficult. In addition, systems need to be adapted to major changes in IT architecture, such as the transition to enterprise and Internetworking systems.[1]

Bringing about these conversions, which are increasingly urgent as we move to real-time infrastructures, has been very expensive. They strain IT staff resources and at the same time effectively starve other departments of resources. It also is common for IT departments to expend significant resources to maintain and enhance existing systems but keep only a few resources available for developing and deploying new systems. To make matters worse, the most challenging, high-status, and high-paying IT jobs in the industry tend to be with computer vendors and software houses. The most talented members of a company's in-house IT staff are tempted to move to more glamorous jobs. Consequently, sometimes it is easier for IT departments to secure budget money than to find qualified staff. Delays caused by these factors have led to frustration and a strong desire by users to take matters into their own hands. As we shall see, the same factors act as drivers toward outsourcing.

The Need for Staff Flexibility

When an IT department and its vendors appear unresponsive to users' demands, the users see developing systems themselves as a nonconfrontational way to get work done. By deploying their own staff in IT roles or engaging services from outside integration or application service companies, business users significantly speed the process of meeting their requirements for IT functionality. There are benefits from closely linking both physical and operational IT resources and end users. Basing IT staff in the business user's department helps educate users to IT's value-adding potential. It reduces communication problems between developers/deployers and users. It makes employee promotions that involve rotating IT staff to other (non-IT) jobs within the department easier, thus enhancing user-IT coordination, and it facilitates moving end users to IT positions.

Growth in the IT Services Industry

Thousands of commercial off-the-shelf software packages are now available for specific IT applications. These packages range from simple accounts payable products to complete enterprise systems products. As we have seen, over-the-Net applications

---

[1] This problem began to emerge in the 1970s, when systems design philosophy shifted from incorporating data into programs to separating data from the processes that use the data.

and other outsourcing options are proliferating as well. To frustrated business users with urgent short-term business needs, these options appear beguiling. These systems are marketed by hardware and software vendors to business managers, and their functional features are emphasized; vendor sales representatives soft-pedal incompatibilities with the firm's existing infrastructure and software upgrade or maintenance problems. Frequently, a proposed point solution to a short-term business problem appears more cost-effective than having the work done or purchased by a central IT department. Often vendors quote a simple up-front price. Such projects seem to hold out the promise of freedom from red tape. Vendors argue, with some justification, that they are able to bring people into the project who are more skilled in current technologies than are those in the IT department.

Users' Desire to Control Their Own Destiny

The idea of regaining control over a part of their business operations, particularly if IT has become mission-critical, greatly appeals to business users. Control in this context has at least two dimensions.

First, users can exercise direct control over systems development priorities. By using either their own staff or software and services companies they select, users hope to obtain a system with vastly improved features in less time than it would take to navigate the priority-setting process in the corporate IT department. Additionally, development and deployment errors made by a user-managed group are sometimes easier to excuse than those made by a distant, centralized group. As a result, project difficulties may be more openly discussed, which can facilitate experimentation and learning during development.

Second, as business conditions change, business users often wish to control systems maintenance priorities. At the time of installation, users may not have weighed the importance of ongoing systems maintenance sufficiently. When they discover how relentlessly business changes drive system change requests, users become less willing to place their maintenance request in the queue with those of other business groups. If managers are being evaluated by how well their business units perform, the desire to have more complete control over change priorities is not altogether unreasonable.

Fit with the Organization

As companies become more global and their operations become more geographically dispersed, users sometimes feel compelled to control systems development and deployment. Their local concerns increasingly diverge from corporate IT initiatives. Similarly, when divisions adopt highly specialized business models that differ from those of other divisions, choices made by corporate IT staffs seem less consistent with the needs of the division. For example, a division of a pharmaceuticals firm focused on cost leadership in commodity products (such as IV fluid bags or other hospital supplies) will take a different approach to IT than will a division with a more traditional research and development (R&D)-intensive, high-margin business model. If corporate IT is driven by high-margin assumptions, inherent priorities may be poorly suited to a more cost-conscious division. Decentralized IT activities may then gain appeal. Decentralized development, deployment, and management avoid the high levels of coordination effort required to keep centralized IT departments attuned to local needs. Finally, if a company decides to divest a unit, the process will be easier if IT activities are not completely integrated with the rest of the company.

Together, these five drivers represent a powerful argument for a strong user role in systems development and suggest when that role might be dominant. Although benefits sometimes can be achieved, as the earlier examples demonstrated, when business users control development, deployment, and management of IT resources, there also may be a downside. As one might expect, the downside of a decentralized IT structure alternative supports the argument for centralized control of IT projects and resources, to which we now turn our discussion.

Drivers toward a Centralized IT Structure

A number of pressures encourage firms to consolidate IT development resources into a more centralized unit. These pressures can be grouped into the following categories.

Staff Professionalism

Maintaining a central IT department enhances an organization's ability to recruit and retain specialized technical personnel by providing more obvious career paths for talented IT employees. In addition, it is easier to keep centralized staff up to date on the latest technologies and develop the necessary skill sets. Moreover, an IT department serves as the focus of deliberate efforts to maintain certain areas of technical competence or expertise. The employees of a centralized IT group have fewer concerns, therefore, about losing pace with the advance of technology or getting lost in the organization when it comes to career development. The inability of some firms to manage the personal development of the IT staff is a key driver for outsourcing IT activities.

Standard Setting and Ensuring System Maintainability

Many organizations experience periodic swings of the centralize/decentralize pendulum because over time the benefits of change often give way to new problems. As we have seen, standardized computing infrastructure pays dividends by reducing the complexity and cost of maintaining a firm's IT capabilities. When IT resources are centrally concentrated, developing and enforcing standards in infrastructure and in IT management practice are easier. Indeed, if IT resources are not centralized but report directly to business user organizations, setting companywide standards almost always takes a backseat to short-term business concerns. Inefficiency in maintaining the IT infrastructure is the cumulative long-term effect of consistently sacrificing standards in favor of short-term concerns. Ironically, inefficiency is a major reason why IT resources are sometimes not available to address short-term business needs. Conversely, centralized IT management activities can increase efficiency dramatically. For example, a recent study at a manufacturing firm showed that centralizing control of its $16 million investment in networked personal computers yielded maintenance cost savings of 40 percent.

In 1988, a large chemical company faced deteriorating relationships between its central IT department and key business user constituencies. When the situation grew chronic, company managers responded by redistributing 80 percent of IT development staff to four divisions, changing both reporting responsibilities and physical locations. Although the change stimulated new ideas and better relationships with users, by 1993 the need for standards to control the costs associated with proliferating user-driven systems development became so intense that the company instituted significantly tighter standards and management practices. In 1997 company managers outsourced the crash development of Intranets and Extranets. The basic decentralized structure, however, was still in place in mid-2001.

Central staff expertise is particularly important for reviewing user-designed systems before they go live. Lacking practical systems design experience, users often ignore data management and security policies, corporate standards, and costing practices that incorporate the full cost of running an application. The managers at a large financial firm learned this lesson the hard way when they discovered that all the user employees who had developed an essential system had left the company without creating any documentation or operating instructions. Even worse, the system had not been subjected to any version control, and the source code was nowhere to be found. All that remained were machine-readable object programs. The system ran, but no one knew exactly what it was doing, and the managers could not change the system.

Envisioning Possibilities and Determining Feasibility

Not surprisingly, most business users are not adept at envisioning the possibilities inherent in new technologies or expert in judging the feasibility of technical applications. Users often focus on obtaining a specific service to address an immediate need without recognizing the fact that successful first applications tend to generate unanticipated second applications (and then third applications, etc.). Their limited experience with IT makes it difficult for business users to see the full implications of the application of a technology; an example is planning that fails to account for possible growth or future expansion of applications. This problem caused some users to see the Web at first as merely a better way to manage documentation. Inability to envision what a system may someday become and to make choices consistent with those possibilities can make future expansion expensive or even infeasible.

User-driven feasibility studies may contain major technical mistakes. Typical consequences include a system that does not handle growing processing requirements or is not cost-effective in operation. Users are often inclined to acquire products with attractive visible features from unstable vendors. Indeed, users may be unable to see the technological drawbacks of an IT product that may predispose its vendor to fail. Accurate assessment of vendor stability is critical because many systems eventually insinuate themselves into the heart of a company's operations. In many cases, extracting unsupported systems from a company's infrastructure is expensive and exceedingly difficult, as is converting applications to new systems and platforms. A single experience with a failed vendor can be a painful learning process.

Corporate Data Management

As we have seen in earlier chapters, the Internetworking capabilities of today's corporations make it possible to synchronize databases across an enterprise. A modern data management strategy requires central coordination of physically distributed databases so that users, regardless of their physical location, can access data files as needed. A central IT staff provides a focal point for conceptualizing and developing the architecture of these systems.

The need for data sharing varies widely with the nature of a company's activities. A conglomerate usually has much less need for data sharing across the firm than does a functionally organized, one-product company. Most firms, however, need companywide, fully interoperable e-mail, videoconferencing, video streaming, and financial systems, to name only a few. All these applications employ database components. Increasingly, enterprisewide interoperability and data exchange are a part of new IT projects. Only a central IT department can cost-effectively develop and distribute such systems to users or coordinate distributed development projects in a way that assures interoperability.

Whenever the subject of decentralized development within individual business units is broached, a competent IT manager's first concern is that the company may lose its ability to manage and control data flows between disparate applications. The narrow perspective of development driven by the short-term problems of a particular business unit may produce data definitions, structures, and systems that lock up data in a nonstandardized format and in inaccessible locations so that they cannot be used enterprisewide. Modern data management and communication standards make it easier to avoid such outcomes. In fact, effective data management policies and standards make it possible for a company to achieve the best of both organizational worlds: responsive decentralized development and products that interoperate through centralized data management hubs. Databases constructed to be consistent with corporate data standards can exchange data periodically or, in some cases, continuously with physically distant databases, keeping the company's data in sync.

In recent years, finding ways to keep data secure has been a growing concern. Security issues are best addressed through centralized control. And security standards are more easily achieved with centrally organized electronic files. In a world of increasingly clever hackers, a company needs to be sure its data are secure and certainly needs to know where all data stores are located. Indeed, some data are so sensitive that they are best kept off the network entirely.

Cost Estimation and Analysis

Because it has practical experience in a broad range of systems efforts, a centralized IT group usually has a better chance of producing realistic systems development and deployment estimates than do decentralized user-based groups. This is not always the case; estimation is often difficult and poorly done even in the best conditions. Inexperienced estimators tend to be too optimistic. Additionally, during the project changes, they approve insufficient accounts of possible complications that add over-head time and cost to the project.

Users seldom understand the true costs of operating the existing services. In many companies, complicated charge-back schemes for allocating the centralized costs of IT services and facilities back to business user departments add to the confusion about costs. Many charge-back methods are historical remnants of frame-works convenient for cost accountants. Often they present measurements of computer resource use that are unfathomable to the business user; for example, each month an unintelligible bill arrives with an unpredictable amount due. In management control environments, where the business user is responsible for variance from budgets, the unpredictability of the true costs causes frustration. In comparison, a locally developed system exhibits understandable and predictable costs. Because corporate charge-back systems are designed to allocate all centralized costs and be-cause overhead allocation methods are often problematical, charges often appear un-fairly distributed and sometimes very high to business users. Disproportionately high allocations provide some business users with strong but corporately subopti-mal incentives for local development.

In the short run much of a company's IT cost is fixed, but it appears to the in-dividual user, because of the charge-back system, as if it were a variable cost that could be reduced. This representation, especially for overhead allocation, is not accurate and sometimes encourages individual user cost reductions that actually generate cost increases for the company as a whole. Cost analysis and manage-ment, using an activity-based computing utility framework, is the only way to as-sure that local decision making is consistent with overall company objectives. This kind of cost management is best mounted from within a centralized IT group ori-ented toward corporate rather than local objectives.

Long-term perspectives and methodical deployment of architectural ideals char-acterize pressures toward centralized IT control. The benefits of central control are long-term cost avoidance and technological risk reduction. The downside of this ap-proach, however, is lack of short-term responsiveness to local business issues and problems. In this age of Internetworking, stand-alone systems and business units tend to become part of a centralized network. Thus, the tensions involved in man-aging IT development and deployment are fully in play. Policies for managing the trade-offs between the obvious short-term benefits and the long-term risks are nec-essary but delicate to administer.

Coordination and Location of IT Policy

The tension between IT staff and business users can be managed by establishing clear policies that specify the user domain, the IT domain, and senior management's role. Senior management must play a significant role in ensuring that these policies are developed and evolve appropriately over time. Both IT staff and users must un-derstand the implications of their roles and the conflicts that may arise as they work together.

IT Responsibilities

The following tasks constitute the central core of IT responsibilities—the minimum for managing the long-term IT needs of an organization.

1. Develop and manage the long-term architectural plan and ensure that new projects fit within the plan. Periodically review and revise the plan and be sure IT stakeholders agree about the objectives and details of the plan. In today's world of enterprise systems and real-time Internetworking, stakeholder agreement and backing are critical.

2. Develop a process to establish, maintain, and evolve company standards in the following areas:

   • Telecommunication protocols and platforms

   • Client devices and client software configurations

   • Server devices, middleware, and database management systems

   • Programming and configuration languages

   • Documentation procedures and formats

   • Data definitions, especially for data elements used throughout the company

   • Storage redundancy, backup, and disaster recovery procedures

   • Information security policy and incident response procedures

   This process and the resulting standards must accommodate innovation by business users, experimentation that can lead to important learning, and real differences in the business requirements of particular business units.

3. Establish procedures that consider outsourcing options when new IT projects are proposed. Ensure that outsourced or user-executed projects adhere closely to corporate standards, are consistent with overall corporate objectives, and take into account interfaces to corporate systems.

4. Maintain an inventory of installed and planned systems and services. To the degree possible, periodically reexamine the total benefits and costs of operating and maintaining these systems and services for consistency with business objectives.

5. Identify career paths for IT staff. Include lateral transfers within and between IT units, upward movement within the IT organization, and outward movement from IT to other functional units. When IT activities are decentralized, this task takes on special importance because career paths for IT personnel may not seem obvious.

6. Establish internal marketing efforts that help business users understand the challenges of IT support and the hidden costs of maintaining IT systems. Encourage business units to modernize when their systems become expensive to run because of age. Also encourage business units that are pushing too fast into leading-edge technologies to slow down or at least take account of their full exposure to risks and costs.

7. Incorporate, as a standard part of the request for proposal (RFP) process when acquiring new hardware or software, a detailed checklist that includes questions about compatibility with existing architecture and standards. For example:

   • Is the proposed new hardware or software technology consistent with corporate standards? If not, where are the points of departure? Do they have serious consequences?

   • Will the new technology support future growth and does it support information exchange within the company's evolving real-time infrastructure?

   • Is the new technology maintainable over the long term?

8. Identify and maintain relationships with preferred systems suppliers. In entering a relationship with a vendor, be sure that the client company's standards enforcement efforts have a basis in the contract with the vendor and that vendor pricing and planning take into account the need to comply with standards.

9. Establish education programs for business users that introduce the benefits and pitfalls of new technologies. Define users' roles in ensuring the successful introduction of new technology in their departments.

10. Set up a process for ongoing review of legacy systems to determine when they should be redesigned and/or replaced.

The tasks for which IT is responsible are particularly important for systems that will become deeply embedded in a company's day-to-day operations. For less operationally critical systems, IT managers can afford more flexibility with respect to standards and responsibilities, although the increasingly integrated nature of infrastructure imposes additional demands even on systems traditionally considered less mission-critical.

If a company's situation warrants it, these core responsibilities can be expanded significantly to impose much tighter and more formal controls. As we have seen, though, because of the uncertain implications of new technology and the resulting difficulty in fully foreseeing impacts, users must apply standards and responsibilities intelligently. A company (or a division or smaller organizational group) might reasonably choose to depart from standards as it tries a new technology. Because standards and responsibilities are not ends in themselves, they should be reviewed frequently. The tendency in IT is to weigh long-term issues more heavily than short-term business needs. Often this is reasonable, but in some cases, if short-term needs are not addressed adequately, there may not be long-term benefits. IT managers therefore must remain flexible as they carry out their duties.

User Responsibilities

To identify IT opportunities, implement new IT services, and understand the uses, costs, and impacts of IT on an organization, business users should take on the following responsibilities:

1. Seek to understand the scope of all IT activities supporting business users. As much as possible, figure out the IT charge-back system and pressure the IT department to

establish an activity-based overhead allocation system that users can understand and use in decision making.

2. Develop realistic estimates of the amount of user personnel investment required for new projects both during development/deployment and in ongoing operation and use. Business users have a tendency to underestimate or even ignore new project costs of this type.

3. Ensure comprehensive user input for all IT projects that support vital aspects of the unit's operations. Take a strong interest in how the service will operate, how it will be introduced, and the level of user training required for both staff and managers.

4. Ensure that the nature of staffing interfaces is consistent with a new technology's strategic relevance to a business unit. If a new technology project is very important, the staffing interface must be close, customized, and based on personal relationships. If the new project is not strategically important, staffing interfaces can be more arm's-length and standardized.

5. Periodically audit system reliability standards, communications services performance, and security procedures.

6. Participate in developing and maintaining IT plans that set new technology priorities, schedule the transfer of IT among groups, and evaluate projects in light of the company's overall strategy.

These responsibilities represent the minimum advisable level of user involvement in a company's IT activities. Depending on a firm's geography, corporate management style, degree of reliance on IT capabilities, stage of IT evolution, mix of technologies, and a variety of other factors, more extensive levels of user involvement may be appropriate. In general, more user involvement is preferable to less. Many companies have come to associate the assignment of full-time user staff to IT projects with expectations of project success.

General Management Support and Policy Overview

In most companies there is a cluster of IT policy and directional activities that require a senior management perspective. In the past these activities were carried out within a central IT organization. Today, because IT has become so critical a part of strategy and day-to-day operational capabilities for so many companies, these activities are carried out at a higher level, in the context of a broader business discussion. In many companies, then, long-range IT planning activities are separated from day-to-day operational activities. Increasingly, the long-range discussions involve senior general managers supported by talented technology specialists.

A chemical company, for example, reorganized in 1990 to establish a 500-person systems and operations department reporting directly to the head of administrative services. This department oversees the company's implementation and operational IT work on a month-to-month, year-to-year basis. At the same time, a 25- to 30-person IT policy group, which reports directly to the head of research, works on overall IT policy and long-range IT strategy for the firm. Similarly, a major conglomerate whose development staff and hardware are distributed in business units still maintains a small but important policy-oriented group at the headquarters level. Even firms that outsource most or all of their IT development and operations need such a policy group to facilitate senior management involvement in vital IT strategy issues.

The key responsibilities of a corporate IT policy group include the following:

1. Ensure an appropriate balance between IT and business users to prevent one group's perspective from dominating. Transfer personnel, reorganize, or create new organizational bodies to keep tensions in balance. For example, an executive steering committee might provide more user input and thus might rectify a situation where the balance had tipped too far toward IT control.

2. Make sure the company has a comprehensive corporate IT strategy. Base the strategy on an overview of technology trends, assessment of the company's current IT capabilities, and the potential of IT initiatives to support overall corporate goals. Such a strategy is particularly important in companies with decentralized IT resources.

3. Manage the inventory of hardware and software systems and services and assure that a corporate orientation extends to purchasing relationships and contracts. In most companies a corporate group is the appropriate place to identify and manage standard policies for relationships with vendors.

4. Establish standards for acquisition, development, and IT systems operation. Ensure that the standards are applied appropriately. With standards adherence, corporate policy groups sometimes play a combined role as consultant and auditor. Hence, a corporate policy group needs to have a technically competent and interpersonally sensitive staff.

5. Facilitate the transfer of technology from one unit to another. Successful corporate policy groups will develop a knack for spotting synergistic technology and system opportunities. The tools the policy group can use to facilitate technology transfer include staff visits across business units, periodic corporate conferences on IT themes, and other communication means, such as newsletters and streamed audio or video programs.

6. Actively encourage technical experimentation. A limited program of research is a very appropriate part of the IT function. An important role of the corporate policy group is to ensure that research and scanning for new technology opportunities do not get swept aside by urgent operational issues. Further, a corporate policy group is in a position to encourage and coordinate patterns of experimentation that smaller units might consider too risky without corporate support.

7. Develop an appropriate planning and control system to link IT to a company's goals. The policy group should monitor planning, system appraisal, charge-back, and project management processes.

As these responsibilities imply, the corporate IT policy group needs to be staffed with people who have broad technical backgrounds and extensive practical IT administrative experience. Perhaps the most important talent, however, is the ability to engage senior business managers so that they can make strategic decisions about proposed IT applications. Attention to IT issues is not a natural inclination for many senior managers, especially in long-established companies. Many senior managers came of age before the current explosion in IT opportunities and therefore are not comfortable in IT discussions. Nevertheless, in most companies IT issues have broadened to the point where they are very important to general management. A company's success, then, may well be tied to general managers becoming involved in IT discussions.

IT Leadership and the Management of Budgets

In most companies organizational structure is an obvious determinant of control over priorities and resources, but there are others. Budgets are an important control mechanism. By adjusting the size of budgets and defining their range of acceptable use, companies can increase or decrease constituencies' control over priorities and resources. For example, giving business users a larger budget to allocate for IT expenditures increases user power over IT decisions. Limiting the portion of the budget that can be used for, say, outsourcing or for technology that does not conform to corporate standards reduces control. Only companies with the most decentralized IT management award IT budget control to business units with no strings attached.

Many firms allocate a certain portion of the IT budget to users while retaining another portion for the IT department. The guiding principle is to place decision rights in the hands of those best capable of making certain classes of decisions. A rule of thumb many companies follow calls for deeply technical or infrastructure expenditures to be decided by the IT group, while IT expenditures that directly affect the frontline business remain under the control of business users. Setting the relative proportions of the budget for IT and user control involves the same tensions and pressures previously discussed, as the following example illustrates.

The IT department in a large manufacturing company was interested in phasing out an obsolete computing platform that each year was harder to support and more expensive to maintain. The user community listened to the IT department's concerns about this platform, agreed that the concern was legitimate, and understood that the higher costs were being charged back to them. But the day-to-day functionality of the system was adequate, and while users supported the idea of phasing out the platform, it was not a high priority for them. The users were inclined, therefore, toward spending their limited IT budgets on initiatives other than the phase-out of the obsolete systems platform.

In a company in which the whole IT budget was under user control, the phase-out of this platform might not have occurred until the aging systems began to perform badly. Because direct business needs were their primary concern, users might have made resource allocation decisions that were less than ideal for the firm by investing in initiatives with direct business impact but less benefit to the company than eliminating the aging computing platform. In a company in which the IT department retained control of some of the IT budget, however, resources could be allocated according to IT priorities and the aging platform might be retired. In the company in question, IT successfully lobbied senior management for a larger portion of budget allocation in one year, which it used to retire the obsolete platform. Senior managers, by controlling the portions of budget under the control of these two constituencies—IT and users—can seek a balance of control that is best for the company as a whole.

Summary   This chapter focused on key issues surrounding the organization and leadership of IT activities over the next decade. What is considered good managerial practice in this field is undergoing a revolution. Changes in recommended management practice are driven by new technologies and possibilities and by the accumulation of management experience with IT. As we have seen, new technologies have the potential for different types of services that will be delivered in a wide variety of ways. The revolution seems likely to continue. Organizational structures put in place in the 1970s were found wanting in the 1990s. Those that worked well in the early 1990s show signs of serious strain as we embrace an Internetworked early 21st century.

Determining the appropriate distribution of IT resources within an organization is a complex task. The way a general manager manages the tensions involved depends a great deal on many non-IT aspects of the corporate environment. The leadership style of the person at the top of a company, especially that person's view of the company's future, provides important guidance. A management vision ideal of strong central control presents a different context for IT organization, resource allocation, and prioritization of decisions than does a vision emphasizing the autonomy of business units. Corporate organizational structure and culture matter, as does the geographic dispersion of business units. The corporate headquarters of a large domestic insurance company imposes a different decision context than do the worldwide plants and sales companies of an international automobile manufacturer.

The quality and location of existing IT resources are the basis for future change. According to business users, how responsive and competent are existing IT resources? If the answer to this question is "not very," some adjustments may be needed whether or not the complaint is fair or accurate. Similarly, the existing and perceived appropriate roles of IT on the strategic grid dimensions have important organizational implications. If a firm is in the "support" quadrant, for example, the IT policy unit must be placed lower in the organization's hierarchy to deal with its perceived lack of urgent relevance to corporate strategy.

In dealing with these forces, managers must seek an appropriate balance between innovation and control and between the perspectives of IT specialists and those of business users. There are questions that can be asked, but there are no right answers to them. An identifiable but very complex series of forces, if well analyzed, will determine for each organization the direction in which the correct answer lies—for now, anyway. Executives can answer the following questions to assess whether they are adequately addressing issues of leadership and organization of IT activities:

1. What is the appropriate balance of emphasis between innovation and control in your organization? Do your IT budgets and organizational structures fit well with that balance?

2. To what degree is the success of your company's business driven by factors local to geographies or business units? Conversely, to what extent is success driven by common factors across geographies and business units? Does the degree of centralization/decentralization of your IT activities fit well with the nature of your business?

3. Have the IT staff or business user perspectives become too dominant in the organization? Is senior management engaged in maintaining an appropriate balance of power between these two perspectives?

4. Are there standards and processes in place to assure efficient data interchange between different business units regardless of the degree of centralization or decentralization of IT resources now or in the future?

5. Does your company have a central IT policy group? Is it successful in enlisting senior managers in IT policy discussions?

Chapter

Managing IT Outsourcing[1]

Increasingly, companies are outsourcing all or significant parts of their management of information technology (IT). The reasons include concern for cost and quality, lagging IT performance, supplier pressure, access to special technical and application skills, and other financial factors. From a relatively unusual entrepreneurial activity in the past, IT outsourcing has in the last five years exploded across the global corporate landscape. Xerox, United Technologies, Commonwealth Bank (Australia), Nortel, and Nedcor are just a few megaalliances. Like marriages, however, outsourcing arrangements are much easier to enter than to sustain or dissolve. The special economic technology issues surrounding outsourcing agreements necessarily make them more complex and fluid than an ordinary contract. For outsourcing to be successful, both parties must make a sustained effort to work together. Indeed, in the long term the management of a strategic alliance is *the* dominant challenge of effective IT outsourcing.

In this chapter we identify the characteristics of situations where outsourcing major portions of a firm's IT activities or infrastructure makes sense and discuss how to structure and manage the resulting alliance. Moreover, we provide a concrete framework to help senior managers think about IT outsourcing. Although many aspects of the framework are relevant to incremental outsourcing, as was discussed in Chapter 7, we concentrate here on programs that involve major, long-term alliances between customer and vendor firms. Major outsourcing programs typically involve larger investments, higher stakes, and greater overall management complexity than does incremental outsourcing. Usually they are born of strategic rather than operational motivations, and their impacts on outsourcing customers are much broader. However, the two approaches are complementary and often are used together. Ultimately, the distinction between

[1]This chapter is adapted from F. Warren McFarlan and Richard L. Nolan, "How to Manage an IT Outsourcing Alliance," *Sloan Management Review* 36, no. 2 (Winter 1995).

major programs and incremental outsourcing may blur, but in today's business settings, the unique challenges posed by strategic alliance-based programs consitute a subject deserving of its own discussion.

Why Outsourcing Alliances Are So Difficult

Many major outsourcing contracts are structured to expand over long periods of time. However, these agreements exist in a world of fast-moving technical and business change. Eight to 10 years is the normal length of a contract in an environment in which computer chip performance is improving by 20 to 30 percent per year. The standard contract length addresses the customer's difficulties in switching vendors as well as economic issues. But a deal that made sense at the beginning of the contract may not make economic sense three years later and may require adjustments to function effectively.

The timing of benefits to the customer and the vendor exacerbates the situation. Benefits in the first year are clear to the customer, who often receives a one-time capital payment in exchange for assets that are being transferred to the vendor. Having been paid and having shifted problems and issues to the vendor, the customer firm may feel relieved. Moreover, the tangible payments in the first year occur in an environment where the outputs most closely resemble those anticipated in the contract. In each subsequent year, however, the contract payment stream becomes less and less tied to the initial set of planned outputs (as the world changes) and thus more subject to negotiation and possible misunderstanding between the customer and the vendor.

From the outsourcing vendor's perspective, the situation is the reverse. The first year may require a heavy capital payment followed by the extraordinary costs of taking on responsibility for the customer's IT operations and executing agreed-upon cost reduction and quality control initiatives. All this is completed in anticipation of a back-loaded profit flow. At precisely the time the vendor is finally moving into its planned profit stream, the customer, perhaps feeling the need for new services, is chafing under the monthly charges and anxious to move to new IT architectures. If the customer is not experienced in partnering activities, profound tensions may develop in the relationship.

A further complication is the fact that only a few outsourcing vendors have the critical mass and access to capital markets to undertake large contracts. Electronic Data Systems (EDS), Computer Sciences Corporation (CSC), and IBM constitute the bulk of the current market. A much larger group of firms, such as Lockheed Martin, Perot Systems, Cap Gemini, and a whole group of application service providers (ASPs), specialize in certain niches in the outsourcing market. ASPs provide special industry skills, small contracts, or specific subfunctions such as network operations. If an alliance is not working, a customer company's options for resolving the situation are limited, particularly because outsourcing is relatively easy but insourcing is very difficult. The most common situation is typified by a major international packaging company that was forced on short notice to transfer its relationship to another outsourcing vendor when the original arrangement no longer fit the strategy of that outsourcing vendor.

Finally, the evolution of technologies often changes the strategic relevance of IT to a firm. From the customer's viewpoint, assigning a commodity service to an outsider is very attractive if the price is right. But delegating a firm's service differentiator is another matter (this, however, is increasingly being done, as will be described later).

Outsourcing in Retrospect

Outsourcing IT has been used by organizations for a long time. In the mid-1960s, for example, computer services bureaus ran a variety of programs whose applications focused heavily on the financial and operations support areas (general ledger, payroll, inventory control, and so on). The programs were both customized and general-purpose, and the individual firm had to accommodate its operations to the standard options in the package. Service bureau customers were mostly small and medium-size firms, although some large firms used them for specialized needs or highly confidential items such as executive payroll.

ADP is a good example of a provider in the outsourcing industry. In 1949 ADP began as a small punch card payroll company. By 2001 it had grown into a $7 billion organization that specialized in large-volume, standard transaction-type activities such as payroll and handling proxy solicitations (almost 100 percent of the industry). Other categories include software contracting companies such as Accenture in the private sector and CSC in the public sector. These firms developed large turnkey applications for organizations that required either a large or a specialized staff, either of which the organization deemed inconvenient, imprudent, or impossible to retain. EDS, in the state and local government sector, provided full outsourcing for organizations whose cultures and salary scales made it impossible to attract people with the necessary skills in a competitive job market.

Despite these examples, before 1990 the general trend was in-house development of IT. At that time, the major drivers for outsourcing were primarily

- Cost-effective access to specialized or occasionally needed computing power or systems development skills.

- Avoidance of building in-house IT skills, primarily an issue for small and very low-technology organizations.

- Access to special functional capabilities. Outsourcing during this period was important but in retrospect largely peripheral to the main IT activities that took place in midsize and large organizations.

In 1990, Kodak's decision to outsource IT was the seminal event that legitimized the idea of allowing a vendor to provide major components of IT services. Kodak's chief information officer (CIO), who had been a general manager rather than a computer professional, took an aggressive position in outsourcing mainframes, telecommunications, and personal computer (PC) maintenance and service. Until then, outsourcing for mid-size to large companies had been mostly a sideshow, and outsourcing generally was reserved for small and medium-size companies with problematic, grossly mismanaged informations systems (IS) departments.

Outsourcing in the 21st Century

As we enter the 21st century, it has become abundantly clear that IT outsourcing is not a transitory management fad. IT outsourcing, a harbinger of traditional IT department transformation, provides a glimpse at the emerging organizational structures of the networked economy. By 1995, more than half of midsize to large firms had outsourced or were considering outsourcing significant IT activities. And this phenomenon is not limited to the United States. Novartis (Switzerland), British Aerospace (the United Kingdom), and the AMP Insurance Company in Australia, for example, have all outsourced substantial parts of their IT activities.[2]

Two factors affect the growth of IT outsourcing: acceptance of strategic alliances and changes in the technological environment.

Acceptance of Strategic Alliances

The value of strategic alliances is widely recognized, and interrelated forces motivate their creation. On one level, finding a strong partner to complement an area of weakness gives an organization an island of stability in a turbulent world. Alliances allow a company to simplify its management agenda safely and gain access to higher-quality resources. On another level, alliances allow a firm to leverage a key part of its value chain by bringing in a strong partner that complements its skills. Such a partner may create an opportunity to innovate synergistically, with the two companies working together so that the whole becomes greater than the sum of the parts. Also, early and successful experiences with alliances increase a firm's confidence in undertaking new alliances in other parts of the value chain as a profitable way to do business. The early experience provides insight into ways to increase the likelihood of a successful alliance.

For an alliance to be successful and endure for the long term, both firms must believe they are winners because they benefit from the synergistic potential of the relationship and the opportunity to specialize. As we suggested in Chapter 7, a vendor that concludes that a deal has become a loser will, reasonably enough, divert resources to other, more promising opportunities. The mutually beneficial economics of a successful alliance therefore must outlast the careers of the participants who put the deal together.

IT's Changing Environment

As we have observed throughout this book, today's firms are not limiting IT only to internal transaction processing systems. Instead, they are integrating internal sys-

---

[2]McFarlan and Nolan, op. cit.

TABLE 9.1 IT Markets

Location	Physical Aspects	Information
Internal	*Automating:* Computerizing physical and clerical processes	*Informating:* Leveraging knowledge workers with computers
	Data Processing (DP) era (1960–1980)	Networking era (1990–?)
	• Dominant use of mainframes and minicomputers • Operational-level systems automated primarily with COBOL • Process controls automated primarily with machine language • Standard packages for payroll and general ledger • Applications portfolio consists of millions of lines of code, with 50% typically purchased from outside	• User tasks leveraged through direct use of microcomputers enabled by graphical user interfaces (GUI) and purchased software such as word processing, spreadsheet, graphics, and computer-aided design and manufacturing • Local area networks (LANs)—user-oriented software for e-mail, database sharing, file transfer, and groupware for work teams • Microcomputer software consists of millions of lines of code, almost 100% purchased from other companies
External	*Embedding:* Integrating computers into products and services.	*Networking:* "The Information Highway"
	Micro era (1980–1995)	Network era (1990–?)
	• Specialized code embedded in products and services to enhance function • Microcomputers in physical products such as automobiles and "smart cards" in services • Thousands of lines of code developed by both specialized internal programmers and outside contract programmers	• Wide area networks (WANs) networking workers, suppliers, and customers • Internet for commercial use • Millions of lines of code, almost 100% purchased from and maintained by outside software firms

tems with those of their customers and suppliers and in the process changing their organizational structure to compete efficiently in the global marketplace. As we also have seen, this integration places extraordinary pressures on firms trying to keep the old services running while developing the interconnections and services demanded by the new environment. Thus, outsourcing has become a viable way for firms to access appropriate skills and speed the transition reliably and cost-effectively.

In fact, as shown in Table 9.1, the development of most of the code that companies now use is already outsourced. A distinct minority of the code in operating systems, e-mail systems, word processing packages, and spreadsheet software actually has been developed within the firm (with a much smaller percentage expected in the future). This trend, which occurred for obvious reasons of economies of scale and scarcity of competent staff, will continue. Currently, Computer Associates, IBM, Microsoft, and a few enterprise software vendors are the de facto software providers to most companies. The internal IT organization is already a selector and integrator of code rather than a developer.

In addition, many organizations see outsourcing as a means to transform legacy applications so that they interact effectively as part of real-time Internetworking infrastructure. Companies look to vendors for low-cost maintenance of the old systems to ensure that they operate reliably as well as for access to the new skills that permit their transformation to the new model. Some companies outsource the operation of old systems and use internal staff to develop new IT capabilities; others do the opposite. This shift toward outsourcing as a major source of new capabilities is as significant today as the move from tabulating equipment was 40 years ago.

What Drives Outsourcing?

Despite the mix of factors that suggests outsourcing varies widely from one company to another, a series of themes in the aggregate explains most of the pressures to outsource.

General Managers' Concerns about Costs and Quality

The same questions about IT costs and responsiveness come up repeatedly when managers consider outsourcing: Can we get our existing services for a reduced price at acceptable quality standards? Can we get new systems developed faster? An outsourcing vendor can save money for a customer in several ways:

- Tighter overhead cost control of fringe benefits. On balance, outsourcing vendors run much leaner overhead structures than do many of their customers.

- More aggressive use of low-cost labor pools by using geography creatively. Frequently, the outsourcing vendor moves data centers and gives portions of the development activity to low-cost areas such as India and Northern Ireland (modern telecommunications make this possible).

- Tough world-class standards applied to the company's existing staff, all of whom have to requalify for appointment at the time of outsourcing. Maintaining high standards keeps employees from losing their skills in leading-edge IT practices.

- More effective bulk purchasing and leasing arrangements for all aspects of the hardware/software configuration through discounts and better use of capacity.

- Better management of excess hardware capacity. By combining many firms' work in the same operations center, an outsourcing vendor actually can use less hardware. One small firm's online operations (a $27 million, 10-year contract) were transferred to a larger data center at no extra cost to the outsourcing vendor. Capacity was simply better used.

- Better control over software licenses through both negotiation and realistic examination.

- More aggressive management of service and response time to meet, but not wildly exceed, corporate standards. Tighter control over inventories.

- Hustle. Outsourcing vendors are professionals. Outsourcing is their only business, and their success is measured by satisfied customers who recommend them to others, bottom-line profitability, and stock market performance.

- The ability to run with a leaner management structure because of increased competence and critical-mass volumes of work.

- The ability to access higher levels of IT staff skills, IT application skills (such as SAP, Oracle, and People Soft), or special customer industry skills.

- Creative and more realistic structuring of leases.

While the cumulative impact of these savings can be significant, there are a few caveats. Unless several knowledgeable bidders closely analyze an existing operation before proposing an alliance, the true picture will not be revealed. An IT efficiency study funded by the IT department and performed by a consulting company hoping to get future business is self-serving and inadequate. Equally important is assessing whether the outsourcing vendor can mobilize its staff rapidly for quick-response development jobs when a customer needs to get products and services to market much faster.

Breakdown in IT Performance

Failure to meet service standards forces general management to find other ways to achieve reliability. As we reflect on the last 30 years of computer growth in most companies, it is not unusual to find a company in which cumulative IT management neglect eventually culminated in an out-of-control situation. For example, Massachusetts Blue Cross and Blue Shield's decision to outsource to EDS was triggered by the failure of three major systems development projects (and losses in the tens of millions of dollars). It saw outsourcing as a way to fix a broken department. Similarly, a midsize bank's interest in outsourcing came after a one-day total collapse of its automated teller machine (ATM) network. Faulty software patches, which had been designed internally, caused the failure.

An additional driving factor toward outsourcing is the need for companies to rapidly retool backward IT structures in order to remain competitive. In one firm general managers thought the internal IT culture was both frozen and backward; it needed to leap forward in performance. The general managers, who lacked both the time and the inclination to undertake the task personally, found outsourcing a good choice for making a rapid transition.

Intense Vendor Pressures

Kodak's decision to outsource its data center and telecommunications to IBM, DEC, and Businessland was, as we have noted, a flash point. Suddenly many general managers saw outsourcing as a highly viable, if often misunderstood, alternative. At the same time, IBM was looking for new value-added services to reach its customer base and compensate for declining hardware margins and sales. It moved aggressively into the field with an expanded and highly energetic sales force. EDS, the largest independent firm in the field, used its General Motors operations center to demonstrate its expertise. CSC, which was strong in the federal sector, built a bridge to the commercial sector with its General Dynamics contract. The visibility of these and other arrangements, combined with the vendors' aggressive sales forces, enabled vendors to approach general managers with compelling reasons to outsource. Today numerous large and small vendors serve the industry.

Simplified General Management Agenda

A firm under intense cost or competitive pressures which does not see IT as its core competence may find outsourcing a way to delegate time-consuming, messy problems. The firm then can focus its energy on other competitive differentiators. If managers perceive the outsourcing vendor as competent and are able to transfer a noncore function to reliable hands, they will not hesitate to choose outsourcing. These IT activities must perform reasonably well, but the firm's long-term competitive differentiation does not come from these activities.

Financial Factors

Several financial issues make outsourcing appealing. One is the opportunity to liquidate the firm's intangible IT asset and thus strengthen the balance sheet and avoid a future stream of sporadic capital investments. An important part of many arrangements has been the significant up-front capital paid by the outsourcing vendor to the customer for both the real value of the hardware/software assets and the intangible value of its IT systems. General Dynamics, for example, received $200 million for its IT asset.

Outsourcing can turn a largely fixed-cost business into one with variable costs. This change is particularly important for firms whose activities vary widely in volume from year to year or which face significant downsizing. The outsourcing vendor can make the change much less painful to a downsizing firm. It can broker the slack more effectively and potentially provide greater employment stability for the company's IT employees (who are there because of the outsourcing vendor's ability to handle multiple operations). In fact, staff members transferred to a vendor as part of an outsourcing deal often view the deal positively for some of the same financial reasons. They see themselves leaving a cost-constrained environment with limited potential for promotion and entering a growth environment where IT (their core competence) is the firm's only business.

A third-party relationship also brings an entirely different set of dynamics to a firm's view of IT expenditures. The company is now dealing with a hard-dollar expenditure that all users must take seriously (it is no longer soft-dollar allocation). There is a sense of discipline and tough-mindedness that even an arm's-length, fully charged-back internal IT department has trouble achieving. Further, firms that do not see IT as a high-leverage function may perceive outside professionals as adding special value.

For a firm considering divestiture or outright sale of one or more of its divisions, outsourcing liquidates and gets value for an asset unlikely to be recognized in the divestiture. It gives the acquirer fewer problems to deal with in assimilating the firm. Also, the outsourcing contract may provide a very nice dowry, particularly if the firm is small in relation to the acquirer. With little or no additional expense, the firm can phase out the contract neatly and add the IT transaction volume to the firm's internal IT activities.

Corporate Culture

Sometimes a company's values make it hard for managers to take certain actions that make business sense. Consider, for example, a firm with several internal data centers and an obvious and compelling case for consolidating them. The internal IT department simply lacked the clout to pull off a centralized strategy in what was a highly decentralized firm built up over the years by acquisitions. The firm saw the decentralized culture as a major strength, not subject to reconsideration. Outsourcing, driven by very senior management, provided the fulcrum for overcoming this impasse, since it was not directly associated with any division or corporate staff.

Eliminating an Internal Irritant

No matter how competent and adaptive a firm's IT management and staff are (and usually they are very good), tension often exists between the end users of the resources and the IT staff. The different language IT professionals use, lack of career paths for IT staff across the organization, perceived high IT costs, perceived unresponsiveness to urgent requests, and perceived technical obsolescence frequently exacerbate this tension. In this context the notion of a remote, efficient, experienced outsourcing vendor is particularly compelling even though the internal perceptions are not necessarily realistic.

Other Factors

A variety of other drivers for outsourcing appear in specific situations. At one midsize high-tech firm, for example, outsourcing provided access to skills the company needed to run a series of critical applications. The firm's managers felt that outsourcing had substantially reduced their corporate risk while providing needed access to specialized knowledge. In another example, a large firm received a level of commitment and energy that it felt would not have been forthcoming from an inhouse unit. Still another firm obtained an infrastructure modernization "adrenaline boost" from outsourcing that netted a two-thirds improvement in time to market.

When to Outsource

When do the benefits of outsourcing outweigh the risks? Five factors tip the scale one way or the other.

Position on the Strategic Grid

As shown in Figure 9.1, for companies in the support quadrant, the outsourcing presumption is yes, particularly for large firms. For companies in the factory quadrant, the presumption is yes unless they are huge and are perceived as exceptionally well managed. For firms in the turnaround quadrant, the presumption is mixed; it may represent an unnecessary, unacceptable delegation of competitiveness, although conversely, it may be the only way to acquire those skills. For companies in the strategic quadrant, the presumption also is mixed. Not facing a crisis of IT competence, some companies in the strategic quadrant find it hard to justify outsourcing; others find it indispensable for gaining access to otherwise unavailable skills. Also, having a subcritical mass in potentially core differentiating skills for the firm is an important driver that has moved companies to outsourcing.

FIGURE 9.1 **Strategic Grid for Information Resource Management**

High

Factory—uninterrupted service-oriented information resource management *Outsourcing presumption:* Yes, unless company is huge and well managed Reasons to consider outsourcing: • Possibilities of economies of scale for small and midsize firms • Higher-quality service and backup • Management focus facilitated • Fiber-optic and extended channel technologies facilitate international IT solutions	*Strategic information resource management* *Outsourcing presumption:* Mixed Reasons to consider outsourcing: • Rescue an out-of-control internal IT unit • Tap source of cash • Facilitate cost flexibility • Facilitate management of divestiture • Provide access to technology applications and staffing skills otherwise not available
Support-oriented information resource management *Outsourcing presumption:* Yes Reasons to consider outsourcing: • Access to higher IT professionalism • Possibility of laying off is of low priority and problematic • Access to current IT technologies • Risk of inappropriate IT architecture reduced	*Turnaround information resource management* *Outsourcing presumption:* Mixed Reasons to consider outsourcing: • Internal IT unit not capable in required technologies • Internal IT unit not capable in required project management skills • Access to technology applications and staffing otherwise not available

IT Impact on Core Operations

Low   *IT Impact on Core Strategy*   **High**

For larger multidivisional firms, this analysis suggests that various divisions and clusters of application systems can be treated differently. For example, an international oil company outsourced its operationally troubled Brazilian subsidiary's IT activities but kept in-house the IT activities of a subsidiary in another country. Similarly, because of the dynamic nature of the grid, firms under profit pressures after a period of sustained strategic innovation (in either the turnaround or the strategic quadrant) are good candidates for outsourcing as a means to clean up their shop and procedures. This was true for one large high-technology organization that saved over $100 million per year by outsourcing.

Development Portfolio

The higher the percentage of IT resources working on maintenance or high-structured projects is, the more the portfolio is a candidate for outsourcing. By high-structured projects we mean those in which the end outputs are clearly defined; there is little opportunity to redefine them and little or no organizational change involved in implementing them. Outsourcing vendors with access to high-quality cheap labor pools (in, for example, Russia, India, or Ireland) and good project management skills consistently outperform, on both cost and quality, local units that are caught in a high-cost geographic area but still have the contacts, skills, and confidence to manage extended relationships. The growth of global fiber-optic networks has made conventional thinking on where work should be placed obsolete. For example, Citibank, based in New York, does much of its processing work in South Dakota. Further, literally hundreds of thousands of programmers are working in India on software development for U.S. and European firms.

High-technology, highly structured work (e.g., building a vehicle-tracking system) is also a strong candidate for outsourcing because this type of work requires staff with specialized, leading-edge technical skills. These skills are widely available in Ireland, India, and the Philippines.

Conversely, large, low-structured projects pose difficult coordination problems for outsourcing. In low-structured projects the end outputs and processes are susceptible to significant evolution as the project unfolds. Design is iterative because users discover what they really want by trial and error. Design work requires that key elements of the design infrastructure be physically closer to consumers. It can, of course, be outsourced, but that requires more coordination to be effective than do the projects described above. One firm outsourced significant design work to a very standards-oriented outsourcing vendor as a way of bringing discipline to an undisciplined organization.

Organizational Learning

A firm's organizational learning ability influences whether it can manage an outsourcing arrangement effectively. Many firms' development portfolios include a large number of projects aimed at process reengineering and organizational transformation. Process reengineering seeks to install very different procedures for handling transactions and doing the firm's work. Organizational transformation tries to redesign where decisions in the firm are made and what controls are used. The success of both types of projects depends on having the internal staff radically change the way it works. It often involves significant downsizing as well.

Responsibility for development work is the hardest to outsource. In gauging the responsibility for success, a firm with substantial experience in restructuring will have less difficulty drawing a dividing line between the outsourcing vendor and the customer. Firms that have not yet worked on these projects will find that outsourcing significantly complicates an already difficult task.

A Firm's Position in the Market

The world of real-time infrastructure is so different from the large COBOL systems and stand-alone PCs of the 1980s and earlier that it is often prohibitively challenging for a firm to modernize by itself. Firms that are far behind their peers often do not have the IT leadership, staff skills, or architecture to upgrade quickly to state-of-the-art technology. The outsourcing vendor, in contrast, cannot afford to keep old systems running but must go forward with contemporary practice and technology. For a firm whose IT capabilities have become obsolete, it is not worth dwelling on how the firm got where it is but vital to determine how it can extricate itself.

Current IT Organization

The more IT activities are already segregated in organizational and accounting terms, the easier it is to negotiate an enduring outsourcing contract. A stand-alone IT unit has already developed the fundamental integrating and control mechanisms necessary for an outsourcing contract. Where such mechanisms do not exist, developing an enduring contract is much more complex because the firm must establish both the framework for resolving issues and the specific technical approaches.

Structuring the Alliance

Successful outsourcing begins by carefully crafting the structure of an outsourcing arrangement. The right structure is not a guarantee of success, but the wrong structure will make the governance process almost impossible. Several factors are vital to a successful alliance.

Contract Flexibility

Most outsourcing deals change over time, often radically. Kodak, for example, repeatedly altered its outsourcing contracts because both business circumstances and technologies changed. Evolving technology, changing economic conditions, and new service options make change inevitable. Outsourcing contracts therefore must be written to allow for evolution. Because contracts often need adjustments, the noncontractual aspects of the relationship are extremely important. If there is mutual interest in the relationship and if there are shared approaches to problem solving, the alliance is more likely to be successful. If this is not the case, trouble may arise.

No matter how much detail and thought go into drafting a contract, it will not provide total protection if things go wrong. Indeed, the process of drafting the contract, which often takes six to eight months, is likely to be more important than the contract itself. During the process each side gains insights into the other's values. When the process is successful, it is a basis for personal relationships that go beyond the written contract.

Standards and Control

Companies are understandably concerned about the prospect of handing control over an important part of a firm's operations to a third party (such as an outsourcing vendor), particularly if IT innovation is vital to the firm's success or if the firm is very dependent on IT for smooth operations. The outsourcing agreement must address these concerns.

Control is in part a state of mind. Most organizations are accustomed to lacking direct control over certain segments of the business. Vendors already control many vital aspects of a firm's day-to-day operations. For example, third parties normally provide electricity and telephone services, and the interruption of those services can cripple an organization in a short time. Providing sustained internal backup for these services is often impractical or impossible. As we have seen in some cases, vendors are better able to provide highly reliable services than are their customers.

Putting innovation and responsibility for new services and products in the hands of a third party is correctly seen as more risky and high-stakes than outsourcing operations. Concerns about outsourcing responsibility for new services and products are more easily resolved for firms in the factory and support quadrants of the strategy grid, where innovation is much less important, than they are for firms in the turnaround and strategic quadrants. Whatever a firm's grid location, however, it must carefully develop detailed performance standards for systems response time, availability of service, responsiveness to systems requests, and so on. These standards must be explicitly written into the contract.

Areas to Outsource

A company can outsource many aspects of IT activities. Broken Hill, for example, outsourced all of its IT activities. Kodak kept systems development but outsourced data center operations, communications, and PC acquisition, each to a different vendor. As we noted earlier, significant portions of firms' IT activities have been outsourced for years. What is at stake here is a discontinuous shift to move additional portions of a firm's IT activities outside the firm. Between the current situation and total outsourcing lie a variety of scenarios. When assessing incremental outsourcing, managers should ask the following questions:

- Can the portion of IT proposed for outsourcing be separated easily from the rest of the firm, or will the complexities of disentangling systems absorb most of the savings?

- Do the activities proposed for outsourcing require particular specialized competencies that we do not possess or lack the time to build?

- How central are the activities to be outsourced to the strategy of our firm? Are they more or less significant to the firm's value chain than the other IT activities?

In outsourcing smaller portions of IT activities, it is important to take into account coordination costs. Companies whose outsourcing approaches over time became fragmented experience enormous coordination costs as they attempt to manage relationships with a large number of vendors.

Cost Savings

Some CIOs believe that the firm's IT activities are so well managed or so unique that there is no way to achieve savings through outsourcing or for the vendor to profit. Skepticism about such beliefs is often warranted, however. The IT department often has a vested interest in status quo organizational arrangements and may resist outsourcing at every turn. Thus, carrying out an objective assessment of the benefits of outsourcing can be very difficult. At one company an internally initiated study done by a consultant retained by the IT department showed that the firm's IT operations were 40 percent more efficient than the average in its industry. The results from a subsequent study refuted that claim.

If properly engaged by a firm's senior managers, however, outsourcing consultants can make a real contribution to efforts to evaluate cost savings as well as in negotiating a contract with an outsourcing vendor. Customer firms outsource infrequently, in some cases only once. Outsourcing vendors are more practiced at negotiating outsourcing deals. Without outside assistance, a customer firm can be overmatched in an unbalanced negotiating process.

Supplier Stability and Quality

During the typical 10-year term of an outsourcing contract, technologies will evolve. A supplier that pays insufficient attention to ongoing modernization and retraining will become a liability as a strategic partner. The stability of the outsourcing vendor's financial structure is also critical. Vendor cash crunches, Subchapter 11, and worse situations are nightmares for customers. Once a firm outsources, it is very hard to bring the applications back to the company. Key aspects of the firm's technical and managerial competence will have evaporated since the outsourcing deal was consummated. Although it is difficult to move quickly from one outsourcing vendor to another (usually the only practical alternative), if it considers the possibility in advance, a firm can mitigate the risks.

Problems are intensified if the way a firm uses technology becomes incompatible with the outsourcing vendor's skill base. For example, a firm in the factory quadrant that selects an operationally strong outsourcing vendor may be in trouble if it suddenly moves toward the strategic quadrant and its partner (the outsourcing vendor) lacks the necessary project management and innovation skills to operate there.

The firm and the outsourcing vendor must manage any potential conflict of interest carefully so that it does not ruin the relationship. The outsourcing vendor makes money by lengthening leases, driving down operational costs, and charging premium prices for new value-added services. The outsourcing customer has little interest in harvesting old technology benefits; old technology is usually one reason the firm outsourced in the first place. The mechanisms for managing potential tensions must be written into the contract. Both firms must make a profit. The more the customer moves to the strategic quadrant, however, the more challenging it is to design a good fit with an outsourcing vendor.

Management Fit

Putting together a 10-year, flexible evolving relationship requires more than just technical skill and contract wizardry. A shared approach to problem solving, similar values, and good personal chemistry among key staff people are critical determinants of long-term success. Outsourcing vendors have very different management cultures and styles. It is often worthwhile for a customer firm to give up something in price to engage an outsourcing partner that will work well over the long term. The information gained in a tortuous six- to eight-month process of putting an alliance together is crucial for identifying the likelihood of a successful partnership. Personal chemistry is a necessity, but it is an insufficient condition for success. Corporate culture fit is the most important factor. Years after the people key to establishing the initial relationship have moved to other assignments, the outsourcing relationship will remain in place.

Conversion Problems

The period of time during an outsourcing study and conversion is one of great stress for a company's IT staff. Uncertainties about career paths and job security contribute to the potential for problems. The sooner plans and processes for dealing with staff career issues, outplacement processes, and separation pay are addressed, the more effective the results will be. Fear of the unknown is almost invariably worse than any reality.

Managing the Alliance

The ongoing management of an alliance is the single most important aspect of the success of outsourcing. There are four critical areas that require close attention.

The CIO Function

The customer firm must retain a strong, active CIO function. The heart of the CIO's job is planning—ensuring that IT resources are at the right level and are appropriately distributed. This role has always been distinctly separate from the active line management of networks, data centers, and systems development, although this has not always been recognized. Line activities can be outsourced, but sustained internal CIO responsibility for the following critical areas must be maintained even in a company that has fully outsourced its IT function.

- *Partnership/contract management.* An informed CIO who monitors performance against the contract and plans for and deals with issues that arise helps an outsourcing alliance adapt to change. The outsourcing experiences of Kodak and J. P. Morgan/Chase provide clear evidence of the need for this ongoing role.

- *Architecture planning.* A CIO's staff must visualize and coordinate a long-term approach to networks, hardware and software standards, and database architectures. The firm can delegate execution of these areas but not its assessment of what it needs to support the firm in the long term. A staff roughly 5 percent the size of the outsourced IT organization is the norm, although in practice the percentage may vary in either direction. In general, organizations should err on the side of too much coordinating staff.

- *Emerging technologies.* A company must develop a clear grasp of emerging technologies and their potential applications. To understand new technology, managers must attend vendor briefings and peer group seminars and visit firms that currently are using the new technology. Assessing technology alternatives cannot be delegated to a third party. At one large pharmaceutical organization, the CIO's staff was vindicated when it became clear that it had first spotted business process redesign as an emerging area, funded appropriate pilot projects (which were skillfully transferred to line management), and finally repositioned the firm's entire IT effort. Users and an outside systems integrator executed the project, with the CIO playing the crucial initiator role. An outsourcing vendor has an incentive to suggest new ideas that lead to additional work. Delegating responsibility for IT-enabled innovation in strategic and turnaround firms is risky because this is such an important part of the firm's value chain.

- *Continuous learning.* A firm should create an internal IT learning environment to bring users up to speed so that they are comfortable in a climate of continuous change. An aerospace firm felt this was so important that, when outsourcing, it kept the internal learning environment in-house.

Performance Measurement

Realistic measurement of outsourcing success is generally difficult, and so companies must develop performance standards, measure results, and then interpret them continuously. Individual firms bring entirely different motivations and expectations to the table. In addition, many of the most important measures of success are intangible and play out over a long period of time. Concrete, immediate cost savings, for example, may be measurable, at least in the short run, but simplification of the general management agenda is impossible to assess.

The most celebrated cases of outsourcing have evolved in interesting ways. Whereas Kodak's major vendor remains intact, another vendor has gone through several organizational transformations triggered by financial distress. In its first 18 months of outsourcing General Dynamics spun off three divisions along with their contracts. EDS and General Motors (GM) took years to work out an acceptable agreement; ultimately, EDS was spun out as a separate company, and its share of GM's internal IT work has been shrinking.

A major power company postponed an outsourcing study for a year. Its general managers believed their internal IT staff and processes were so bloated that while outsourcing IT would clearly produce major savings, they would still be leaving money on the table. Consequently, they reduced their IT staff from 450 to 250 and reduced the total IT expenditure level by 30 percent. With the "easy" things done, they then entertained several outsourcing proposals to examine more closely what additional savings and changes in their method of operation would be appropriate and then proceeded to outsource.

Mix and Coordination of Tasks

As we noted earlier, the larger the percentage of a firm's systems development portfolio devoted to maintaining legacy systems, the lower the risk of outsourcing the portfolio. The question becomes: Can we get these tasks done significantly faster and less expensively? The bigger the percentage of large, low-structured projects in the systems development portfolio is, the more difficult it becomes to execute a prudent outsourcing arrangement because the necessary coordination work to be done is much more intense. Large systems development projects using advanced technology play directly to outsourcing vendors' strengths. Conversely, issues relating to structure (and thus close, sustained give-and-take by users) require so much extra coordination that many outsourcing benefits tend to evaporate.

If not carefully managed, both the contract and the different geographic locations of the outsourcing vendor's development staff may inhibit discussion and lead to additional costs. Managing the dialogue across two organizations with very different financial structures and motivations is both challenging and, at the core, critical to the alliance's success. Concerns in this area led J. P. Morgan and Dupont not to outsource significant portions of their development activity.

Customer-Vendor Interface

The importance of the sensitive interface between the customer and the outsourcing vendor cannot be overestimated. First, outsourcing cannot imply delegation of final responsibility to the outsourcing vendor. The reality is that oversight cannot be entrusted to someone outside the firm, and as we have mentioned, a CIO and the supporting staff need to manage the agreement and relationships. Additionally, the interfaces between the customer and the outsourcing vendor are very complex and usually must occur at multiple levels. At the most senior levels there must be links to deal with major issues of policy and relationship restructuring, whereas at lower levels there must be mechanisms for identifying and handling more operational and tactical issues. For firms in the strategic quadrant, these policy discussions occur at the CEO level and occasionally involve the board of directors.

Both the customer and the outsourcing vendor need regular full-time relationship managers and coordinating groups lower in the organization to deal with narrow operational issues and potential difficulties. These integrators are crucial for managing different economic motivations and friction. The smaller the firm is in relationship to the outsourcing vendor's total business, the more important it is that these arrangements be specified in advance before they get lost among other priorities.

During the last 10 years an entirely different way of gaining IT support for outsourcing has emerged. While outsourcing is not for everyone, a number of very large and sophisticated organizations have made the transition successfully, and the practice is growing rapidly. What determines success or failure is managing the relationship less as a contract and more as a strategic alliance.

Summary

In this chapter we described a framework for managing large outsourcing programs. The framework identifies the characteristics of situations in which outsourcing makes sense and the issues involved in structuring and managing outsourcing alliances. Many aspects of the framework are relevant to the earlier discussion of incremental outsourcing, but the unique challenges posed by strategic alliance-based programs require special attention. Executives can use the following questions to assess whether they are seizing the opportunities provided by outsourcing and managing the associated risks:

1. Have you assessed the case for outsourcing some or all of your company's IT activities? If past studies indicated that outsourcing did not make sense, how confident are you of the objectivity of those studies?

2. If you are engaged in outsourcing relationships, have you built the need to change the relationship over time into the contract? Do you have specific mechanisms in place to indicate when an adjustment to the contract might be called for?

3. Do your outsourcing arrangements provide profits for both parties to the agreement?

4. Have you retained an internal CIO function to perform the IT planning and contract monitoring functions that cannot be delegated? Have you adequately funded and staffed this internal group?

5. Do you have practices in place to nurture and maintain the health of the outsourcing relationship?

Chapter

10

A Portfolio Approach to IT Projects

A division of a major chemical company halts its SAP installation and takes a major write-off. Although the company had successfully implemented SAP before, this time an inexperienced project manager misjudges the amount of change management necessary. The company starts over with an experienced project manager and a change management consultant. Losses are in the millions.

A major credit card company underestimates processing requirements by more than tenfold as it moves its online credit card processing to a new service provider. The system crashes. One and one-half million accounts are at risk. Service levels plunge. Both the chief information officer (CIO) and one of his direct reports lose their jobs.

A manufacturing company consolidates activities from more than 50 plants, field offices, and order entry points into a national service center. Only after consolidation is well under way does the company realize that wait time to confirm orders averages 25 seconds. In the estimation of firm managers, any wait longer than 2 seconds makes the system unusable.

Two major insurance companies attempt to install the same software package to solve an identical problem with their field sales forces. In one company, the new technology generates a 46 percent increase in sales from one year to the next. In the other, all the money is wasted; $600 million is written off with no benefit.

Horror stories from the late 1960s and early 1970s? Hardly. These examples are disturbingly recent. Most date from the end of the 1990s, and some from the 21st century. Despite 40 years of accumulated experience in managing information technology (IT) projects, the day of the big disaster on a major IT project has not passed. Why? An analysis of these examples and a preponderance of research over the last 10 years suggest three serious deficiencies that involve general and IT management: (1) failure to assess the implementation risk of a project at the time it is funded,

(2) failure to consider the aggregate implementation risk of a portfolio of projects, and (3) failure to recognize that different projects require different managerial approaches. In this chapter we examine the sources of implementation risk and suggest strategies for managing and mitigating it.

Sources of Implementation Risk

In discussing implementation risk, we assume that IT managers have brought appropriate methods and tools to bear on a project. Implementation risk, as we define it here, is what remains after the application of the proper methods and tools. While mismanagement is another source of risk, it is not included in our notion of implementation risk because it is not inherent in the nature of a project. Risk, however, is a necessary part of a project experience. It follows that risk itself is not inherently bad; rather, it is an essential characteristic of projects that promise benefits. The idea of taking on higher risk for a higher return is basic to business thinking. All beneficial business activities undertake risk, and project management is no different.

Project feasibility studies typically provide estimates of financial benefits, qualitative benefits, implementation costs, target milestone and completion dates, and staffing levels. Developers of estimates often provide voluminous supporting documentation. Only rarely, however, do they deal frankly with the risks of slippage in time, cost overruns, technical shortfalls, and outright failure. Usually they deny or ignore such possibilities. Ignoring project risk is a profound error with significant consequences, such as the following:

- Failure to obtain anticipated benefits due to implementation difficulties

- Higher than expected implementation costs

- Longer than expected implementation time

- Resulting systems whose technical performance is below plans and requirements

- System incompatibility with selected hardware and software

Three important project dimensions influence *inherent* implementation risk:

Project size. The larger the project in monetary terms, staffing levels, duration, and number of departments affected, the greater the risk. Multimillion-dollar projects obviously carry more risk than do $50,000 efforts and tend to affect the company more if the risk is realized. Project size relative to the normal size of an IT development group's projects is also important. A $1 million project in a department whose average undertaking costs $2 million to $3 million usually has lower implicit risk than does a $250,000 project in a department whose projects have never cost more than $50,000.

Experience with the technology. Project risk increases when the project team and organization are unfamiliar with the hardware, operating systems, database systems, and other project technologies. New technology projects are intrinsically more risky for a company than are projects that use familiar technologies. A project posing a slight risk for a large, leading-edge systems development group may be highly risky for a smaller, less technically advanced group. By hiring systems integration consultants with expertise in those technologies, a company can potentially reduce the risk associated with unfamiliar technologies. Accenture, CSC, EDS, IBM, and a host of smaller competitors offer services of this kind.

Project structure. In some projects, which we term *high structure,* the nature of the task fully and clearly defines project outputs. From the project's beginning throughout its duration, outputs remain fixed. Inherent stable requirements make these projects easier to manage. Similarly, projects that require little organizational change are much less risky than are projects that require substantial modification of the organization and employee work habits. We contrast high-structure projects with low-structure projects, which do not have such convenient characteristics. Requirements for low-structure projects are difficult to determine, and they tend to evolve throughout the project. To realize benefits, they typically require organizational change.

An insurance company's project to create a laptop computer–based version of an agent's rate book provides an example of a highly structured project. At the beginning of the project, the planners reached an agreement on the product lines to be included, the layout of each page screen, the process of generating each number, and the type of client illustration that would be possible. Throughout the life of the project these decisions were never altered. Consequently, the team organized itself to reach a stable, fixed output rather than to cope with a potentially mobile target. The key risk, effectively managed, was training the agents to operate in these new ways.

Project Categories and Degree of Risk

Figure 10.1, which combines in a matrix the various dimensions influencing risk, identifies eight distinct project categories with varying degrees of implementation risk. Figure 10.2 gives examples of projects that fit in those categories. Even at this grossly intuitive level, this classification is useful to separate projects for different types of management review. Innumerable IT organizations have used the matrix successfully for understanding relative implementation risk and for communicating that risk to users and senior executives. The matrix helps address the legitimate concern about whether all the people viewing a project will have the same understanding of its risks.

Assessing Risk for Individual Projects

Figure 10.3 shows excerpts from a questionnaire one company developed for assessing project implementation risk. In total, the project manager[1] must answer 42

---

[1]Actually, both the project leader and the key user answer these questions, and then they reconcile the differences in their answers. Of course, the questionnaire data are no better than the quality of thinking that goes into the answers.

FIGURE 10.1 Effect of Degree of Structure, Company-Relative Technology, and Project Size on Project Implementation Risk

		Low Structure	High Structure
Low Company-Relative Technology	Large Project	Low risk (very susceptible to mismanagement)	Low risk
	Small Project	Very low risk (very susceptible to mismanagement)	Very low risk
High Company-Relative Technology	Large Project	Very high risk	Medium risk
	Small Project	High risk	Medium-low risk

FIGURE 10.2 Project Examples by Implementation Risk Categories

	Low Structure	High Structure
Low Company-Relative Technology	Spreadsheet support for budgeting	Year 2000 compliance work
High Company-Relative Technology	Online graphic support for advertising copy	Artificial intelligence (AI)–driven bond trading

FIGURE 10.3   Project Implementation Risk Assessment Questionnaire (Sample from a Total of 42 Questions)

Risk Factor			Weight
1. Total development work-hours for system*			5
100 to 3,000	Low	1	
3,000 to 15,000	Medium	2	
15,000 to 30,000	Medium	3	
More than 30,000	High	4	
2. Estimated project implementation time			4
12 months or less	Low	1	
13 months to 24 months	Medium	2	
More than 24 months	High	3	
3. Number of departments (other than IT) involved with system			4
One	Low	1	
Two	Medium	2	
Three or more	High	3	

Structure Risk Assessment

Risk Factor			Weight
1. If replacement system is proposed, what percentage of existing functions are replaced on a one-to-one basis?			5
0–25%	High	3	
25–50%	Medium	2	
50–100%	Low	1	
2. What is the severity of user department procedural changes caused by the proposed system?			5
Low		1	
Medium		2	
High		3	
3. What is the degree of needed user organization structural change to meet requirements of the new system?			5
None		0	
Minimal	Low	1	
Somewhat	Medium	2	
Major	High	3	
4. What is the general attitude of the user?			5
Poor, against IT solution	High	3	
Fair, sometimes reluctant	Medium	2	
Good, understands value of IT solution		0	
5. How committed is upper-level user management to the system?			5
Somewhat reluctant or unknown	High	3	
Adequate	Medium	2	
Extremely enthusiastic	Low	1	
6. Has a joint IT-user team been established?			5
No	High	3	
Part-time user representative appointed	Low	1	
Full-time user representative appointed		0	

FIGURE 10.3 Project Implementation Risk Assessment Questionnaire (Sample from a Total of 42 Questions) *(continued)*

Technology Risk Assessment		
Risk Factor		**Weight**
1. Which of the hardware is new to the company?[†]		5
None		0
CPU	High	3
Peripherals and/or additional storage	High	3
Terminals	High	3
Mini or macro	High	3
2. Is the system software (nonoperating system) new to IT project team?[†]		5
No		0
Programming language	High	3
Database	High	3
Data communications	High	3
Other (please specify)	High	3
3. How knowledgeable is user in area of IT?		5
First exposure	High	3
Previous exposure but limited knowledge	Medium	2
High degree of capability	Low	1
4. How knowledgeable is user representative in proposed application area?		5
Limited	High	3
Understands concept but has no experience	Medium	2
Has been involved in prior implementation efforts	Low	1
5. How knowledgeable is IT team in proposed application area?		5
Limited	High	3
Understands concept but has no experience	Medium	2
Has been involved in prior implementation efforts	Low	1

Note: Since the questions vary in importance, the company assigned weights to them subjectively. The numerical answer to a question is multiplied by the question's weight to calculate the question's contribution to the project's risk. The numbers are then added to produce a risk score for the project. Projects with risk scores within 10 points of each other are indistinguishable in their relative risk, but those separated by 100 points or more are very different in their implementation risk to even the casual observer.

*Time to develop includes system design, programming, testing, and installation.

[†]This question is scored by multiplying the sum of the numbers attached to the positive responses by the weight.

Source: This questionnaire is adapted from "Dallas Tire," Case No. 180-006 (Boston: Harvard Business School Case Services, 1980).

questions about a project before senior managers will approve it. The company drew up these questions after analyzing its experience with successful and unsuccessful projects. Although these questions may not be appropriate for all companies, they provide a good starting point for thinking about implementation risk. A number of other companies have used the questionnaire in developing their own instruments for measuring risk.

The questions not only highlight the sources of implementation risk but also suggest alternative routes to conceiving the project and managing it to reduce risk. If the initial aggregate risk score seems high, analyses of the answers can suggest ways of reducing the risk, for example, by reducing project scope, using more familiar technology, or breaking the project into multiple phases. Managers should not consider risk unalterable; instead, its presence should encourage better approaches to project management. Questions 5 and 6 in the "Structure Risk Assessment" section are good examples of questions that could trigger changes.

The higher the assessment score, the greater the need for very senior approval. In the company that developed this questionnaire, only the executive committee can approve projects with very high scores. This approach ensures that top managers are aware of significant hazards and are making appropriate trade-offs between risk and strategic benefits. Managers should ask themselves the following questions:

1. Are the benefits great enough to offset the risks?

2. Can the affected parts of the organization survive if the project fails?

3. Have the planners considered appropriate alternatives?

The questionnaire is readministered several times during the project to reveal any major changes in risks as it unfolds. Ideally, risk assessment scores decline throughout implementation as the number and size of the remaining tasks dwindle and familiarity with the technology increases.

When senior managers believe a project has low implementation risk yet IT managers know it has high implementation risk, horror stories sometimes result. The questionnaire helps prevent potential misunderstandings by encouraging a common understanding among senior management, IT managers, and user managers about a project's relative implementation risk.

Portfolio Risk

In addition to determining relative risk for single projects, a company should develop a profile of aggregate implementation risk for its portfolio of systems projects. Different portfolio risk profiles are appropriate to different companies and strategies.

For example, in an industry where IT is strategic (such as retailing or catalog sales), managers should be concerned if there are no high-risk projects in the project portfolio. Such a cautious stance may open a product or service gap through which the competition may seize advantage. A portfolio loaded with high-risk projects, however, suggests that the company may be vulnerable to operational disruptions if projects are not completed as planned. Referring back to the strategic grid discussed in earlier chapters, for "support" companies, heavy investment in high-risk projects may not be appropriate; they should not be taking strategic gambles in the IT arena. Yet even these companies should have some technologically challenging ventures to ensure familiarity with leading-edge technology and maintain staff morale and interest.

These examples suggest that the aggregate implementation risk profiles of the portfolios of any two companies can legitimately differ. Table 10.1 lists the issues that influence companies toward or away from high-risk efforts. The risk profile

TABLE 10.1   **Factors that Influence Implementation Risk Profile of Project Portfolio**

	Portfolio Risk Focus	
Factor	**Low**	**High**
Stability of IT development group	High	Low
Perceived quality of IT development group by insiders	High	Low
IT critical to delivery of current corporate services	No	Yes
IT an important decision support aid	No	Yes
Experienced IT systems development group	Yes	No
Major IT fiascoes in last two years	No	Yes
New IT management team	No	Yes
IT perceived as critical to delivery of future corporate services	No	Yes
IT perceived as critical to future decision support aids	No	Yes
Company perceived as backward in use of IT	No	Yes

should include projects executed by outside systems integrators as well as those of the internal systems development group. As the table shows, IT's aggregate impact on corporate strategy is an important determinant of the appropriate amount of implementation risk to undertake.

Project Management: A Contingency Approach

Conventional wisdom and much of the literature on how to manage projects suggest that there is a single right approach to project management. The implication of this way of thinking is that managers should apply the same tools, project management methods, and organizational linkages to all such efforts. We disagree.

Although there may indeed be a set of general-purpose tools that can be used in managing IT implementation (we describe some later), the contribution each makes to project planning and control varies widely according to the project's characteristics. Further, the means of involving the user—through steering committees, representation on the team, or as a team leader—should also vary by project type; in short, there is no universally correct way to run all projects.

Management Tools

The general methods (tools) for managing projects are of four principal types:

External integration tools include organizational and other communication devices that link the project team's work to users at both managerial and lower levels.

Internal integration devices, which include various personnel controls, ensure that the project team operates as an integrated unit.

Formal planning tools help structure the sequence of tasks in advance and estimate the time, money, and technical resources the team will need for executing them.

TABLE 10.2 Tools for Project Management

Integration Tools/Techniques, External	Integration Tools/Techniques, Internal
Selection of user as project manager	Selection of experienced IT professional to lead team
User steering committee (which meets frequently)	Team meetings
User-managed change control process	Distribution within team of information on key design decisions
Distribution of project team information to key users	Technical status reviews/inspections
Selection of users as team members	Human resources techniques to maintain low turnover of team members
User approval process for system specifications	Selection of high percentage of team members with significant previous work relationships
Prototyping with users	Participation of team members in goal setting and deadline establishment
Progress reports	Obtaining outside technical assistance
User involvement/responsibility in other key decisions and actions	

Formal Planning Tools	Formal Results Control Tools
Project management software	Status-versus-plan reports
PERT, CPM	Change control disciplines and systems
Milestone selection	Milestone review meetings
Systems specifications	Analysis of deviations from plan
Project approval processes	
Postproject audit procedures	

Formal results-control mechanisms help managers evaluate progress and spot potential discrepancies so that corrective action can be taken.

Results controls have been particularly effective in project settings with the following characteristics:[2]

1. There is clear knowledge in advance of the desired results.

2. The individuals whose actions are influenced by the formal mechanisms can control the desired result, at least to some extent.

3. Results can be measured effectively.

Highly structured projects involving a low degree of technology satisfy these conditions very well; formal results-control mechanisms are very effective in these settings. For low-structure projects involving a high degree of technology, none of the above conditions apply; consequently, results control can make only a limited contribution. In those settings, major contributions can be derived from internal integration devices (personnel controls). Table 10.2 provides examples of commonly used types of integration and control tools.

[2]Kenneth A. Merchant, *Control in Business Organizations* (Marshfield, MA: Pitman Publishing, 1985).

Influences on Tool Selection

Different project types call for the use of different management tools. Using the project categories in Figure 10.1, we describe the tools most suitable for each project type below.

High-Structure/Low-Technology Projects

Highly structured projects that present familiar technical problems have the lowest risk and are the easiest to manage of the projects described in Figure 10.1. Unfortunately, they are the least common. High structure implies that the nature of the task defines its outputs, the possibility of users changing their minds about the desired outputs is practically nonexistent, and significant change management issues are not present. Project leaders do not have to create extensive administrative processes just to get a group of users to agree to maintain commitment to a design. External integration practices such as assigning IT systems analysts to user departments, mandating heavy representation of users on the design team, and requiring formal user approval of design specifications are cumbersome and unnecessary for this type of project. Other integrating actions, however, such as training users how to operate the system, remain important.

Since the system's concept and design are stable throughout the duration of this type of project and since the technology involved is familiar to the company, the project can be staffed with people with average skill levels. The project leader does not need extraordinary IT skills. This type of project readily provides opportunities to the IT department's junior managers, who can gain experience that will be applicable to more ambitious tasks in the future.

With their focus on defining tasks and budgeting resources against them, formal planning tools (such as program evaluation and review technique [PERT]) and critical path method [CPM]) are likely to work well on this type of project. They force the team to develop a thorough and detailed plan that exposes areas of "soft" thinking. Such projects are likely to meet the resulting milestone dates and adhere to the target budget. Moreover, the usual results-control techniques for measuring progress against dates and budgets provide reliable data for spotting discrepancies and building a desirable tension within the design team in regard to working harder to avoid slippage.

A portfolio in which 90 percent of the projects are of this type should produce little unplanned excitement for senior and user managers. It also requires a much more limited set of skills for the IT organization than would be needed for portfolios with a different mixture of project types.

High-Structure/High-Technology Projects

Projects in this category are vastly more complex than the high-structure/low-technology projects just discussed. Projects with high structure and high technology call for significant elaboration on the practices outlined in most project management handbooks. Converting a mainframe system to run on client-server architecture is a good example of a high-structure/high-technology project so long as the objective is replicating the same functions on the new platform. Another example is a firm's initial efforts at Web-enabling access to key content for internal use by company employees.

For this type of project to succeed, interaction between the project team and the users is not crucial. The outputs are so well defined by the nature of the undertaking that obtaining user input and dealing with changes that users request are unimportant. Interaction with users, however, is important in two respects: (1) to ensure coordination on any changes in input/output or any other manual procedure changes necessary for project success and (2) to deal with any systems restructuring that must follow from unexpected shortcomings in the project's technology.

In this kind of project, it is common to discover during implementation that the selected technology is inadequate for the task, which forces a long postponement while new technology is chosen or vital features of the system are modified to make the task fit the available technology. This was true of the firm described at the beginning of the chapter that consolidated activities from over 50 plants into a national call center. In a similar experience, an industrial products company temporarily returned to processing some order-entry procedures manually so that the rest of an integrated materials management system could be shifted to purchased hardware.

For this type of project, technical complexity drives the characteristics of a successful manager. The manager should have a strong background in high-technology projects (preferably, but not necessarily, in an IT environment) and should be able to "connect" with the deep technologists the project will require. The ideal manager will foster an atmosphere of communication within the project that will help anticipate difficulties before technologists understand they have a problem. When managing large projects in this category, an effective project leader must establish and maintain teamwork, develop a record of all key design decisions, and call subproject meetings as needed.

Formal planning methods that identify tasks and set completion dates will have much less predictive value. The team will not understand key elements of the technology in advance. All too often seemingly minor bugs will have major financial consequences.

At one company an online banking system generated "garbage" (Os and Xs) across all the computer screens roughly once each hour. One keystroke erased the "ghost," but it remained a disconcerting aspect of a banking system. Four months and more than $200,000 were dedicated to eliminating the mysterious quirk. Solving the problem involved uncovering a complex interaction of hardware features, operating system functions, and application traffic patterns. Indeed, a vendor ultimately had to redesign several microprocessor chips to solve the problem once and for all. Formal results-control mechanisms have limits in monitoring the progress of such projects, and personnel controls become more important.

In summary, technical leadership and internal integration are the keys in this type of project; external integration plays a distinctly secondary role. Formal planning tools yield estimates that may contain major inaccuracies, and great danger results when neither IT managers nor high-level executives recognize this. Managers who do not acknowledge the inherent level of uncertainty may believe they have precise planning and close controls in place when in fact they have neither.

Low-Structure/Low-Technology Projects

When low-structure/low-technology projects are well managed, they present low-risk profiles. Too often, though, such projects fail because of inadequate understanding and focus on business requirements. Indeed, the key to operating this kind of project lies in effective efforts to involve the users in design, development, and implementation.

Developing substantial user support for a system design and keeping the users committed to that design are critical. Such projects therefore benefit from the following:

1. A user as project leader or as the number two person on the team.

2. A user steering committee to evaluate the design periodically.

3. Breaking the project into a sequence of small, discrete subprojects.

4. Formal user review and approval on all key project specifications.

5. Distributing minutes of all key design meetings to the users.

6. Adhering, when possible, to all key subproject time schedules. Low turnover among users is important here; a consensus reached with a user manager's predecessor is of dubious value.

The SAP debacle described in the beginning of the chapter illustrates what can happen when a project in this category does not benefit from adequate user involvement. End-user requirements for the system were unclear from the beginning. The project manager and his staff paid little heed to communications with users or to change management. In the middle of the project people with limited technical backgrounds and no familiarity with the division's operations replaced key users. Although the technology was familiar to the company, a mismatch grew between the design of the system and the needs of the organization. Eventually the mismatch became impossible to ignore. At a cost of millions of dollars, the project was halted, restaffed, and restarted.

Once the design is finalized, the importance of user leadership increases. At some point after the design is finalized, users almost always come up with "great new ideas." Unless the alternatives they suggest are critical to the business (a judgment best made by a responsible user-oriented project manager), the change requests generated by great ideas must be addressed in a formal change-control process. Unless change control follows a disciplined process, users will make change after change. When this happens, a project evolves rapidly into a state of permanent deferral, its completion forever six months in the future.

If the project is well integrated with users, formal planning tools are very helpful in structuring tasks and removing the remaining uncertainties. Target completion dates can be quite firm as long as the system's target remains fixed. Similarly, the formal results controls afford clear insight into progress to date, flagging both advances and slippages (as long as the systems target remains fixed). Personnel controls also are vital here. If integration with user departments is weak, for example, excessive reliance on results controls will produce an entirely unwarranted feeling of confidence in the project team. By definition, however, the problems of technology management are usually less difficult in a low-structure/low-technology project than in high-technology ventures, and a staff with a normal mixture of technical backgrounds should be adequate.

In almost every respect a low-structure/low-technology project differs from other types. The key to success is close, aggressive management of external integration, supplemented by formal planning and control tools. Leadership must flow from users rather than from technologists.

Low-Structure/High-Technology Projects

Projects in this category have outputs not clearly defined at the project's start. Such projects are also technically complex. Managers therefore require technical expertise and an ability to communicate with users about business needs. The same intensive external integration needed for low-structure/low-technology projects is necessary here. Total user commitment to a particular set of design specifications is again critical. At the same time, strong technical leadership and internal project integration are vital. This effort requires highly experienced project leaders, and those leaders need wholehearted support from the users. Before undertaking such a project, managers should seriously explore whether the project can be divided in smaller parts or can employ less innovative technology. Low-structure/high-technology projects are extremely difficult and should not be undertaken lightly.

Although formal planning and results-control tools are useful here, in the early stages they contribute little to reducing uncertainty or highlighting problems. Planning tools do allow the manager to structure the sequence of tasks. Unfortunately, new tasks crop up with regularity, and those that appear simple and small can suddenly become complex and protracted. Further, unsuspected interdependencies between tasks often become apparent. Time, cost, and the resulting technical performance are almost impossible to predict simultaneously. In NASA's Apollo moon project, for example, technical performance was key and cost and time were secondary. In the private sector, cost and timing usually cannot be considered secondary.

Relative Contribution of Management Tools

Table 10.3 shows the relative contribution each of the four groups of project management tools makes to maximizing potential project success. It reveals that different management styles and approaches are needed for managing the different types of projects. The usual corporate handbook on project management, with its single-minded prescriptive approach, fails to deal with the realities of the tasks facing today's managers, particularly those dealing with information technology. The right approach to managing a project flows from the specific characteristics of the project.

Additionally, the need to deal with the corporate culture within which both IT and the project team operate further complicates the project management problem. Formal project planning and results-control tools are much more likely to produce successful results in highly formal environments than they are in companies where the prevailing culture is more informal. Similarly, selecting and effectively using integrating mechanisms is very much a function of the corporate culture. Too many former IT managers

TABLE 10.3 Relative Contribution of Tools to Ensuring Project Success by Project Type

Project Type	Project Description	External Integration	Internal Integration	Formal Planning	Formal Results Control
I	High structure–low technology, large	Low	Medium	High	High
II	High structure–low technology, small	Low	Low	Medium	High
III	High structure–high technology, large	Low	High	Medium	Medium
IV	High structure–high technology, small	Low	High	Low	Low
V	Low structure–low technology, large	High	Medium	High	High
VI	Low structure–low technology, small	High	Low	Medium	High
VII	Low structure–high technology, large	High	High	Low+	Low+
VIII	Low structure–high technology, small	High	High	Low	Low

have made the fatal assumption that they were in an ideal position to reform the corporate culture.

Emergence of Adaptive Project Management Methods[3]

The trend in the last decade has been toward projects that challenge traditional tools for project management and entail very high implementation risk. Business requirements for many enterprise systems are not well defined in advance and also involve new technologies. As investments, these systems have unattractive profiles. They require large investments, most of which must be spent up-front, to achieve uncertain (because of their inherently high implementation risk) benefits.

As we have noted, results-control tools and traditional planning methodologies do not work well in the presence of so much outcome uncertainty. Project managers who are expert in communicating with the user and in project technologies can help mediate the risks. Increasingly, however, outcome uncertainty and difficulty in determining system requirements in advance are leading to evolution in the project management process.

An emerging response to these conditions is *adaptive methods:* approaches to design, deployment, implementation, and investment that assume a need to gather information and to learn as one goes. To be used successfully, adaptive methods require that project staff be able to experiment during a project without incurring prohibitively high costs. Although evolving prototyping technologies allow low-cost project experimentation, adaptive methods are not yet universally applicable. To understand adaptive methods, consider the methodologies they are intended to replace.

[3]The materials on "adaptive methods" are based on work by Professor Austin.

Software Development Life Cycles

Traditionally, the activities necessary to design, implement, and operate information systems have been combined into a methodology that is sometimes called the system development life cycle (SDLC).[4] SDLC represents IT projects in a sequence of phases. The names of the phases vary across SDLC examples, but most are more or less consistent with the following:

Analysis and design. The traditional process begins with a comprehensive analysis of requirements, followed by documentation of the desired capabilities of the system in a form that can be used by system developers to code and implement the system. Either a user request or a joint IT department/user proposal which includes a formal statement of costs and benefits often initiates the process. IT professionals typically manage the design process. Today business users and technology specialists—often supported by vendors and/or consultants—determine the requirements for developing a new system or adapting a software package or in-place system.

Construction. Once requirements, costs, and benefits are defined and specifications are developed, the system can be coded. Traditionally, construction was a highly specialized activity that combined high levels of technological skill with a large dose of art, experience, and logic. Today, system construction involves selecting appropriate computer equipment and then creating, buying, and adapting the computer programs needed to meet system requirements. The final step is to test the system both in the laboratory (often called alpha testing) and in the real-world user environment (often called beta testing). Intense coordination and control are required to assure that the project remains on track, within budget, and focused on user requirements. Even the best designs require numerous interdependent decisions that must be made in real time as the system is being constructed. Large, often dispersed project teams must coordinate closely to ensure that the system components will work together flawlessly. The decision to outsource portions of the project or the entire project markedly increases coordination and control costs, because all technical decisions and tasks still must be managed, but this time across firm boundaries.

Implementation. Implementing a new IT system involves extensive coordination between the user and the technologist as the transition is made from the predominantly technical IT-driven task of construction to user-driven ongoing management of the completed system. Whether the system is bought or made, the implementation phase is very much a joint effort. Extensive testing, which may disrupt normal business operations, must be performed; training is

---

[4]It is worth noting that the list of responsibilities inherent in this methodology remains with the firm regardless of whether all or a portion of the system development process and IT operations/management is outsourced. The job of IT and business management is to ensure that those tasks are performed in the most effective and efficient manner regardless of where or by whom they are performed.

required; and work procedures and communication patterns may be disrupted. Often achieving the benefits of the system is dependent on the ability of individuals and groups to learn to use information from the system to make better decisions and add value to the business. It is essential to shape the organization's operational and management structure, processes, and incentives to exploit the potential of an IT system. In this world of electronic commerce, the impact of the system often extends to groups and individuals outside the organization, which further complicates implementation.

Operation and maintenance. To avoid ongoing problems, operation and maintenance are planned in advance, ideally during the early stages of requirements definition and design. Maintenance is complex, particularly for older systems. It requires highly competent professionals to perform the necessary changes safely and in a way that does not bring the system (and the firm) to a crashing halt.

Adaptive Methodologies

Adaptive and prototyping intensive methodologies call for quickly building a rough preliminary version of the system without going through a lengthy or formal requirement definition or design phase. Interacting with an early prototype makes the system easier to visualize for both users and developers. Thus, adaptive approaches iterate quickly through the traditional phases of design, construction, implementation, and operation, improving the performance of the product each time. Instead of moving slowly and deliberately through development phases, adaptive projects try to loop through each phase every week or even every day. Early prototypes are typically crude, but they are an excellent basis for discussions about system requirements between developers and users throughout development.

Companies that have implemented large enterprise systems successfully, such as Cisco and Tektronix, have tended to restructure projects to formally incorporate the idea of in-progress learning and midcourse adjustment. Although adaptive projects are carried out in a variety of ways, they share five basic characteristics:

1. They are iterative. Design, construction, and implementation occur in small increments that result from each iteration so that outcomes and interactions can be tested as they appear.

2. They rely on fast cycles and require frequent delivery of value so that incremental implementation does not slow down a project. Long lead times and variable delivery timing are discouraged.

3. They emphasize early delivery to end users of functionality, however limited, so that feedback can be incorporated into learning and improvement cycles.

4. They require skilled project staff capable of learning and making midcourse adjustments in the middle of deployment.

5. They often resist return on investment (ROI) and other similar tools for investment decision making that implicitly assume predictability of outcomes, instead emphasizing "buying of information" about outcomes as a legitimate expenditure.[5]

Although Cisco's managers did not explicitly identify their project management approach as "adaptive," they explicitly emphasized "rapid, iterative prototyping" as the basis for their approach. Tektronix divided its project into more than 20 "waves" that provided formal opportunities for deliberation, adjustment, and learning.

In recent years adaptive methods have made significant inroads into the ways in which developers create systems and software. As more off-the-shelf system components and more over-the-Net IT services become available, many firms are doing less and less software development internally. But even installing vendor software requires systems development. "Extreme programming" (or XP)[6] and "adaptive software development"[7] are examples of popular adaptive development approaches. Open-source software development, a technique that has led to the development of widely used infrastructure components such as the Linux operating system and the Apache Web server, also has adaptive characteristics.[8]

Adaptive methods emphasize low-cost experimentation and rapid delivery of system prototypes. They deemphasize up-front planning intended to "get it right the first time." In essence, the adaptive approach is to create something that works roughly as quickly as possible, begin to experience unexpected effects as soon as possible, and then change and improve the system rapidly. Adaptive methods are designed to offset the inevitability of unexpected outcomes.

It is worth noting that formal results-oriented controls not only work badly for large, risky projects but also can lead to dysfunction and disaster. For example, holding tightly to early schedule and functionality promises can provide project managers with incentives to downplay or ignore complicating factors that come to light as a project unfolds. Within an adaptive framework, unexpected complications are learning inputs that prompt midcourse adjustments. In a traditional results-oriented

---

[5]Robert D. Austin and Richard L. Nolan have suggested in the paper "Manage ERP Initiatives as New Ventures, Not IT Projects" (Harvard Business School Working Paper 99–024) that very large IT projects have risk profiles that resemble those of new ventures more than those of traditional IT projects. Venture investors cope with risky venture profiles by using a variety of adaptive techniques that legitimize the notion of buying information about the new venture. Large IT projects must adopt a similar approach that recognizes the impossibility of knowing everything in advance and the importance of in-progress learning.

[6]Kent Beck, *Extreme Programming Explained: Embrace Change* (Reading, MA: Addison-Wesley, 1999).

[7]James A. Highsmith III, *Adaptive Software Development: A Collaborative Approach to Managing Complex Systems* (New York: Dorset House, 1999).

[8]Eric S. Raymond, *Cathedral & the Bazaar: Musings on Linux & Open Source by an Accidental Revolutionary* (O'Reilly & Associates, 2001).

framework, complications often are swept under the rug because they interfere with the achievement of preset project milestones and because implementation team members are reluctant to admit that they failed to anticipate the complications. This dysfunctional dynamic can be especially significant if a company has hired expert consultants to assist with implementation. Consultants hired as experts dread admitting that they did not foresee complications, and client company managers often assume that experts must have anticipated all the possible complications. In this situation an unexpected complication can translate into systemic lack of communication between consultants, who do not want to admit what they did not anticipate, and client managers, who have unrealistic expectations about what the consultants should have foreseen.

Adaptive Methods and Change Management

Earlier in this chapter we noted the importance of exercising discipline when considering the system changes that users suggest once a design is finalized. Adaptive methods do not aspire to finalize a design in a discrete early phase of a project; instead, adaptive methods call for an acceptable design to emerge gradually during the development process. It would be a serious mistake, however, to conclude that change management is less important for adaptive projects.

Adaptive projects achieve change management in part by intensely involving users in evaluating the outcome of each development iteration and deciding on the next enhancement to be introduced into the system. Users are forced to confront at every iteration trade-offs between delay in obtaining useful results and implementation of their "great ideas." When the development process is an active collaboration between users and the IT staff, a natural discipline evolves to control unreasonable user requests.

But change management becomes important for adaptive projects in a different sense as well. Adaptive methods are an emerging response to outcome uncertainty in systems development. Rigorous *change management* is the corresponding response to the same kind of uncertainty when one changes existing systems vital to a company's operations. The approaches are two halves of a management system for balancing IT systems agility with rigorous operational control.

The essence of sound change management is to strictly control the migration of system features from development, through testing, into production with a clear understanding of the benefits and the potential for unanticipated problems at each stage. Successful change managers introduce new system features into production infrastructure with high confidence in the changes. They know at all times exactly what is running in their production environment and are therefore better able to diagnose problems and respond to incidents quickly. Effective change management in fact makes adaptive development possible by insulating the production environment from adaptive experimentation. Adaptive methods make sense only when the experiments do not result in catastrophic consequences, and effective change management prevents that situation.

Process Consistency and Agility in Project Management[9]

In practice, project management always involves balancing a tension between process consistency and process agility. Project managers need to ensure a thorough and disciplined approach to make sure that no balls are dropped, all requirements are met adequately, and no important details go unnoticed. This usually is accomplished through formal specification of project steps, required documentation, and compliance mechanisms (such as reviews or progress reports). At the same time, however, companies need to retain an ability to change direction, in the middle of a project if necessary, when business conditions require it. The tension arises from the fact that the tools used to improve consistency—specifications, documentation, compliance mechanisms—often are perceived as encumbrances that work against project responsiveness and agility. A firm that is well practiced and expert in its established routines may have trouble changing them. A firm that has grown accustomed to using certain tools may continue to try to use them in business conditions in which they are less appropriate.

In the last decade many companies have struggled with this issue, including many technology companies for which responsiveness to market and time to market were overriding concerns. For the most part, these companies resisted full-fledged adoption of traditional project methodologies because they perceived that adoption as too damaging to project agility. In place of traditional project management methodologies, many Network Economy companies have attempted to develop "light" methodologies that contain the essential elements of "heavy" methodologies but are not as cumbersome.

A Minimalist Approach to Process Formalization

The companies that have been most successful in balancing discipline and agility have neither eschewed process formalization altogether nor let process formalization efforts overwhelm them. Rather, they have developed simple process management tools based on the idea that the best balance is one that includes the minimum formal specification critical to the success of a project. These simple tools fall into three categories:

Flow. People working on projects need to understand the relationships between their activities and those of others. That is, they need to understand the overall process "flow." Process tools in this category can be simple depictions of the process context that are intended to give decision makers at specific points in the process a sense of the overall business picture. Deep detail is not required or recommended. Simple schedules and flowcharts work well here.

Completeness. People working on projects need to be sure that everything is being done, that no ball is being dropped. This is where detail comes into the picture. Tools in this category can be simple lists to convey what needs to be

[9]The materials in this section are based on a note by Professor Austin.

done, when it needs to be done, by whom, and whether it is complete. Simple checklists work well here.

Visibility. People working on projects need to be able to review processes while they are being executed to get status information. Ideally anyone, whether from engineering, marketing, or elsewhere, can review the same "picture" and come away with the information he or she needs. Visibility is not easy to achieve. Computerized status-reporting systems can provide this kind of visibility, but some of the best solutions are simple wall charts that allow status to be tracked in a way that everyone (in one physical location, anyway) can see.

In some contexts, another category of tools must be added: tools to ensure that project activities are auditable. This may be true of projects that will result in government systems or safety-related systems.

Managing the tension between consistency and agility is for most companies a general process issue that extends well beyond project management. Process frameworks from earlier times, when systems were proprietary and the common Internet platform was not available for commerce, significantly encumber many Industrial Economy firms. As these companies work to make the transition to the Network Economy, they face the difficult task of distilling processes down to essential elements to reclaim lost project and organizational agility.

Summary

The last decade has brought new challenges to IT project management and new insights into the management process. Our research in these areas leads us to three conclusions:

1. Firms will continue to experience major disappointments as they push into new application areas and technologies. Today, however, the dimensions of implementation risk can be identified in advance, and this information can be included in the decision process. If a firm implements only high-risk projects, sometimes it will fail.

2. A firm's IT development projects in the aggregate represent a portfolio. Just as financial fund managers calculate and manage the risks within their portfolios, general management must make critical strategic decisions on the aggregate implementation risk profile of the IT portfolio.

3. Project management in the IT field is complex and multidimensional; different types of projects require different clusters of management tools.

As we have seen, progress in understanding how to manage projects continues. The emergence of adaptive methods is an interesting development, but we are still evaluating its ultimate applicability. Executives can use the following questions to assess whether they are managing the risks inherent in IT projects to maximize gain:

1. Have you established risk assessment procedures (such as the questionnaire in Figure 10.3) to evaluate the risk of individual projects? Is such a procedure a standard part of project approval and status reporting at the company?

2. Do our project planning, tracking, and control processes account adequately for differences in types of projects (high/low structure, high/low technology)? Are our management expectations about projects sufficiently contingent on inherent project risk factors?

3. Have we performed a risk analysis on our portfolio of application projects? If so, is the portfolio risk profile appropriate to the quadrant of the strategic grid in which we operate? Is it a good fit with our business objectives and strategies?

4. Are we exploring emerging project management methodologies to determine their applicability to our business?

Conclusion

The Challenges of Managing in a Network Economy Revisited

> Prediction is hard, especially of the future.
> —*Yogi Berra, hall of fame baseball player and manager*

In 1943 Thomas Watson, the venerable chairman of the IBM Corporation, predicted that there would be a world market for "maybe five computers." Today there are hundreds of millions of computers worldwide. The magnitude of the error in this "expert's" forecast stands as a reminder that it is difficult to see far into the future. A quick glance backward reinforces the point. In 1992 there were no Web browsers. Before 1995 Amazon.com was but a glimmer in Jeff Bezos's eye. Five years ago who would have foreseen the rapid rise—and fall—of the "dot-com bubble"? Much has changed very quickly, and nothing has happened to suggest that the IT industry is on the verge of slowing down its pace of evolution and change. There is surely more excitement ahead.

The objective of this book has been to provide its readers with a better understanding of the influence of 21st-century technologies on executive decisions. While this kind of understanding may help sharpen our predictions, our aim has not been to arm you to engage in future thinking for prediction's sake alone. Instead, we have focused on providing analytic frameworks and an overview of the issues involved in using those frameworks to identify opportunities, design and deploy new technology-based businesses, and create business value in the Network Economy. These frameworks are based on concepts and theory that have withstood the test of time and remain relevant despite radical changes in the business environment. We have dealt with enduring practical questions from the point of view of the executives who are grappling with them. Not long ago, many predicted the death of traditional economic and management principles. The subsequent fall in technology market stocks suggests that we should not be too quick to throw out fundamental management principles as we embrace the new.

Markets and models, capabilities and organization, networked infrastructure and operations, and leadership of the IT organization are core subject areas that can be used to organize the management issues discussed in this book. Within these subject areas we explored the following key themes:

1. The continuous pace of technology evolution requires that we confront new choices for designing and building industries, markets, and organizations.

2. The business models that dominated the Industrial Economy are evolving to take advantage of the new technologies and business practices of the Network Economy, giving rise to new sources of power and differentiation.

3. The types of opportunities pursued and the technology employed strongly influence the approach to developing, operating, and managing IT.

4. As IT infrastructure becomes more standardized, modular, and scalable, we are seeing a shift in IT investment priorities and decisions from a cost-avoidance, project-centered approach to an asset-based, strategic option approach.

5. The time required for successful organization learning and assimilation of rapidly changing technologies limits the practical speed of change.

6. External industry, internal organizational, and technological changes are increasing the pressure on organizations to buy rather than make IT applications and services.

7. The ability to exploit 21st-century technology demands high levels of engagement and cooperation among four key constituencies: business executives, IT executives, users, and technology providers/partners.

8. The ability to ensure high levels of security, privacy, reliability, and availability is a core capability that determines an organization's ultimate success and survival.

9. Over the last decade there has been a fundamental shift in IT that has dramatically changed the way people access and use technology, the way organizations exploit it, and the way it is developed and managed.

As we have demonstrated, the effect of the new technologies on markets and industries will be to alter competitive positions and frame new strategic imperatives that require new capabilities. The new technologies have enabled new business models and improved the viability of old ones; executives in established firms that do not seize the business model opportunities presented by new technologies will find their market positions threatened.

New networked infrastructures interweave complex business-technical issues that general managers dread but that ultimately make the difference between a rigid and constraining IT capability and a flexible and dynamic one. These infrastructures come with many layers of relationships, technology models, and risk management processes that ultimately determine the IT possibilities that dramatically affect the ability to compete today and the business opportunities that can be pursued in the future. Finally, there are the challenges of executing technology-based strategic initiatives, an area that many companies cannot seem to master. The projects grow larger and harder, and decisions must be made ever more quickly. Most executives express concern that this relentless change is occurring much too fast to enable them (and their organizations) to learn. Yet this is an area that must be mastered if disasters are to be averted and returns are to be realized from IT investments.

Annotated Bibliography

General Management Bookshelf

Ackoff, Russell L. *Creating the Corporate Future: Plan or Be Planned For.* New York: Wiley, 1981. An important book that provides a broad context for IT planning.

Anthony, Robert N. *The Management Control Function.* Boston: Harvard Business School Press, 1988. This book introduces the framework of operational control, management control, and strategic planning relative to the area of IT application and its management problems.

Argyris, Chris. *On Organizational Learning.* Cambridge, MA: Blackwell Business, 1993. Explores how to achieve organizational effectiveness by managing through improved communication processes.

Bartlett, Christopher A., and Sumantra Ghoshal. *Managing across Borders: The Transnational Solution.* Boston: Harvard Business School Press, 1991. A succinct and mind-expanding discussion of the impact, true costs, and strategic value of computer systems and their notable future influence.

Beer, Michael, Russell A. Eisenstat, and Bert A. Spector. *The Critical Path to Corporate Renewal.* Boston: Harvard Business School Press, 1990. Through an in-depth analysis of six companies that have undergone fundamental changes, the authors describe what works and what does not in corporate renewal.

Bower, Joseph L. *Managing the Resource Allocation Process: A Study of Corporate Planning and Investment.* Boston: Division of Research, Harvard Business School Classics, 1986. This in-depth analysis of corporate planning and capital budgeting provides critical insights relevant to both the role of steering committees and how IT planning can be done effectively.

Bradley, Stephen P., and Richard L. Nolan, eds. *Sense and Respond: Capturing the Value in the Network Era.* Boston: Harvard Business School Press, 1998. This book captures the tremendous shift in the adaptiveness of management control systems and organizations in an information-mediated world.

Brealey, Richard, and Stewart C. Myers. *Principles of Corporate Finance,* 6th edition. New York: McGraw-Hill, 2000. Describes the theory and practice of corporate finance. Discusses why companies and financial markets behave the way they do.

Brynjolfsson, Erik, and Brian Kahin, eds. *Understanding the Digital Economy: Data, Tools and Research.* Cambridge, MA: MIT Press, 2000. Considers new types of data collection and research that might help public and private organizations analyze the economic impact of the Internet and electronic commerce in the United States and internationally. Main areas of discussion include market structure, competition, and organizational change.

Bunnell, David, and Adam Brate. *Making the Cisco Connection: The Story behind the Real Internet Superpower.* New York: Wiley, 2000. A detailed story of the most Internet-enabled company in the world. It both describes its accomplishment in great detail and identifies what it did to get there.

Burgleman, Robert A., and Modesto A. Maidique. *Strategic Management of Technology and Innovation.* New York: McGraw-Hill Higher Education, 1992. Using a combination of text, readings, and cases, this book discusses how general managers can augment and develop a firm's capabilities for managing technological innovation.

Burt, Ronald S. *Structural Holes: The Social Structure of Competition.* Cambridge, MA: Harvard University Press, 1992. The basic element in this account is the structural hole: a gap between two individuals or organizations that have complementary resources or information. When the two are connected through a third individual, an entrepreneur, or an organizational market, the gap is filled, creating important advantages for the intermediary. Competitive advantage is a matter of access to structural holes in relation to market transactions.

Cairncross, Francis. *The Death of Distance: How the Communications Revolution Will Change Our Lives.* Boston: Harvard Business School Press, 1997. This far-reaching book describes the societal transformation that is being enabled by cheap, ubiquitous global bandwidth.

Champy, James, and Michael Hammer. *Reengineering the Corporation.* New York: Harper Collins, 1993. This pathbreaking book discusses the practical barriers and problems in achieving reengineering success.

Chandler, Alfred D., and James W. Cortada, eds. *A Nation Transformed by Information: How Information Has Shaped the United States from Colonial Times to the Present.* New York: Oxford University Press, 2000. A 250-year history of the information revolution. It is perhaps the most thoughtful book written on the roots of the information economy.

Christensen, Clayton M. *The Innovator's Dilemma: When New Technologies Cause Great Firms to Fail.* Boston: Harvard Business School Press, 1997. An explosive best-seller that highlights the perils of slow-moving change-resistant corporate cultures in a fast-moving technical world.

Copeland, Tom, Tim Koller, and Jack Murrin. *Valuation: Measuring and Managing the Value of Companies.* New York: Wiley, 2000. Provides insights and information on value creation and measurement, valuing start-ups and other hyper-growth companies, valuing cyclical companies and companies in emerging markets, and calculating the cost of capital and option pricing methods to value flexibility.

Davenport, Thomas H., and John C. Beck. *The Attention Economy: Understanding the New Currency of Business.* Boston: Harvard Business School Press, 2001. A thoughtful book that captures the importance of knowledge management in an information-overloaded world.

Hamel, Gary, and C. I. Prahalad. *Competing for the Future.* Boston: Harvard Business School Press, 1994. How to develop core competencies to implement a future-oriented strategy.

Kuhn, Thomas S. *The Structure of Scientific Revolution.* Chicago: University of Chicago Press, 1970. Thomas Kuhn (1922–1996) argued that scientific advancement is not evolutionary but rather is a "series of peaceful interludes punctuated by intellectually violent revolutions." In those revolutions "one conceptual world view is replaced by another."

Leonard, Dorothy A. *Wellsprings of Knowledge: Building and Sustaining the Sources of Innovation.* Boston: Harvard Business School Press, 1998. Focuses on the knowledge-creating activities and behaviors that managers guide, control, and inspire: developing problem-solving skills, experimenting to build for the future, integrating information across internal project and functional boundaries, and importing expertise from outside the firm.

Nolan, Richard L., and David C. Croson. *Creative Destruction: A Six-Step Process for Transforming the Organization.* Boston: Harvard Business School Press, 1995. This book analyzes the very different organization structures that are made possible by new information technology and the problems involved in implementing those structures.

Nolan, Richard. *Dot Vertigo: Doing Business in a Permeable World.* New York: Wiley, 2001. A fast-moving book on the special issues of doing business in an Internet-linked customer-supplier world.

Porter, Michael. *Competitive Strategy.* New York: Free Press, 1995. This widely read book provides a disciplined structure to the question of how firms achieve superior profitability. Porter's rich frameworks and deep insights provide a sophisticated view of competition.

Porter, Michael. *Competitive Advantage: Creating and Sustaining Performance,* New York: Free Press, 1985. A complement to *Competitive Strategy,* this book explores the underpinnings of competitive advantage in the individual firm. Now an essential part of international business thinking, *Competitive Advantage* takes strategy from broad vision to an internally consistent configuration of activities. Its powerful framework provides the tools needed to understand the drivers of cost and a company's relative cost position.

Shapiro, Carl, and Hal R. Varian. *Information Rules: A Strategic Guide to the Network Economy.* Boston: Harvard Business School Press, 1998. The first book to distill the economics of information and networks into practical business strategies.

Shell, G. Richard. *Bargaining for Advantage: Negotiation Strategies for Reasonable People.* New York: Viking Penguin, 1999. This book provides a realistic, powerful framework for business and consumer negotiations that will help everyone from the inexperienced anxious negotiator to the seasoned veteran.

Simons, Robert. *Levers of Control.* Boston: Harvard Business School Press, 1995. Provides a refreshing and new way to think about management control.

Slywotsky, A., and D. Morrison. *Profit Patterns: 30 Ways to Anticipate and Profit from Strategic Forces Reshaping Your Business.* New York: New York Times Business, 1999. Extrapolating from the painter Pablo Picasso's work, the authors theorize that by recognizing industry patterns—by seeing the order beneath the surface chaos—managers, investors, and entrepreneurs can prepare for change before it occurs.

Tapscott, Don, David Ticoll, and Alex Lowy. *Digital Capital: Harnessing the Power of Business Webs.* Boston: Harvard Business School Press, 2000. A book on the implications of a digitized, totally wired world.

Timmons, Jeffry A. *New Venture Creation: Entrepreneurship for the 21st Century.* New York: McGraw-Hill/Irwin, 1999. Covers the process of getting a new venture started, growing the venture, successfully harvesting it, and starting again.

Treacy, Michael, and Fred Wiersema. *Disciplines of Market Leaders: Choose Your Customers, Narrow Your Focus, Dominate Your Market.* Reading, MA:

Addison-Wesley Publishing Co., 1994. This book presents a view of what needs to be done for firms to be successful in the market.

Williamson, O. E., and Sidney G. Winter, eds. *The Nature of the Firm: Origins, Evolution, and Development.* New York: Oxford University Press, 1993. Develops Ronald H. Coase's theory, first presented in his 1937 article "The Nature of the Firm," that raised fundamental questions about the concept of the firm in economic theory. The book contains the original article as well as a series of lectures by Williamson and Coase's Nobel Prize in Economics acceptance speech.

Yoffie, David B., ed. *Competing in the Age of Digital Convergence.* Boston: Harvard Business School Press, 1997. An important set of essays on the implications for corporate strategy of computing in a digitized world.

Technology Management Bookshelf

Baldwin, Carliss Y., and Kim Clark. *Design Rules: The Power of Modularity.* Cambridge, MA: MIT Press, 2000. Argues that the computer industry experienced previously unimaginable levels of innovation and growth because it embraced the concept of modularity, building complex products from small subsystems that could be designed independently yet function together as a whole.

Beck, Kent. *Extreme Programming: Embrace Change.* Reading, MA: Addison-Wesley, 1999. Provides an intriguing high-level overview of the author's Extreme Programming (XP) software development methodology, a controversial approach to software development which challenges the notion that the cost of changing a piece of software must rise dramatically over the course of time.

Brooks, Frederick. *The Mythical Man-Month: Essays on Software Engineering.* Reading, MA: Addison-Wesley, 1995. One of the classics in the field of program management. The author draws on his experience as the head of operating systems development for IBM's famous 360 mainframe computer and distills his wisdom in an easily accessible form.

DeMarco, Tom, and Timothy Lister. *Peopleware: Productive Projects and Teams.* New York: Dorset House, 1999. Using a conversational and straight-forward style, the authors assert that most projects fail because of failures within the teams running them.

Feghi, Jalal, Jalil Feghi, and Peter Williams. *Digital Certificates: Applied Internet Security.* Reading, MA: Addison-Wesley, 1999. An excellent reference on the subject of encryption and digital certificates.

Forcht, Karen A. *Computer Security Management.* Danvers, MA: Boyd & Fraser, 1994. A practical book that describes the multiple aspects of computer security and the steps to be taken to gain good results.

Highsmith, James III. *Adaptive Software Development: A Collaborative Approach to Managing Complex Systems.* New York: Dorset House, 1999. Provides a series of frameworks to help an organization employ adaptive principles, establish collaboration, and provide a path toward using an adaptive approach on large projects.

Hoch, Detlev J., Cyriac R. Roeding, Gert Purkett, and Sandro K. Lindner. *Secrets of Software Success: Management Insights from 100 Software Firms around the World.* Boston: Harvard Business School Press, 1999. A practical book that focuses on the issues that must be resolved for a successful software implementation.

Lawrence, Paul R., and Jay W. Lorsch. *Organization and Environment: Managing Integration and Differentiation.* Boston: Harvard Business School Classics, 1986. This classic presents the underlying thinking of the need for specialized departments and how they should interface with the rest of the organization. It is relevant for all IT organizational decisions.

Lucas, Henry C., Jr. *Information Technology and the Productivity Paradox: Assessing the Value of Investing in IT.* New York: Oxford University Press, 1999. An interesting analysis of how one goes about justifying IT investments.

McKenney, James L. *Waves of Change: Business Evolution through Information Technology.* Boston: Harvard Business School Press, 1995. This book captures the long-term dynamics of an evolving information architecture as it traces more than 30 years of the history of information technology in four organizations.

Perrow, Charles. *Normal Accidents: Living with High Risk Technologies.* Princeton, NJ: Princeton University Press, 1999. Looking at an array of real and potential technological mishaps—including the Bhopal chemical plant accident of 1984, the *Challenger* explosion of 1986, and the possible disruptions of Y2K and genetic engineering—Perrow concludes that as our technologies become more complex, the odds of tragic results increase.

Raymond, Eric S., and Bob Young. *The Cathedral and the Bazaar: Musings on Linux and Open Source by an Accidental Revolutionary.* Sebastapol, CA: O'Reilly and Associates, 2001. A text defining the open source revolution in computing, discussing the advantages of open source computing with such technologies as Perl, Linux, and Apache. Offers a glimpse into the future of these types of technologies and their uses in the digital age.

Smith, H. Jeff. *Managing Privacy Information Technology and Corporate America.* Chapel Hill: University of North Carolina Press, 1994. A very practical book that talks about information technology privacy, current practices, and issues for the future.

Upton, David. *Designing, Managing, and Improving Operations.* Upper Saddle River, NJ: Prentice-Hall, 1998. An example of Upton's writings on the benefits of incremental improvement strategies and especially the need to design operational infrastructures so that they can be improved incrementally.

Utterback, James. *Mastering the Dynamics of Innovation: How Companies Can Seize Opportunities in the Face of Technological Change.* Boston: Harvard Business School Press, 1994. An analysis of the forces to manage in developing new products and processes as a strategic force.

Wheelwright, Steven C., and Kim B. Clark. *Leading Product Development.* New York: Free Press, 1995. A focused view on senior management's role in shaping strategy based on continuous product development as a competitive means. Time from concept to market is the critical success factor.

Yates, Joanne. *Control through Communication: The Rise of System in American Management.* Baltimore: Johns Hopkins University Press, 1993. Traces the evolution of internal communication systems through the late 19th century and into the 20th century through a focus on innovative companies such as DuPont.

Zwicky, Elizabeth D., Simon Cooper, and D. Brent Chapman. *Building Internet Firewalls,* 2nd edition. Sebastapol, CA: O'Reilly, 2000. An excellent reference on firewalls and their capabilities.

Index